T0347261

Risk, Global Governance and Security

This book applies risk society theory to the 'War on Terror', steering the discussion away from the militaristic discourse of the Bush era towards an emphasis on global cooperation and a new cosmopolitan agenda.

The literature and rhetoric of the war on terror has been dominated by dramatic high-profile military campaigns and division in the international community. This overlooks the various multilateral practices and cooperative processes that are emerging to combat global terrorism. President Bush himself had initially been at pains to stress that his 'war' on terror would be like no other; it would involve not just military tools but financial, intelligence, police and diplomatic measures too. More than seven years since Bush's proclamation, and with a new occupant in the White House, the time is right for an in-depth evaluation of how this 'other' war on terror has developed. Yet these relatively mundane regulatory dimensions have received much less attention than the 'hot' wars in Afghanistan and Iraq, where ongoing difficulties suggest that military force alone is inadequate in controlling globalised terrorism.

This book aims to redress this imbalance, by foregrounding these initiatives, tracing their implementation and reflecting on the implications for international relations. Adopting an analytical approach that seeks to incorporate theories of risk, global governance and security, this book aims to explore the overlapping multilevel and multilateral dynamics of the emerging global security architecture that have remained neglected and unmapped thus far in the war on terror.

This book will be of interest to students of risk politics, security studies, global governance and international relations in general.

Yee-Kuang Heng is Lecturer in International Relations, University of St Andrews, UK. **Kenneth McDonagh** is Lecturer in International Relations in the School of Law and Government, Dublin City University.

Routledge global security studies
Series editors: Aaron Karp, Regina Karp and Terry Teriff

Risk, Global Governance and Security

The other war on terror

**Yee-Kuang Heng and
Kenneth McDonagh**

Routledge
Taylor & Francis Group

LONDON AND NEW YORK

First published 2009
by Routledge
2 Park Square, Milton Park, Abingdon, Oxon OX14 4RN

Simultaneously published in the USA and Canada
by Routledge
711 Third Avenue, New York, NY 10017, USA

Routledge is an imprint of the Taylor & Francis Group, an informa business

© 2009 Yee-Kuang Heng and Kenneth McDonagh

Typeset in Times by Wearset Ltd, Boldon, Tyne and Wear

British Library Cataloguing in Publication Data
A catalogue record for this book is available from the British Library

Library of Congress Cataloging in Publication Data
A catalog record for this book has been requested

ISBN10: 0-415-47196-6 (hbk)
ISBN10: 0-203-87822-1 (ebk)

ISBN13: 978-0-415-47196-1 (hbk)
ISBN13: 978-0-203-87822-4 (ebk)

Contents

Acknowledgements

We would like gratefully to acknowledge the encouragement of our editor Andrew Humphrys. The very useful suggestions and comments of three anonymous reviewers also helped us immensely in writing this book. Any errors or omissions of course remain our responsibility alone. We also wish to acknowledge that some of the material in Chapter 3 is drawn from 'The other war on terror revealed: Global governmentality and the Financial Action Task Force's campaign against terrorist financing', *Review of International Studies*, July 2008, published by Cambridge University Press. Chapter 5 also draws from material previous published in 'Governing global security in the departure lounge', *Journal of Global Change and Governance*, Vol. 1 No. 3, 2008. We would like to thank the anonymous reviewers of both those articles for their constructive comments and criticisms. Elements of this research have also been presented at the ISA Annual Convention in San Francisco, March 2008, and the CISS Conference in Paris, June 2008. Again thanks go to the chairs, discussants and other participants of those panels for their comments. We would also like to acknowledge the Institute for International Integration Studies, Trinity College Dublin for financing part of the research presented here.

Yee-Kuang Heng would like to express heartfelt thanks to colleagues at the School of International Relations, University of St Andrews, UK. They have made him feel truly at home in a short space of time. The financial assistance of the British Academy, which enabled an earlier version of this book to be presented at the International Studies Association Annual Convention 2008, must also be acknowledged. Last but not least, this book is dedicated to his Mum and Dad, as well as Chihiro and Hiroko who have shown tremendous bravery in coping with extremely trying circumstances. Of course, he would like to thank his wife Akiko for her love, patience and help, which often went unacknowledged.

Ken would also like to thank his colleagues at the School of Law and Government, Dublin City University and at the Department of Political Science, Trinity College Dublin for their feedback and support at various stages of this research. Ken would also like to thank his parents, John and Toni McDonagh, and family. Finally, he would like to thank his wife Katya for her love and support without which this work would not have been possible.

Abbreviations

ACLU	American Civil Liberties Union
ACSIF	Air Cargo Security Industry Forum
AML	anti-money laundering
APEC	Asia Pacific Economic Cooperation
APIS	advanced passenger information system
ATF	anti-terrorist financing
AU	African Union
CCTV	closed-circuit television
CIA	Central Intelligence Agency
CSI	Container Security Initiative
CTBT	Comprehensive Test Ban Treaty
CTC	Counter-Terrorism Committee (UN)
CTF	counter-terrorist finance
DHS	Department of Homeland Security (US)
DoD	Department of Defence (US)
EASA	European Aviation Security Association
ECAC	European Civil Aviation Conference
FATF	Financial Action Task Force
FBI	Federal Bureau of Investigation (US)
FSRB	FATF-style regional body
G7	Group of 7
G8	Group of 8
GASAG	Global Aviation Security Action Group
IAEA	International Atomic Energy Agency
IATA	International Air Transport Association
ICAO	International Civil Aviation Organisation
ICC	International Criminal Court
ICJ	International Court of Justice
IMF	International Monetary Fund
IOSA	IATA Operational Safety Audit
IPE	International Political Economy
IR	International relations
ISO	International Organisation for Standardisation

KYC	know your customer
MNC	multinational company
MoD	Ministry of Defence (UK)
NAFTA	North American Free Trade Area
NATO	North Atlantic Treaty Organisation
NCCT	Non-Cooperating Countries and Territories Initiative (FATF)
NGO	non-governmental organisation
NPT	Non Proliferation Treaty
NWS	nuclear weapons states
PMC	private military contractor
PNR	Passenger Name Records
PSI	Proliferation Security Initiative
RBA	risk-based approach
SALT	Strategic Arms Limitation Talks
SARP	Standards and Recommended Practices (ICAO)
SEMS	Security Management System
SSI	Strategic Surveillance Initiative (FATF)
START	Strategic Arms Reduction Treaty
SWIFT	Society for Worldwide Interbank Financial Telecommunication
TSA	Transport Security Administration (USA)
UN	United Nations
UNCLOS	United Nations Conference on the Law of the Sea
UNSC	United Nations Security Council
WMD	weapons of mass destruction

1   The other war on terror

Introduction

This book is aimed at the less visible, lower-profile aspects of global cooperative counter-terrorism strategies. It argues that the highly visual violent events
of Abu Ghraib, Guantanamo and extraordinary rendition that have, for better
or worse, come to define the war on terror, in fact have their more 'ordinary'
mundane and barely visible counterparts that are in need of more attention.[1]
In so doing, we seek to provide a fresh theoretical perspective of risk, global
governance and security, on what we term the 'other war on terror', a campaign
that has been ongoing beneath our very noses with relatively less scrutiny. To
illustrate our point by way of contrast, in the years since the tragic events
of 11 September 2001 (hereafter 9/11), most retrospective evaluations of the
ensuing war on terror will inevitably, and rightly, roll out the unfortunately
long list of eye-catching landmark events that have dominated headlines. These
range from dramatic high-profile military campaigns in Afghanistan and Iraq,
accusations of American unilateralism, secret 'extraordinary rendition' flights
and extra-judicial killings of Al Qaeda suspects by CIA drones, controversy
over the 2002 National Security Strategy's emphasis on pre-emptive strikes.
Guantanamo Bay and Abu Ghraib are now bywords for American apparent disregard of international law and human rights since 9/11. Wiretaps, snooping
and infringements of civil liberties, 'waterboarding', torture, the list goes on.
Who can forget as well the bitter division in the international community, even
amongst erstwhile NATO allies, the US, France and Germany, over the controversial war on Iraq in 2003 and subsequent failure to unearth weapons of mass
destruction?

Yet despite years of the most powerful country in the world applying military
force and pressure in 'a no-holds-barred, global war on terrorism', noted terrorism analyst Bruce Hoffman wrily observed in February 2007 that 'Al Qaeda is
on the march, rather than on the run', contrary to President Bush's rhetoric.[2] A
year later in February 2008, Director of National Intelligence John McConnell
warned that despite losing many of its senior operational planners, 'Al Qaeda
and its terrorist affiliates continue to pose significant threats to the United States
at home and abroad, and al Qaeda's central leadership based in the border area

of Pakistan is its most dangerous component.'[3] Another August 2008 assessment by the US intelligence analyst in charge of transnational threats continues this line of argument about Al Qaeda's resilience in the face of military attempts at eliminating its leaders: 'in spite of successful U.S. and allied operations against al-Qaeda, especially the death of important al-Qaeda figures since December, the group has maintained or strengthened key elements of its capability to attack the United States in the past year'.[4] Notwithstanding the increasingly bitter debate in Washington on just how strong Al Qaeda is or whether it has splintered into what Marc Sageman terms 'leaderless jihad',[5] it has become clear that the use of dramatic highly visible military force, while a useful and indispensable instrument in the counter-terrorism tool kit, is not always the right solution all the time. Furthermore as Amoore and de Goede point out, although the oft-cited Abu Ghraib, Guantanamo and extraordinary rendition flights are intolerable examples that deservedly attract attention,

> there are other violences at work in the war on terror that are relatively unacknowledged and perhaps as a result, are in danger of being accepted as uniquitious features of contemporary life … concealed in the actions taken on the basis of the minutiae of daily life.

They seek to provide 'a glimpse of the otherwise concealed, ordinary everyday security practices of the war on terror'. Amoore and de Goede suggest these developments constitute a relatively unacknowledged dimension in the war on terror, which is in need of critical questioning.[6] While power might be exercised overtly in the use of dramatic military force, it might also be deployed in less overt and more subtle ways in the everyday dimensions of the 'other' war on terror.

In light of the unsatisfactory nature of visible military force, coupled with a need to interrogate relatively unremarkable security practices in the war on terror, this book poses its central question in two parts. Empirically, have there been any alternative non-military policies pursued and how effective are they? Theoretically, how might one think about such alternatives? In this introductory chapter, therefore, we seek first to establish the academic and strategic context within which we position ourselves. In order to do so, we outline three important developments in academic and policy debates that we suggest are intertwined in recent thinking about the war on terror, and how they have motivated us in writing this book. The first involves recent debates within the US foreign policy community on the best way forward for American grand strategy in the twenty-first century, notably the suggestion that a new more complex form of global governance might be the way of the future. As Winston Churchill once famously quipped, 'it is better to jaw-jaw than to war-war'. Although Al Qaeda is far from being Nazi Germany, the legendary wartime British prime minister's words do still resonate in an age of terror. Indeed, might not the shared global nature of risks also bring the world together into greater communication and cooperation as a counter-terrorism strategy? Second, there is increasing recognition of the need to move away from reliance on military force, leading to examination of alternative less-noticed non-military aspects of the war on terror so far: what we call the 'other' war on terror. And the third and final development we shall discuss concerns the prominence of risk in attempts to conceptualise the war on terror, both by policy makers and academics. What particularly intrigue us are the unexplored convergences and synergies between these three developments that we have outlined. We argue that these, taken together, might help us to achieve a more complete understanding of the war on terror, in particular its less noticed dimensions.

The first issue we wish to begin with relates to recent debates within the US foreign community on the best way forward for America's role in the war on terror. After all, 'most of the avalanche of books after 9/11 on America's grand strategy condemn Washington's penchant for bellicose unilateralism and assert that a better way is possible'.[7] In order to illustrate this ongoing debate, consider two recent musings by leading protagonists in the US foreign policy community – one by John Bolton and the other by Strobe Talbott. These two books, according to Joseph Nye, 'serve as bookends in our current debate about America's role in the world'.[8] Both represent rather different strategic visions geared towards achieving the same desired goal of managing security in a global age of risks and uncertainty. Talbott, President Clinton's deputy secretary of state and current president of the Brookings Institution, strongly endorses global governance as the way of the future: 'individual states will increasingly see it in their interest to form an international system that is far more cohesive, far more empowered by its members, and therefore far more effective than the one we have today'. Talbott however is not so sure about whether the United Nations (UN) in its current form should provide the central pillar of this global governance. Instead, he argues 'the U.N. needs to be incorporated into an increasingly variegated network of structures and arrangements – some functional in focus, others geographic; some intergovernmental, others based on systematic collaboration with the private sector, civil society, and NGOs'. His vision is of a flexible mesh of international agreements and organisations that operate at different levels mutually to support one another. Bolton, on the other hand, is the leading neo-con hawk of the first Bush administration appointed as US ambassador to the UN. Arguing to the complete opposite, he decries the European inclination and preference for multilateral bodies to create 'norms' in international practice. This, Bolton claims, lessens and undermines America's flexibility and freedom for unilateral action, as it becomes mired in endless diplomatic wrangling. Which vision is the appropriate strategy to adopt? While both Talbott and Bolton have their strengths and weaknesses, this book builds upon Talbott's notion of overlapping multilevel global governance and how that might have a crucial role to play in the war on terror.

This brings us to the second development we wish to highlight: an increasing awareness of the need to develop cooperative non-military alternatives to military force as a counter-terrorism strategy. As Chairman of the US Joint Chiefs of Staff Admiral Mike Mullen put it in his September 2008 Congressional testimony, 'we cannot kill our way to victory'.[9] Academics too have also been paying more attention to such less-noticed dimensions and their moral, political and policy implications. Particularly, the campaign to curtail terrorist finances has recently generated a fair bit of buzz among researchers.[10] There has also emerged a body of literature that analyses counter-terrorism in non-militaristic terms. These include works ranging from dataveillance, data mining, surveillance, the analysis of ordinary transactions data of various kinds, to urban landscape design.[11] There is also no shortage of prescriptions on how better to fight global jihad, for instance those by Daniel Byman.[12] Wynn Rees too has detailed the impressive level of counter-terrorism occurring at the trans-Atlantic level, particularly on issues of homeland security. Yet as Cortwright and Lopez recently argued, 'America's reliance on military approaches and the Bush administration's avowal of a constant state of war have overshadowed non-military, multilateral efforts, and there has been an analogous neglect of these alternative strategies in the literature on terrorism.'[13] Clearly, we would certainly not lay claim to being the first to highlight such issues or that these have been completely overlooked, to the contrary. But we would at the same tim, though, point out that many of these efforts seem to be more empirical policy oriented and neglect theoretical engagement with broader concepts and ideas relating to risk and global governance. That is where we could claim some form of novelty, particularly in the mode of analysis operationalising Ulrich Beck's *World Risk Society* thesis and his particular understanding of global cooperation as a counter-terrorism tool: the third development we shall introduce later. At this point, it is worth pointing out that we consciously eschew commonly held criticisms of American unilateralism and its predominant focus on military force, and recognise that, at times, force when properly applied is warranted and absolutely crucial to preventing terrorism. The problem with military force however is that controversies over the war in Iraq and US unilateralism have simply become a 'lightning rod for criticism of US foreign policy', and in the process has 'overshadowed a more pragmatic and multilateral component of the Bush administration's grand strategy ... this unheralded move is well intentioned and well advised'.[14] Drezner suggests that because Washington's attempts to accommodate rising powers through reshaping international institutions 'have focused more on so-called low politics than on the global war on terrorism, they have flown under the radar of many observers'. Adopting a similar thread of argument, this book argues that within the global war on terror, there is also a tendency to overlook the various multilateral practices and cooperative processes that have emerged, indeed often under active American encouragement and plodding. The analysis of the war on terror at the current time is therefore somewhat incomplete, for these processes have quietly slipped under the radar screen of public opinion, which has been more attuned to what Drezner terms the 'rhetorical excesses of former UN Ambassador John Bolton and former Secretary of Defence Donald Rumsfeld'.[15]

Such relative neglect is strange and puzzling, because right from the beginning the US administration has actually made a point of how the war on terror was not just a military struggle but rather a campaign waged on many fronts. President Bush himself had initially been at pains to emphasise that:

> this 'war' would be like no other ... fought on a variety of fronts ... the front lines will look different from the wars of the past ... it is a war that will require the United States to use our influence in a variety of areas in order to win it.[16]

America's latest 2006 *National Strategy for Combating Terrorism* reiterated the point that the 'War on Terror is a different kind of war'.[17] To his credit, Bush had stressed right from the word go that the war on terror would be waged and prosecuted on many fronts, often without the visible titanic military battles reminiscent of 'old wars'. The president's address to the Joint Session of Congress on 20 September 2001 made clear that some actions would of course include dramatic military strikes but other policies would be less publicised, 'secret even in success'. Not everything that was going on would be shown on TV, or even necessarily entail the dramatic use of military force. The 2003 *National Strategy for Combating Terrorism* hammered home this point: 'we will not triumph solely or even primarily through military might. We must fight terrorist networks ... using every instrument of national power – diplomatic, economic, law enforcement, financial, information, intelligence, and military.'[18] The strategy also emphasised the need for a multilateral approach, noting that denying terrorist organisations sponsorship and sanctuary required working with willing and able states, enabling weak states, persuading reluctant states and compelling unwilling states.[19]

Despite presidential reminders of their importance, these non-military dimensions have neither caught the public eye nor imagination. The reason for this above all lies mainly in the administration's widely derided use of the word 'war' in the first instance, conjuring up public expectations of military force and titanic battles.[20] In 2005, even America's top military officer, General Dick Myers, then chairman of the Joint Chiefs of Staff, resisted using the phrase 'war' because 'if you call it a war, then you think of people in uniform as being the solution' when in truth 'it is more diplomatic, more economic, more political than it is military'.[21] While the pros and cons of uttering the 'war' word constitutes in itself a much deeper debate that we shall not go into, the administration did unveil a new and controversial Bush Doctrine on preventive war, and literally put that doctrine into practice by invading Afghanistan and Iraq: significant events that naturally elicit the attention of international relations scholars.[22] But, now that the pitfalls of relying on military force have been highlighted so drastically in Iraq as well as the continued instability in post-Taliban Afghanistan, it seems more appropriate than ever perhaps to examine some less-noticed alternative means and non-kinetic (to use the Pentagon's jargon) strategies employed in the war on terror. After all, the US 2006 *Quadrennial Defence Review* and the *National Military Strategic Plan for the War on Terrorism* both stress that transnational terrorists 'cannot be defeated solely through military force'.[23] But, as

Jonathan Stevenson has convincingly pointed out, the *Quadrennial Defence Review* still seems to retain an 'implicit faith' and 'indulges this temptation' in military power, especially in designating special operations forces as the primary counter-terrorist instrument:

> although the Pentagon does recognise the non-military imperatives of the counter-terrorism effort, it still appears inclined to believe that the application of military power – albeit unconventional military power – will ultimately dictate victory ... such an attitude could lead to the downplaying of paramount non-military aspects of counter-terrorism to the detriment of national and international security.[24]

As Stevenson suggests, we really do need to focus on 'demilitarising the war on terror'. Stevenson prescribes placing a premium on 'infiltration and information – that is intelligence and law enforcement countering the jihadist message of victimisation, rather than on military war-fighting capabilities'. He further recommends that 'US defence posture should expressly subordinate military measures to diplomacy and civilian law enforcement and intelligence.'[25] As a result, State Department activities such as public diplomacy and psychological operations would take the lead. We expand Stevenson's argument further by exploring how multilateral cooperative initiatives and even non-state private actors such as global industry organisations might have a useful counter-terrorism role to play as well. Our purpose therefore is to move away from what Stevenson labelled 'the military temptation', by examining more cooperative multilateral 'soft' initiatives against global terror that have emerged, tracing their implementation and reflecting on the implications for international relations (IR) theory and global politics. Special operations forces such as the Green Berets who often refer to themselves as 'quiet professionals' actually have got the general approach to counter-terrorism and the big picture right: quiet actions sometimes do have a greater impact than visible bombs and air strikes. However, special operations forces still tend to 'militarise' the war on terror, albeit in a more quiet way. Truly non-military 'quiet' counter-terrorism strategies that emphasise steady patient cooperation over direct kinetic action deserve more attention in their own right. Indeed, recent discussions seem to be moving in this direction with talk of Morocco's own 'Gentle War on Terror' or the 'Quiet War on Terror' being waged by the US in the Horn of Africa.[26] The time is ripe for an in-depth evaluation of this 'other' war on terror. As US Homeland Security czar Michael Chertoff observed:

> our ultimate goal is a time when security measures are a comfortable, convenient part of our routine; a time when people go about their daily lives mindful of risks but not encumbered by fear, unwavering in their resolve and full participants in their own protection.[27]

This is especially so when scholars working in IPE are now suggesting that we should adopt a bottom-up perspective as 'our everyday actions shape and transform the world economy'; and not just powerful states and multinational corporations. Small-scale local actors and everyday people too have agency in shaping their political and economic environments.[28] Similarly, our goal here is also to suggest that the 'other' war on terror too has its 'everyday' dimensions that equally shape political and strategic environments.

The notion of 'pre-emptive security' too plays a role not just in relation to the Iraq war, 'but manifests itself in everyday life through controversial policy measures, including pre-emptive arrest, monitoring library records, the analysis of telephone and other communications data, border control, and the mining of financial data for suspicious transactions.'[29]

It should be sufficiently clear by now that we desire to steer existing academic discussions on the war on terror away from the somewhat militaristic and negative tinge it has unfortunately acquired so far and position it within emerging debates in the US foreign policy community on global governance as the way forward for America's role in the world. The third and final related development we wish to address involves the increasing prominence of risk in attempts to conceptualise the war on terror, both by academics and policy makers. Risk, after all, has been suggested by the *New Scientist*, as one of the 'World's 10 Biggest Ideas'.[30] John Adams suggests that 'God and bad luck have been banished. Large armies are employed in the production of risk assessments, whose purpose is the identification and avoidance of all conceivable sources of misfortune.'[31] One of these of course is terrorism. As the UK's 2006 counterterrorism strategy recognises, 'the aim is to reduce the risk from international terrorism, so that people can go about their daily lives freely and with confidence'.[32] The UK 2008 National Security Strategy too announced the establishment of a *National Risk Register*, which assesses the 'likelihood and impact of a range of different risks that might directly affect the UK'.[33] This indicates the importance of risk as a concept in the forefront of official thinking about security today, but also as the UK *National Security Strategy* stresses with its subtitle 'security in an interdependent world'.[34] Faced with globalisation, the sociologist Ulrich Beck has also described global terror, together with ecological conflict and financial crises, as one of the three pillars underpinning his 'World Risk Society'.[35] Therefore, in terms of the overarching theoretical framework underpinning this book, we see ourselves located within a fast-growing body of recent literature on risk, global governance and security, particularly its implications for understanding the global war on terror. Since 9/11, an eclectic body of literature has recognised the timely relevance of risk in multiple fields. These range from biopolitics, criminology and surveillance studies, dataveillance and governance, the use of risk profiling technologies such as biometrics, global health and Foucauldian accounts of governmentality, to name but a few.[36] Others focused on military strategy, security and war.[37] While scholars, such as Amoore and de Goede for instance, have found that new techniques of data mining constitute a new system of 'risk governing',[38] relatively less attention has been lavished on the notion proposed by other risk scholars including Ulrich Beck and Anthony Giddens that global governance and cooperation might in itself help serve as a global risk management strategy in the war on terror. To the extent that cooperative non-military strategies to manage global terrorism risks have been studied by Cortwright and Lopez who fill the gap to some degree, these have not yet been assessed in light of a theoretical framework informed by Beck and risk studies. In this book, therefore, we argue for shifting the emphasis of academic attention more broadly towards a critical assessment of the potential benefits and pitfalls in deploying cooperative multilevel global governance as a strategy to managing global terrorism risks. One might justifiably call such attempts 'global risk governance'.[39] After all, if one agrees with Michael Power that 'the risk management of everything holds out the promise of manageability in new areas',[40] why not also consider the theoretical and empirical implications of attempts to manage global systemic risks such as terrorism by way of global governance? To do so, we adopt an interdisciplinary analytical approach that explores and builds on theoretical synergies that might exist between risk studies and more established mainstream IR theories on global governance and security. As a result, it is hoped this book is able to uncover the overlapping multilevel and multilateral dynamics of the emerging global risk governance architecture that have remained relatively unmapped thus far in the 'other' war on terror.

Yet, one does not usually automatically equate global governance with orthodox counter-terrorism strategies: so what is the relationship between the two? How might a broadly conceived global governance approach described above differ from orthodox forms of counter-terrorism and how it might serve useful functions as global risk management? Counter-terrorism involves political, military, diplomatic, financial, intelligence and police tools of statecraft in response to terrorist acts or threats. It is designed to deny terrorists successful use of the terrorist tactic. In our case, we are concerned with strategies adopted in response to 9/11 and the desire to avoid a repetition. Counter-terrorism can be broad-ranging and multifaceted: addressing root causes, prevention and preparedness and strengthening the international framework for multilateral action. In America, 'the paradigm for combating terrorism now involves the application of all elements of our national power and influence'.[41] The four principal strands of the UK 2006 counter-terrorism strategy are as follows:

1   preventing terrorism by tackling the radicalisation of individuals,
2   pursuing terrorists and those that sponsor them,
3   protecting the public, key national services and UK interests overseas,
4   preparing for the consequences.[42]

Similarly, the US 2006 *National Strategy for Combating Terrorism* stresses priorities of action, among which include preventing attacks by attacking terrorists and degrading their capacity to operate and deny weapons of mass destruction (WMD) to terrorists and safe havens of any sort.[43] These various priorities and strands of national counter-terrorist strategies are then translated into action and made practicable in different ways. For example, the second strand of the UK's strategy mentioned above emphasises gathering intelligence, disrupting terrorist activity through various means and international cooperation, to strengthen intelligence gathering and terrorist disruption. Translated into action, the most visible to the public eye of course would be dramatic police swoops by masked elite counter-terrorist units on terrorist safe houses to break up secret cells, for instance those in Bradford or North London. Even more eye-catching would be the 2003 deployment of tanks at Heathrow Airport, or air strikes and the use of ground troops to eliminate terrorist safe havens in places like Afghanistan or Iraq. Or one might point out the stepped-up security at airports with machine-gun-toting police officers to prevent and deter possible attacks. These are just some of the images we have in mind when we think of counter-terrorism strategies. In fact, the 2006 US *National Strategy for Combating Terrorism* argues that 'we have broken old orthodoxies that once confined our counterterrorism efforts primarily to the criminal justice domain'.[44] For instance, the law enforcement/criminal justice approach emphasised a fundamentally reactive approach to counter-terrorism. That is to say, law enforcement and investigative efforts were usually engaged only after a terrorist act had been committed. It was essentially a law enforcement matter for the courts where terrorists or their state sponsors are retaliated against retrospectively *after* they committed terrorism. It was retrospective in the sense of dealing with the aftermath: the goal was to arrest and bring terrorists to justice and to be tried and convicted in a court of law. Critics complain that this usually only nets the low-level operatives while leaving the masterminds alone. This paradigm also views terrorism more as a criminal act, rather than an act of war. The events of 9/11 seem to have changed all that, not least through the use of the word 'war' on terror. The legislation put in place afterwards, particularly the USA Patriot Act, represents a 'radical shift from the policy of "consequence management" in dealing with the terrorist threat. The law, in short, is proactive and attempts to prevent acts of aggression before they materialise.'[45]

However, while the criminal justice paradigm has by no means been completely displaced, counter-terrorism in truth now spans a much wider range of activity and, we argue, a global governance perspective is also able to encapsulate these myriad activities. While multilateral cooperation has always been a key part of counter-terrorism in terms of intelligence sharing or freezing of terrorist assets, a global governance perspective emphasises taking a more broad-ranging and multilevel approach. In doing so, it is more sensitive and attuned to the increasingly diverse range of actors and activities involved, involving states, regional organisations, transnational NGOs and private firms to global businesses. These all now come together in a hodgepodge of activities at various levels to regulate terrorism. What we are interested in is how such processes emerge, their basis for cooperation and how these initiatives serve counter-terrorism functions. Such an approach is never going realistically to compete with air strikes or police raids for news headlines. Indeed, it is far from the seemingly heavy-handed Orwellian imagery conjured up above. One result is often 'routinised' low-key initiatives that are more or less incrementally integrated into our everyday routines. Indeed, one might argue that such 'everyday' dimensions and implications of the war on terror deserve more academic attention. Take, for instance, passing through airport security scanners and the restrictions on liquids. Or having your data taken each time your credit card is swiped. Subcontracted out to private security companies, these processes have also become part of the counter-terrorism repertoire. Similarly, each time we go to our high street banks and send money overseas, we are regulated by a set of global risk-based standards designed to reduce the risks of terrorist financing. As we will show, such private actors have an increasingly important part to play in a more inclusive notion of global governance and counter-terrorism.

Thinking about the 'other' war on terror

At 08:46:40, American Airlines Flight 11 crashed into the North Tower of the World Trade Center (WTC) in New York City. Approximately 17 minutes later, a second aircraft, United Airlines Flight 175, crashed into the South Tower. A third aircraft, American Airlines Flight 77, crashed into the Pentagon, Washington DC, just over half an hour later. The fourth and final aircraft, United Airlines Flight 93, came down in a field in Shanksville, Pennsylvania, apparently as a result of passenger intervention in the hijacking at 10:02:23. At 09:59 the South Tower of the WTC collapsed, followed by the North Tower just under half an hour later. A total of 2973 were killed in New York, Washington and Pennsylvania on the morning of 11 September 2001,[46] a day that would enter the political lexicon as 9/11.[47] However, there is a degree of uncertainty as to what extent the events of 9/11 constituted an act of war at least in any conventional sense. Indeed President Bush's initial response indicated the degree of this uncertainty. At about 09:30, the president addressed the nation for the first time, speaking from the elementary school where he had been engaged in a photo opportunity with school children to promote his child literacy programme. The address took place after the towers had been struck but before the Pentagon had been hit and before either tower had collapsed. In the statement President Bush called on the Federal Bureau of Investigation (FBI) to conduct 'a full-scale investigation to hunt down and to find those folks who committed this act'.[48] At this stage at least it appeared that the attacks were to be treated as a criminal act requiring law enforcement and not as an act of war mandating a military response. However by evening this had shifted, though specific mention of the attacks being an act of war was left out in order to avoid unnerving the American people.[49] Bush was later to claim that as soon as he had been told that the second tower had been hit he knew he was at war.[50] But what form was such a war likely to take? Have IR scholars paid sufficient analytical attention to the drastically different nature and shape that this 'war on terror' was to take and has taken since then?

Although for many the first visible steps of the war on terror came on 7 October, when US-led forces began bombing raids against Taliban and Al Qaeda targets in Afghanistan, in fact the first blow had come earlier. Two weeks earlier on 24 September 2001, President George W. Bush announced what he termed 'a major thrust of our war on terrorism'.[51] Executive Order 13224 on freezing terrorist financing was touted as the first major step, to be pursued with equal vigour and publicity as the military initiatives, which at that time, one should add, had not yet publicly commenced.

The importance of these non-military aspects of the campaign should not be underestimated; indeed by some accounts the financial front has emerged as one of the most crucial and successful in the war on terror.[52] Additionally, the ongoing difficulties in Afghanistan and Iraq serve as a reminder that unilateral military force alone is woefully inadequate in controlling globalised terrorism. As a result, alternative multilateral approaches might come increasingly to the fore to be considered. Multilevel cooperative and regulatory measures such as those entailed in curtailing terrorist financing thus seem to offer a suitable complement to, rather than a replacement for, the military means adopted so far. These and other similar less noticeable initiatives are important in that they potentially provide a plausible multilevel global governance framework for managing the complex transnational nature of global terrorism today.

Rather than being focused and predicated only on a single military strand, the global war on terror has in actual fact manifested itself in a number of non-military, multilateral, multilevel strategies. For instance, in relation to the reform of everyday banking practices to curtail terrorist financing and attempts at global harmonisation of aviation security standards, the US and other governments engaged in the fight against Al Qaeda have actually been rather resourceful in seeking out diverse approaches to managing the problems of counter-terrorism, often in cooperation with an array of non-state actors. Furthermore, we suggest that these lower profile 'routinised' strands of the war on terror, which do not capture headlines, are likely to have more profound and long-lasting impact on IR in the future, challenging as they do traditional concepts of sovereignty, power and the state. This book is therefore an attempt to refocus the gaze of IR theory on these practices in prosecuting the war on terror. We next provide some background to the issues and cases we will address, highlighting the questions and puzzles that concern us. We then turn to discuss how emerging theoretical perspectives in risk studies and developments in global governance theory might prove to be potentially complementary tools in answering the questions we raise. By way of squaring the theoretical circle, we then take one further crucial additional step that both risk scholars and global governance theorists have left mostly unaddressed: how might global governance actually work in practice to manage risks? We argue that once translated into practice, global governance initiatives in the war on terror also reflect key risk management strategies and characteristics such as reducing vulnerabilities and re-engineering of terrorist operating environments. The final part of this chapter then supplies a brief outline of the structure of the book as a whole, drawing a conceptual roadmap to where we are going, and how we intend to arrive there.

Less-noticed dimensions of the 'other' war on terror

As we shall demonstrate here, apart from military campaigns, the war on terror has also witnessed several multilateral cooperative attempts at overlapping levels – from global to regional, formal to informal, public to private – all in order to regulate terrorism in its various guises. Three main issues concern us in this 'other' war on terror: the campaign against terrorist financing by the Financial Action Task Force (FATF), the ad hoc US-led informal 'coalition of the willing' in the Proliferation Security Initiative (PSI) and the cooperation of state and private sector actors in issues relating to aviation security. These cases were selected with a common set of criteria in mind: they demonstrated a flexible mix of less-noticed initiatives to manage global terrorism that emerged at different levels of analysis with a range of actors (state and non-state, public and private) operating with varying degrees of formality. These case studies also reflect the 2006 *United Nations Global Counter-terrorism Strategy*'s new initiatives calling for 'involving civil society, regional and sub-regional organizations in the fight against terrorism and developing partnerships with the private sector to prevent terrorist attacks'.[53] While we recognise the UN remains a central actor in global governance, we are more interested in initiatives that develop outside the more formalistic UN framework. In terms of theory, these cases also appear, at least ostensibly at face value, to be quite close to what both Talbot and Beck would recognise from their broader conceptions of multilayered governance and cooperation. Furthermore, these cases also illustrate the complexity of counter-terrorism today by highlighting a selection of the various issue areas and dimensions in which concerns about terrorism are able to manifest, from terrorist finances to WMD proliferation and airline security. Above all, what interests us is how and to what extent these initiatives, taken together, can be viewed as a nascent risk-based platform for global risk governance of systemic risks such as terrorism that an individual actor alone cannot manage. The selection of case studies is also designed to reflect the various ways and means in which cooperation can help. As the US 2006 *National Strategy for Combating Terrorism* put it:

> We will ensure that such international cooperation is an enduring feature of the long war we will fight. We will continue to leverage the comparative advantage of these institutions and organizations – drawing on what each does best in counterterrorism, from setting standards to developing regional strategies to providing forums for training and education.[54]

To begin with setting standards, according to Daniel Benjamin, the financial front has been 'the most successful part' of the war on terror so far.[55] Yet, where scholars have attempted to examine these cooperative multilateral dimensions, they have mostly confined themselves to regulatory or legal loopholes in specific issues.[56] A broader theoretical approach remains to be undertaken, examining the implications for questions of global governance, global security and the overall attempt at managing risks. Yet this financial 'war' has been overshadowed by public and media fixation on military force, although academics have admittedly been quicker to focus their attention on it. When Donald Rumsfeld spoke of the mission determining the coalition, this was usually assumed to refer to cooperation among states in military and defence issues. However, the aftermath of 9/11 has also witnessed 'the creation not only of international military and political coalitions but of a global financial coalition as well'.[57]

One such coalition was the Financial Action Task Force (FATF) established by the then-G7 summit in Paris in 1989 to tackle criminal money laundering, particularly in the drug trade. After 9/11, its mandate was extended to terrorist financing, as the money trail behind the atrocities highlighted the vulnerabilities of the international banking system. What is even more interesting is how thinking in terms of risk has been incorporated and institutionalised into the FATF. For instance its 40+9 Framework is essentially a risk-based approach representing the benchmark gold standard of global best practices that states and financial actors should implement to reduce their risks of exposure to terrorist financing. Yet the term 'task force' implies that it is informal, flexible and finite, and not a permanent 'international organisation' with associated bureaucracy and formal treaty mandate. This was part of its appeal.

While there are certainly questions being raised about its efficacy and implementation problems, the FATF is interesting to us in that it appears to reflect an overlapping and interlinked global counter-terrorist architecture being assembled at multiple levels. In cooperation with states and with significant input from non-state actors such as NGOs, global businesses and international banking consortiums, the FATF can be viewed as cooperative attempts with one goal in mind: to manage shared global risks through universal standards-setting and capacity-building.[58]

The Proliferation Security Initiative (PSI) represents yet another piece in the multilateral jigsaw being put in place and assembled for waging the war on terror. This time, the comparative advantage of cooperation lies in not just standards-setting but also joint platforms for training and education including expanding partnership capacity. As the UN *Global Strategy for Combating Terrorism* recognises, 'capacity-building in all States is a core element of the global counter-terrorism effort to prevent and combat terrorism and crimes that may be connected with terrorism, including the smuggling of WMD materials'.[59] Indeed, contrary to popular assumptions about US unilateralism, the US-led war on terror thus far has in truth relied, to a large degree, on a variety of multilateral counter-proliferation mechanisms such as the PSI. In 2002, President Bush approved the *National Strategy to Combat Weapons of Mass Destruction*, which outlined a comprehensive approach for combating the world's most dangerous weapons. The strategy set forth three pillars – non-proliferation, counterproliferation, and consequence management – and emphasised the importance of international cooperation, along with intelligence, research and development and targeted strategies to securing our future. The strategy also stated:

> One of the most difficult challenges we face is to prevent, deter, and defend against the acquisition and use of WMD by terrorist groups. The full range of counterproliferation, nonproliferation, and consequence management measures must be brought to bear against the WMD terrorist threat, just as they are against states of greatest proliferation concern.[60]

The PSI is one such attempt at counter-proliferation and mitigating the risks, and basically reflects the strategy's claim that 'we will also promote new agreements and arrangements that serve our non-proliferation goals'.[61] It was first announced by President George Bush on 31 May 2003, basically aiming to stop, interdict and prevent shipments of WMD and relevant parts worldwide. Some authors considered it to be a direct reaction of the American government to the interdiction of a North Korean ship (*So San*) transporting Scud missiles to Yemen. Despite stopping the ship it was eventually allowed to continue its journey since there was no international legal authority to seize its cargo.[62] In order to avoid similar occurrences, Undersecretary of State for Arms Control and International Security John Bolton was asked to lead a multilateral response. The result was the PSI. However, in utilising this somewhat different type of informal 'coalition of the willing', the PSI is designed to allow the maximisation of cooperation and flexibility for the minimum of costs. Admittedly, the original founding rationale for the PSI was to stem the flow of WMD-related material to rogue states like North Korea and Iran. However, it has also been accorded a substantial role in the war on terror as part of overall efforts to reduce the risks of terrorists obtaining access to WMD materials. In December 2008, the *World at Risk* report by the commission on the Prevention of WMD Proliferation and Terrorism called for the PSI to be expanded as part of the global effort to prevent WMD-material falling into terrorist hands. As National Security Advisor Stephen Hadley points out:

> In today's world, nation-states are not the only proliferation risk we face – for non-state actors are active on both ends of the supply chain.... On the consumer end of the supply chain, we see global terrorist organizations actively seeking WMD.[63]

Indeed, the US 2006 *National Strategy for Combating Terrorism* identified the denial of WMD to rogue states and terrorist allies as one of four key priorities for action:

> Weapons of mass destruction in the hands of terrorists is one of the gravest threats we face. We have taken aggressive efforts to deny terrorists access to WMD-related materials, equipment, and expertise, but we will enhance these activities through an integrated effort at all levels of government and with the private sector and our foreign partners to stay ahead of this dynamic and evolving threat.

We selected the PSI for our purposes because it represents yet another dimension and manifestation of the wide spectrum and range of cooperative global governance efforts against terrorism, this time in terms of reducing the risks of terrorists obtaining WMD materials. Furthermore, there is clear recognition among the US government and states involved that the risks in question transcend national geographical borders, which in turn require new forms of cross-border cooperation and management, including enlisting the help of the private sector. Interesting comparisons can also be made with the earlier case of the FATF, not just in terms of how they emphasise engagement with private non-state actors but also in terms of the degree of formality. Although the FATF is not a formal treaty-based organisation with physical presence, the FATF 40+9 Framework and associated mutual evaluation processes are somewhat more formalised and institutionalised: it even assumes the trappings of quasi-legality with UN Security Council backing and endorsement through Resolution 1617 in 2005 that 'strongly urges all member states to implement the comprehensive international standards' contained in FATF recommendations.

What is even more striking about the PSI is how it operates on an even more informal, ad hoc, voluntary and loosely organised basis. Much like the FATF, the PSI does not have a formal treaty mandate, permanent physical organisation, nor does it pass binding legislation or rules. But that is as far as the similarities go. Instead of the FATF's more formalistic 40+9 Framework, the PSI simply contains four relatively loose 'principles' that members sign up to voluntarily, which prescribe specific policies to be taken. Unlike the FATF, there are no mutual evaluation processes or public reports. Instead, the PSI is much more action oriented, and involves regular training and interdiction exercises between member states and meetings of experts.

The final case we examine in this book is the issue of aviation security. It serves to the extent of private sector involvement, both independently and as part of public–private partnerships, in the war on terror, particularly in areas traditionally the preserve of the state alone. The overlapping multilevel global aviation architecture emerging to combat terrorism now ranges from the global and international, right down to the private corporate level in order to manage risks. This case study is particularly designed to highlight the fact that the managing of global transnational security risks now needs to be extended beyond merely states alone to incorporate a range of non-state actors, public or private, at global, transnational, national and subnational levels. Most visibly, of course, we know about private contractors and their increasing presence in the war on terror. In Iraq in 2003–04, $750 million was spent on private military contractors (PMCs). By some accounts, death rates have topped 1000, which means that the casualty rates are about a quarter of American military rates. Yet 'this silent surge in contractor armies' has not garnered as much public attention.[64] And that is only at the extreme end of the more visible involvement of private contractors in the wider network of providing global security governance. In line with our broader cooperative approach, our discussion of private actors is limited to their involvement in the 'quieter' aspects of the war on terror, notably aviation security. For the majority of people, contact with this non-state mechanism of governance occurs on a routine basis when passing through airports where airline security, restrictions on liquids and baggage screening is contracted out to private security personnel. It also occurs almost invisibly in the form of data mining activities before citizens even get to the airports. As we will explore later, the design and delivery both of information technologies and the acquisition of the intelligence that guides them is increasingly in the hands of private actors. At the same time, somewhat similar to the FATF, there are multilevel cooperative attempts at global standards-setting. Airport security standards based on a new consensus about global aviation risks are being agreed and established at the national, regional and international level both by 'formal' international organisations like the International Civil Aviation Organisation (ICAO) and the private global trade body International Air Transport Association (IATA). Both ICAO and IATA also help in capacity-building, to assist partners meet these new risk-based standards in order to mitigate the risks posed to aviation security.

Indeed, the cases we select in this book are intended to highlight the fact that the front lines of the 'other' war on terror have now become amorphous and increasingly blurred; these now stretch to cover a wide range of our otherwise 'routine' everyday activities, from financial transactions at our local high street banks and going through airport security, not just the deserts of Iraq or the interdiction of WMD materials on the high seas.

Globalisation, risk and security governance: towards a theoretical synthesis

Mindful of the examples outlined above and associated questions they raise, this book sets out to examine how various strands and developments in IR theory can come together in understanding and explaining these developments. Since the end of the Cold War, IR theory has experienced something of an interregnum in terms of theoretical hegemony, not least within the subfield of security studies where, as Baldwin notes, 'redefining security has become something of a cottage industry'.[65] But what exactly was the nature of this redefinition and what effect does it have on our understanding of security generally, and conceptualising the war on terror in particular? Rothschild suggests that the substantive effect of the redefinition of security in the 1990s is that of 'security in an "extended" sense'.[66] This extension occurs in a number of ways and in a number of directions. First, it is extended downwards from a concern with the security of states to a concern with the security of individuals.[67] Second, it is extended upwards to the security of the global system, from the nation to the biosphere. Third, security is extended horizontally, in that the number of issues that can properly be considered 'security' issues is extended. The first two extensions involve a redefinition of what it is that is to be secured, the third relates to the sorts of security in question. Thus new security items are added to the agenda – political, economic, social, environmental etc. Finally, the responsibility for the provision of security is diffused in a number of directions – upwards towards international organisations, downwards towards regional and local government, sideways to NGOs, to public opinion, the media and the press.[68] The challenge for global security studies is how to deal with this extension of the definition of security in a theoretically consistent and useful manner. A number of attempts to do so have so far been made: balance of power theory, security regimes, security communities, security governance and, most notably for our purposes, risk.[69]

Particularly in the early period after the end of the Cold War, balance of power theory was mobilised to analyse and predict the shape of international relations to come. Mearsheimer for one argued that the likeliest consequence of the end of a bipolar world order would be a return of instability and interstate competition: 'If the Cold War is truly behind us, the stability of the past 45 years is not likely to be seen again in the coming decades.'[70] However, the failure of significant counter-balancing behaviour by the Great Powers to emerge in subsequent years has led other security studies academics to look elsewhere for explanations of the dynamics of global security in the twenty-first century.[71] Two competing but not necessarily incompatible approaches are 'security regimes', as developed by Jervis, Krasner and Snyder among others, working from a broadly realist perspective, and 'security communities' from a more constructivist perspective. The main difference between both approaches centres on the relative importance of identity and communication versus more materialist causal forces.[72] The debate between the relative contribution of the material or ideational to the existence of security regimes/communities need not detain us here, as it has been noted in relation to similar debates in another field that such discussions are akin to debating whether the length or the width contributes more to the area of a rectangle.[73] However, Krahmann argues that although the above approaches are more effective than balance of power theory in explaining the changes in the trans-Atlantic security system after the Cold War, there are a number of key features that they cannot effectively explain:

1 new institutions that have been created to deal with specific security needs e.g. the Visegrad 9;
2 the fluid and flexible nature of the issues dealt with by these new arrangements;
3 the emergence of shifting ad hoc coalitions even within existing organisations such as the Combined Joint Task Forces in NATO;
4 the increasing involvement and reliance upon private actors in dealing with and delivering security.[74]

In other words, Krahmann was asking how should we best explain and understand the emergence of the overlapping and interlinked formal, semi-formal and informal security arrangements today.

Furthermore, the shifting terrain in security studies can be linked with broader discussions on the nature of international relations in the late twentieth and early twenty-first centuries. One of the key developments in this period is the increasing challenge to the image of international relations as concerning simply the relationships between sovereign, separate and independent units called states. In other words, that:

> whereas men within each state are subject to a common government, sovereign states in their mutual relations are not. This anarchy it is possible to regard as the central fact of international life and the starting-point of theorising about it.[75]

Clearly such a view would restrict the possibilities for IR theory; the notion of 'sovereign states' would restrict discussion of the international by and large to the established Western states. It would be fruitless to attempt to shoehorn the fragmented sovereignties of the Balkans or Sub-Saharan Africa into this world view. Furthermore, even in the case of relatively stable and established states the notion that they are somehow completely self-contained sovereign, unitary and independent actors is questionable. The growth both of international intergovernmental organisations and of non-state entities from Amnesty to Al Qaeda has undermined the position previously accorded to states in the discussion of the international. This growth of 'supra-territorial' space in the realm of what has until now been known as the international is often described as the process of globalisation. Scholte, for example, characterises the process of globalisation as the 'transcendence (rather than the mere crossing or opening) of borders'.[76] This growth of non-state transnational space has eroded the previously held dichotomy of the domestic and the international that marked the approach and boundaries of traditional IR theory. Globalisation therefore calls for a more open ended and flexible definition of actors in the 'global' than the traditional conception of territorially distinct sovereign states in 'a state of nature' and anarchy.

In response to this challenge, the sociologist Ulrich Beck has inspired a range of authors working to adapt his influential World Risk Society thesis to the study of IR, in particular the changing nature of military strategy and security in such a globalised world. Beck argued that the Hobbesian 'state of nature' needs to be redefined in order to accommodate the radical transformation of the nature of global politics in the late twentieth century:

> Globalization ... has introduced a new space and framework for acting: politics is no longer subject to the same boundaries as before, and it is no longer tied solely to state actors and institutions, the result being that additional players, new roles, new resources, unfamiliar rules and new contradictions and conflicts appear on the scene.[77]

The globalisation of risks and the need to manage properly and regulate risk is highlighted dramatically in the US sub-prime crisis that has spread worldwide and roiled global financial markets in late 2008. Chairman of the US Senate Banking Committee Chris Dodd described this crisis as 'entirely both foreseeable and preventable. This was no act of God; it was no Hurricane Ike. It was created by a combustible combination of private greed and public regulatory neglect.'[78] The implication is clearly that had better governance and standards been put in place, the economic crisis (one pillar of Beck's World Risk Society) could have been averted: the basic premise of risk management that similarly applies to global terrorism as well (the other pillar of global risk).

Beck's proposal of a transnational 'cosmopolitan manifesto' to address global risks is based on the fundamental assumption that global risks create 'risk communities' where people come together to negotiate and manage risks. Beck suggests this was the last bond 'in a world where God, nations and historical purpose are increasingly disavowed'.[79] At this point, it is worth clarifying and stressing here that such a stance does not involve the denial, rejection or even the much-heralded demise of the state as a salient actor, but rather that its role and challenges should not be taken for granted but instead empirically mapped. Beck argues that not only has the nature of global politics and actors been transformed but also that of the nature of threats. In a globalised world, humanity faces globalised threats that undercut the ability of the self-contained nation state to perform the duty of a Leviathan and provide security. As a result, the globality of risks 'melts down the seemingly cast-iron system of international and national politics and makes it open to change, at least for one historic moment in time'.[80] What form such change takes, however, is not predetermined. While Beck argues that a cosmopolitan order must emerge, others have been less optimistic.

Aradau and Van Munster have recently questioned Beck's assertion that expert knowledge will come to the fore and argue that in fact governance in a risk society becomes one of governance of decision. In the absence of either accepted expert knowledge or the time/space to wait for such knowledge, political actors operate to reduce risk based on instinctive rapid responses. As a result democratic oversight and deliberation are sacrificed to the politics of action in the war on terror.[81] Other scholars such as Rasmussen, Coker and Heng have employed Beck's insights to examine the implications for military strategy and the transformation of NATO in the war on terror. They argue that a risk framework utilised in this way, allows us to make sense of ideas such as 'unknown unknowns' and the Precautionary Principle in understanding the rationales and recourse to military force and war in the age of terror. These reflect the increasing prominence of the language and vocabulary of risk in international security.[82]

What we can take from these discussions on risk though is the problematisation of the arbitrary distinction between inside and outside, domestic and international in a world of globalised risks. We will return in depth to these discussions on risk in Chapter 2. For the moment, we suggest that in order to take the debate on risk and security forward, what needs to be explored in greater detail is how synergies can be found to exist between the increasingly lively academic debate on risk, and more established mainstream discussions on approaches to global governance. Jarvis and Griffith find it strange 'that IR as a discipline grapples with one of the most recurrent structural risks, the problem of war and the management of power' and yet IR still is not 'at the forefront of research and theory development into risk and risk studies'.[83]

Partially in response to the problem of dealing with overlapping and interlinked institutions and initiatives, the governance approach has developed on two levels: domestic and international. At the domestic level, the governance literature largely addresses what has been termed the 'hollowing out of the state', that is the increasing delegation of and/or privatisation of functions previously the sole domain of the government.[84] At the international level, despite discussions of the implications of governance for security studies[85] much of the literature on global governance has focused on economic and development issues.[86] One notable attempt to link governance and security through a development lens is Mark Duffield's *Global Governance and the New Wars: The Merging of Development and Security*. Duffield addresses the shifting terrain of humanitarian assistance and liberal war in the post-Cold War period. He argues that a new mode of liberal global governance has emerged that has redefined the concept of development and linked it in direct consequentalist terms to the expanding definition of security. Caroline Thomas similarly examines the linkages between global governance, development, human security and poverty.[87] As a result, development issues have become intrinsically linked to issues of security and stability, particularly the idea of human security as an alternative to state-based conceptualisations of security. Maclean *et al.* for instance examine the implications of human security for global governance and new forms of multilateralism.[88] The interlinking of private, public, governmental and international organisations in this complex system of governance is highlighted. Our purpose here is not just to draw on these themes, but widening the scope to look at how these overlapping systems of governance affect the war on terror. Indeed, a flexible and broad-ranging understanding of global governance and its fluidity is adopted throughout this book. As James Rosenau insists, there exists a continuum or a range of possible global governance arrangements that can manifest in different overlapping forms. These can exist between the transnational and the subnational, the informal and the institutionalised; the state-centric and the multi-centric. The state is simply one element of global governance.[89] Others can include transnational coalitions of social elite forces, such as key business, intellectual and political elites in the G8 zone.

The approach we adopt in this book therefore not only accepts but extends this prevailing set of assumptions about global governance into global security issues. As we have already seen above, in the 1990s within development studies and security studies, a number of research programmes began to take shape. In the former the literature increasingly became concerned with the decentring of the state, the growth of global governance and the privatisation of development, while in the latter a number of different approaches emerged, notably that of risk and security studies concerned with the growth of non-traditional threats, the broadening of the security agenda to include such issues as health and the environment. Despite the possibility of potential synergies existing between the two strands of literature, few works have attempted to draw these perspectives closer together. While the concept of governance has gained ground in the comparative and development literature, it remains relatively under-examined in risk and security studies. On the other hand, the debate on risk has concerned itself with an eclectic range of topics, but has so far not yet seriously engaged with global governance, which ironically seems to be exactly what Beck thinks would help the West win the war on terror. This book therefore aims to map out the implications of taking a global governance perspective to managing security risks in the war on terror. To do so, it first develops a theoretical approach derived from exploring the grounds for potential synergies in the existing global governance, risk and risk management literature. Through a series of case studies, we then test this framework by applying it to the cases we have outlined previously: the

FATF's efforts against terrorist financing, the PSI, the role of private corporate firms in the global war on terror and the intersection of private and public control of airport security. With this theoretical guideline in mind, this book therefore seeks to uncover the various forms of multilevel overlapping global governance strategies unearthed when analysts decentre the state and military force as the locus of examining shifting patterns in the 'other' war on terror. In the process, it asks whether these attempts are driven by a shared collective concern with managing global terrorism risks and how have these cooperative global governance initiatives actually helped in practice to manage the risks of global terrorism. After all, victory was defined in the 2003 US *National Strategy for Combating Terrorism* as the creation of a world in which 'our children can live free from fear and where the threat of terrorist attacks does not define our daily lives'.[90] In operational terms this simply means reducing the scope and capability of terrorist organisations to a point where terrorism is returned to the 'criminal domain', and is in effect unorganised, localised, non-sponsored and rare.[91] These goals seem to hint at a risk management approach, which reduces the risks from terrorism while recognising at the same time that it cannot be completely eliminated. Just as we live with the daily risks of traffic accidents, so too must we adopt the same approach to the risks of terrorism. Homeland Security Secretary Chertoff reminds us that:

> We all live with a certain amount of risk. That means that we tolerate that something bad can happen; we adjust our lives based on probability; and we take reasonable precautions. We all have to live with a certain amount of risk if we don't want to become prisoners in our own homes. When we get into our cars, we take reasonable precautions, but we also go about our lives: We go to work; we drive our children to school; we visit friends. We are managing risk.[92]

Structure

The layout of the book is as follows. In Chapter 2, 'Risk, global governance and security', we propose the theoretical framework we wish to employ. This chapter explores the possible theoretical synergies that might exist between global governance frameworks as suggested by scholars such as Rosenau and Talbott, and those working on risk and security studies, particularly the recent works of Ulrich Beck on the *Cosmopolitan Vision*. These two groups of scholars have worked on similar problems of global security but the linkage between them presently remains limited and underdeveloped. We then move to examine how various approaches to global governance might in fact prove complementary to risk and security studies. In particular, security governance similarly posits the emergence of a complex system of functionally differentiated overlapping networks that involve public and private actors at multiple levels. Hence, we identify and build on existing ideas of a range of authors, such as Elke Krahmann's 'security governance', Renn and Walker's notion of 'global risk governance', to

James Rosenau's notion that governance exists on a broad continuum, from formal to informal cooperative mechanisms. The chapter then concludes by examining practical ways in which these emerging multilevel global security governance frameworks can help manage global terrorism risks. In doing so, we highlight some key benchmark indicators of a risk-based approach, and strategies for risk management such as identifying and reducing vulnerabilities and reshaping operating environments.

Using ideas and concepts we have outlined in Chapter 2 based on Beck's ideas about managing the World Risk Society and from related global governance literature, we then move to discuss in Chapter 3, the multilevel coalitions working against terrorist financing and how the global governance architecture can help to manage risks. We examine in particular the evolution and activities of the relatively 'informal' FATF, and its intersection with global initiatives such as the UN Counter-Terrorism Council (CTC). By examining its flaws, mechanisms and processes, we suggest that despite its numerous downsides, the FATF is also in many ways, an exemplary case of risk-based cooperative multilateral global governance initiatives to reduce terrorism risks. As a risk management strategy, it works to reshape terrorists' global operating environment by raising the bar, adding layers of difficulty and generally making it more difficult and harder for terror networks to obtain and transfer funds. Besides states, global businesses and NGOs have reached a very clear endorsement and utilisation of a shared risk-based approach. These regulatory standards emphasise the identification of risk factors and continuous surveillance to reduce vulnerabilities and likelihoods. Overall, it works on a layered security concept: to add layers of difficulty for terrorist attempts at financing. However, the flip side of the FATF's activities is also indicative of how risk is not a neutral tool of governance despite its claim to be a scienticised mode of analysis. Power relations and powerful actors such as the US and EU still underpin the subjective definition and selection of risks, as well as the regulatory benchmarks recommended. It is often power and coercion rather than voluntary consensus on risk that bring about agreement and compliance. Many negative downsides of FATF regulations also exist, raising questions about the implications of risk management for civil liberties, human rights and questions of inclusion/exclusion.

In Chapter 4, using the same set of concepts drawn from Chapter 2, we assess a rather different case of informal coalitions of the willing: the Proliferation Security Initiative. As with the FATF, the PSI has no formal treaty mandate, but it represents another somewhat different and even looser variant of an informal multilateral perspective concerned with reducing global risks in the war on terror. The PSI adds a further layer of global governance that intersects and overlaps with a variety of other bilateral, multilateral and universal anti-proliferation regimes in order to control security risks. It is a cooperative attempt to harmonise interdiction practices and also disseminate best practices against WMD proliferation worldwide. The PSI also works on capacity-building to help partners manage proliferation risks, by engaging with the private transportation system to help identify 'red flags' and risk factors. More specifically, when construed as a form of global risk management strategy, the PSI works to reduce the likelihood of terrorists obtaining WMD materials, through identifying risk factors, interdiction and reshaping the global risk milieu by constraining terrorists' freedom of movement. Like FATF, the PSI also banks on a layered security system and international cooperation with private actors and state governments to increase difficulties of terrorist proliferation. Once again, however, these cooperative attempts at risk management raise questions about the role of law and international legal implications of such 'informal' governance mechanisms. It also raises concerns and divisions within the international community, rather than generating what Beck might term 'cosmopolitan' consensus on a collective risk.

Global governance theory, when read in conjunction with risk and security studies, reinforces a need for a variety of non-state public and private actors, besides states, to engage with and contribute in the multilevel management of global security risks. We address this issue in the penultimate Chapter 5, by looking at the role of various private non-state actors in global aviation security. Where preceding chapters examine global and international-level efforts led by states, this chapter analyses the other end of the spectrum in multilevel global governance where private trade and industry groups are taking global initiatives. The global airline association IATA, for instance, has played crucial roles in harmonisation of risk-based global aviation security standards, to a larger degree than state-centric ICAO, which faces political obstacles in its activities as we shall see. A variety of airport security functions have already been contracted out to private actors working on risk profiles and risk assessments of passengers and 'risky' individuals before they fly worldwide. There are of course questions to be asked again about the socially constructed and subjective perceptions of aviation security risk, which belie issues of power and stymie attempts at generating a more 'cosmopolitan' global consensus. The combined effect of these new multilevel risk-based initiatives aims to obtain crucial intelligence to supplement official government sources, and once again applying a layered security system to disrupt terrorists' operating environment by generally increasing the number of hoops terrorists have to jump through in order to achieve their goals from their points of origin to arrival. Aviation security has been chosen as the best case to explore these dynamics as it is a site where the global and the local, the public and the private intersect in ways that allow us to explore the dynamics of the interlinking of the public and private management of security risks.

Finally in Chapter 6, we draw together some common threads of the three case studies presented above, and argue that a 'theoretical' framework weaving together insights from risk and global governance theory may prove useful in understanding the medium- to long-term effects of the war on terror. While the impact and perception of risk is of course not uniformly felt across the world, many leading states and a variety of non-state actors are slowly and generally coming around to the 'cosmopolitan' realisation that they share global terrorism risks and need to introduce new transnational overlapping cooperative mechanisms to cope. It highlights a more positive integrative function that can conceivably be served by the global risk society, rather than the dystopian vision of gloom and doom all too often presented by commentators wracked by anxieties, fears, uncertainties and all sorts of worst-case scenarios. By fundamentally altering the global operating environment of terrorists, adding layers of difficulty and chipping away at their operational and planning capability, global governance can generally make it harder for terror cells not only to survive but more crucially, to succeed operationally. That, after all, is the more realistic goal of global risk management, rather than over-inflated expectations of perfect absolute security. When the guns fall silent in Iraq and Afghanistan, this new overlapping multilevel global security architecture now emerging, which operates quietly behind the scenes in the background patiently seeking to reduce global terrorism risks, will most probably remain in place. It is therefore imperative that IR theory will have the requisite tools to analyse this new architecture. This book is simply one small contribution to that ongoing effort.

2 Risk, global governance and security

Being at global risk is the human condition of the 21st century.

(Ulrich Beck, 2006b)

Introduction

The guiding principle and overarching theoretical premise of this book is that global risks such as terrorism that characterise today's 'global risk society' can best be managed by a new culture of multilateral multilevel cooperation between actors of all sorts.[1] Needless to say, this informs the empirical analysis employed throughout our case studies. But what sort of theoretical basis within IR exists for thinking in such terms? The answer might lie in a relatively well-established body of work on global governance theory, which provides a useful starting point, but how might that in turn engage with the fast-growing field of risk and security studies? In this chapter, we set out to explore and consolidate the foundations that might exist for a fruitful theoretical convergence between risk studies and global governance. In order to sketch out the academic environment within which this book positions itself, we begin by discussing the bourgeoning field of risk studies, paying particular attention to the diverse manifestations and usages of risk-related concepts that have emerged so far in the war on terror. Since one of the added-value claims of this book is to operationalise Ulrich Beck's ideas about 'cosmopolitan' cooperation, these will need to be singled out for critical evaluation.[2] In the process, we highlight core themes that will guide our empirical analysis, as well as critique some conceptual drawbacks in Beck's ideas. We then turn to global governance, particularly notions of 'global security governance' and 'global risk governance', demonstrating how shared assumptions and interlocking goals do exist between the two sets of literature: Beck's global risk society on one hand and global governance on the other. Finally, seeing that Beck has remained somewhat silent on the issue, we also assess how global governance strategies can themselves fulfil crucial risk management functions in practice, which have taken on new importance in the war on terror. It remains to be stressed here at the onset that our goal is not so much norma-tive or prescriptive. We are *not* in any way suggesting that the global security architecture we are examining somehow represents or endorses a normative vision for how global governance arrangements *should* be. We do not use global governance as a normative term denoting 'good' or 'bad' practice. By invoking the cosmopolitan in Beck's sense of the word, we are not automatically granting a seal of legitimacy to what are arguably anti-liberal practices such as the sharing of airline passenger data demanded by US authorities. We are simply using theories of risk as a critical conceptual lens to describe and analyse existing global governance practices rather than passing normative judgement on those practices.[3] Furthermore, the multilateral approaches discussed should not necessarily be seen as indicative of Beck's ideas being consciously adopted and implemented. Rather we are simply suggesting that such developments do appear to be moving closer to what Beck had in mind than the more militarised aspects of the war on terror so far.

Risk and security studies in the war on terror

Before we plunge headlong into the world of risk, it is worth noting here at the onset that risk studies have become so broad and wide-ranging that it is difficult to demarcate clearly the boundaries of the field. Such difficulties relate to the contested nature of risk as a concept itself, how it has been defined, understood and deployed by scholars working in different disciplines. One definition of risk, among others, is the probability of contingent harm, assessed in terms of frequency of occurrence, severity of loss and vulnerability. A key element of risk is probability and uncertainty. Terrorism precisely is about 'uncertainty, playing on randomness to keep whole populations in fear'.[4] As Prime Minister Brown argued in November 2007, 'terrorism can hit us anywhere from any place'.[5] Such is its severity that it has been labelled a 'strategic risk', prompting a new chapter to Britain's Strategic Defence Review.[6] Risk here is largely used as a descriptive term referring to a perilous situation, for terrorism is not simply what has happened, but also what *could* happen in future.[7] We are also concerned with how risk also carries policy implications, as Rasmussen argues, 'risk is a scenario followed by a policy proposal for how to prevent this scenario from becoming real'.[8] When security becomes increasingly conceptualised in terms of probabilistic 'what-if' risk scenarios, the importance of risk is further elevated in attempts to 'connect the dots'. As a US Joint House-Senate Inquiry concluded, 'on September 11, enough relevant data was resident in existing databases … had the dots been connected, the events would have been exposed and stopped'.[9] Many differing approaches to risk exist though. Cognitive psychologists focus on subjective cultural perception of risks; risk assessors, econometrists and insurers prefer quantitative approaches, while sociologists study the broader socio-political origins and significance of risks. Scientists attempt an objective 'scientific' understanding of risks such as genetically modified crops. Institutional regulatory approaches such as those in banks address rules, regulations and norms in how organisations should manage risk. The emphasis placed on particular aspects therefore varies according to the idiosyncratic concerns of analysts and inherent limits of case studies in various fields.[10] As Michael Power observed:

> various specialist definitions and classifications exist in the attempt to secure its meaning, and these definitions reflect specific institutional interests. In some traditions (health and safety), risk is equated with hazards and dangers; for others (finance) it is a matter of volatility in expected outcomes, both negative and positive.[11]

With such a wide range of definitions, it is possible that, without necessarily engaging with say the sociological work of Beck, scholars such as Bracken, Bremmer and Gordon can introduce technical risk management and assessment techniques into decision-making theory and foreign policy analysis.[12] As for international finance, Yadav has examined the evolution of the concept of risk in global banking and regulation.[13] Indeed, many in the field of finance use risk concepts derived from econometrics and insurance companies. These are in truth, quite different from the sociological literature on risk that this book relates most closely to. Recognising the impact of risk in variety of subject areas, a diverse group of scholars have come together to evaluate how risk has influenced fields ranging from psychology, social policy, media, to sexuality and the environment.[14] Contributors to a more recent special issue of *Security Dialogue* also highlighted how risk is far from a uniform concept, employing different approaches to the emergence and deployment of risk.[15] Again, these included ideas derived from sociology (Ulrich Beck, Niklas Luhmann, Anthony Giddens), governmentality (Michel Foucault, François Ewald, Robert Castel) and criminology (Pat O'Malley, Richard Ericson). Given such rich diversity, it is therefore not surprising that scholars have attempted to mix and match. Mythen and Walklate take a cross-disciplinary approach in merging Beck's works with Frank Furedi's 'culture of fear' and Foucauldian governmentality, showing how the various theories of risk can help promote understanding of the nature of terrorism.[16] Elbe for his part begins by using Beck to examine the securitisation of health issues such as HIV/AIDS, before concluding that François Ewald's alternative theorisation of risk as 'neologism of insurance' better serves his analytical purpose.[17] Similarly, Aradau and Munster have also utilised Beck as a starting point for understanding security practices in the war on terror but conclude in support of Foucauldian ideas of governmentality and precaution.[18] Continuing with this interdisciplinary approach, Amoore and de Goede too have their contributors consider the various ways in which risk calculation has manifested in areas from biometrics, new technologies of border security, to policing practices in attempts to govern by risk in the war on terror.[19] The increasing concern with risk has meant technologies of imagining the future and scenario planning are becoming more politically significant, particularly pre-mediation and imagination in security practice.[20] Understanding risk as a form of bio-political power or security technology is another important dimension of risk studies that has emerged.[21] For instance, Mick Dillon diverges from the preceding scholars, being more concerned with a Foucauldian understanding of risk as a bio-political security technology.[22] Indeed different angles of risk studies keep emerging; Jarvis and Griffiths in yet another special issue, this time in the journal *Global Society* have introduced risk into the study of another of IR's major subfields, IPE or international political economy.[23] Even scholars working on the IPE of tourism have latched on to the current concern with the globalisation of fear and risk in global travel.[24]

What emerges from the discussion is how scholars employ the concept of risk according to their own particular understanding of the term. Staying faithful to this sociological understanding of risk, yet another group of IR scholars has focused more or less on the implications of ideas derived from the likes of Beck, Furedi and Bauman for thinking about war, military strategy, security and the changing nature of conflict.[25] Perhaps the best illustration of Beck's impact on academia as a whole is his appropriation by other disciplines, besides IR. For instance, his ideas have been applied to issues of governance and sustainable development in development studies.[26] Meanwhile, researchers in criminology have been pondering the suitability of Beck's thesis for the fight against terror.[27] There have also been suggestions that in an age of globalisation, geo-politics is increasingly about managing geographical risks.[28] The link between Beck's thesis and sports has also been made.[29]

Despite a seeming flurry of activity and deluge of edited books and special issues on risk – a sure sign as any that the concept is gaining ground – it is perhaps timely to regroup and take stock of how we have got here and future research directions. This is particularly important as the ever-bourgeoning set of works referred to above all share an abiding interest in how well the study of risk, however it is defined, provides suitable frameworks tailored to their particular research agendas. Yet, this impressive collection of risk literature does not quite engage with Ulrich Beck's pet concern: risk and its relationship with global cooperation. This book is therefore partly motivated by an attempt to reconfigure the existing academic debate, shifting the terms of argument in the process. What follows is a brief critical evaluation of Beck's thoughts on the relationship between risk and global cooperation in the 'other' war on terror. The flaws and critiques of Beck, such as questions on risk definition, perception and patterns of political engagement, have already been addressed by scholars such as Mythen and others.[30] How for instance might Beck's 'manufactured insecurities', which originally related to pollution and global warming generated by industrial and scientific processes, now apply to global terrorism? Mindful of these critiques, we have another specific concern, zeroing in on his ideas on risk and global cooperation, which contain their own conceptual shortcomings.

Global cooperation and the World Risk Society

While risk specialists such as Ulrich Beck and Anthony Gidddens are usually associated with their gloomy conclusion that the post-Cold War world is becoming a global risk society afflicted by a whole plethora of undesirable dangers, what seems to have received less attention is their rather more optimistic vision of the implications for the world. As Power put it, usually 'the image is of a runaway world in need of risk governance'.[31] In fact, Beck is anything but an alarmist and believes that the anticipation of catastrophe can actually help fundamentally change global politics.[32] Beck and Giddens appear to have reached a consensus that positive upsides in the form of intensified cross-border cooperation can result due to a need for effective management of shared risks. In response to new global risks, Beck posits two possible models of global order: *Pax Americana* structured hierarchically based on relations between states, led by America, or a *global cosmopolis* based on the principle of equality and cooperation between a wide range of actors to be realised through corresponding reform of international law and international organisations.[33] Beck clearly plumbs for the latter and, as will be shown later, this line of thought has become particularly pronounced in his most recent works touting 'cosmopolitanism'.

The purpose of this part of the chapter is therefore to reassess the major contours and characteristics of just what global cooperation based on risk might look like, setting the theoretical foundation for discussion. The theme of global cooperation as a way effectively to combat risk is certainly not new or groundbreaking in the risk literature although it remains somewhat under-discussed. After all, Anthony Giddens had suggested as far back as 1998 that 'the expansion of cosmopolitan democracy is a condition for effectively regulating the world economy, attacking global economic inequalities and controlling ecological risks'.[34] In Giddens' view, the European Parliament provided a model for a stronger UN General Assembly and International Court of Justice (ICJ). In his earlier works in the late 1990s, Beck too had proposed a transnational 'cosmopolitan manifesto', where people brought together by shared global risks form 'risk communities' to negotiate on risks.[35] Beck does exceed Giddens in his proposals, ranging from international cooperation to the concept of a transnational state:

> Trans-national states come together in response to globalization and *thereby* develop their regional sovereignty and identity beyond the national level. They are thus cooperative and individual states – individual states *on the basis of* cooperative states. In other words, interstate unions open up new scope for action by post-national individual states.[36]

In reading Beck, it becomes clear that the main gist concerns how political action in the age of globalisation is now motivated by a shared perception of the global nature of dangers: 'being at global risk is the human condition of the 21st century'.[37] Such de-territorialised risks pose problems for the traditional framework of a self-contained nation state. Beck contends that as recognition of global risks increases, so too does the compulsion to arrive at cosmopolitan solutions. This in turn holds the key to reshaping an apparently rigid state-centred international system. The theme of 'transformation' and global governance has dominated his recent musings, although Beck does not phrase it explicitly in such terms. Indeed, tracing Beck's intellectual development over the years, one finds a distinct trend where he is now moving away from simply outlining the causes of the 'risk society' and 'reflexive modernisation' in the 1990s, towards a recent trilogy of books dedicated to 'cosmopolitan realism' and cooperative solutions to the war on terror.[38] This book purposely situates itself in this most recent intellectual phase of Beck's thinking.

Suggesting that there exists a silver lining against the grain of widespread doom and gloom, Beck outlines three possible reactions to risk: denial, apathy, transformation. 'Transformation' opens up the possibility of new cooperative actions across borders. In the face of global terrorism, Beck proclaims that 'the only path to national security is by way of transnational co-operation. The global terrorist threat inaugurates a new era of transnational and multilateral co-operation.'[39] States must both *de*nationalise and *trans*nationalise to protect their own national interests. In other words, dilute their hitherto absolute conceptions of sovereignty in a globalised world, to deal with these global problems. This leads to *cooperative transnational states*. The strictly national outlook, what Beck calls 'methodological nationalism', becomes an impediment to the transnational reinvention of statehood to cope better with the impact of globalisation: 'the great political challenge of our time'.[40] Such an approach cannot reconcile the fact that risks know no borders, and can only be answered through cooperation.[41] New thinking is crucial because the global risk society faces a temptation to 'normalise' the risk into established frameworks. For instance the wars in Afghanistan and Iraq are the first wars waged against a global risk.[42] Yet terrorism became 'territorialised' within rogue states, causing policy makers mistakenly to opt for habitual solutions in interstate warfare.[43] Instead, the global dangers of climate change, terrorism and economic globalisation demand a transnational mindset of 'cosmopolitics'.[44] To be cosmopolitan is 'no longer simply to feel a citizen *of* the world but above all a citizen *for* the world'.[45] It is important though to stress that Beck does not imply undermining, let alone abolishing nation states. Rather, he emphasises restoring their capacity to manage global risks effectively – in collaboration with one another and in fact actually increasing their powers.

The cosmopolitan outlook

Such collaboration is indispensable because, as Beck puts it, 'cosmopolitanism has left the philosophical realm and entered reality'.[46] In this way, he is claiming the human condition itself has become cosmopolitan. A central feature of this is how the 'shared experience of crisis in world society, awareness of interdependence of global risks, overcomes boundaries between national and international, us and them'.[47] The three pillars of World Risk Society – ecological, economic and terrorist risks – work to sharpen global consciousness.[48] Such new realities require new thinking, and Beck's solution: a *cosmopolitan outlook*, to grasp new social and political realities, and a 'methodological cosmopolitanism'.[49]

Unlike more conventional Kantian-inspired accounts of 'normative' or 'philosophical' cosmopolitanism that advocate harmony and recognising differences between national and cultural borders, Beck's circumspect understanding of 'cosmos', it must be noted, simply means 'culture, worldview, any horizon wider than that of a nation-state'.[50] Cosmopolitanism for him only serves to highlight uncontrollable liabilities, of something undesirable that might happen that stimulates people to forge new cross-border relationships. Beck is rather realistic in recognising that it does not herald universal love or a utopian 'world republic'. Nor will it replace nationalism. The 'cosmopolitan outlook' above all means recognising that faced with global dangers, previous distinctions between internal and external, national and international, us and them, lose their validity.[51] What defines cosmopolitanism to Beck is a mindset or mentality that accepts the fluid cross-border nature of the globalised world, the 'cosmopolitan outlook' refers to a 'global sense, a sense of boundarylessness where humans are everyday historically alert, demonstrating reflexive awareness of ambivalences in a mileu of blurring differentiations'.[52] The age-old mixing of people and cultures is not new, but what is new is the self-conscious reflexivity and awareness of it.[53] Beck wonders about the implications of this new historical reality where people view themselves as part of the same threatened world. He stresses that the 'walls between them must be replaced by bridges ... such bridges must be erected in human minds, mentalities, and imaginations (the "cosmopolitan vision") ... which search for collective answers to transnational problems such as terrorism'.[54] Interdependencies now exist not only between states but also other actors at different levels.[55]

It is quickly apparent that Beck's 'cosmopolitan outlook' is crucially premised on nations sharing the same perception and concern with global risks, shedding their previous 'national' mindsets for a 'cosmopolitan' world view. The cooperation that results is 'cosmopolitan' only in the narrowly circumscribed way, as Beck describes it, when various actors share the same perceived risks and reflexive awareness that only multilateral cooperation can effectively regulate transnational risks. Risk is touted as something that would somehow overcome national differences, as countries perceive it in their shared interests to cooperate. At the same time, Beck does recognise that risk is produced for political gain, creating fear and inflating a need for security that encroaches on liberty and equality. Furthermore, Beck appears to neglect another controversial issue: the socially constructed nature of risk. Subjective perceptions and cultural contexts shape how a particular risk is assessed, analysed and managed. The difference in perception and hierarchy of concerns and values within different communities helps explain why the 'focus placed on the danger originating from footwear by US airport security was not found at a European airport'.[56] Risk is seldom objective but socially constructed, created and problematised by those seeking to regulate it. As Hulsse argues, this seems to be the case with anti-terrorist financing regulations because just ten or 15 years ago, none existed.[57] Different actors can feel divergent levels of exposure to risk and we discuss in our case studies how significant an obstacle, different subjective perceptions of risk are to global counter-terrorism cooperation. Furthermore, the 'program of cosmopolitan democracy is not politically neutral. Substantial disparities exist in access to global resources ... some already have global fora at their command.'[58] There is also a real concern about the lack of accountable institutions at the global level that need not face their electorates. Indeed, what makes organisations like the FATF or practices like passenger data sharing 'cosmopolitan' when most civil rights groups oppose them? Indeed, many critical analyses have highlighted the negative implications for liberties, freedom and rights.[59] As we shall see in our case studies, these problems plague a nascent 'cosmopolitan outlook'.

Risk-cosmopolitanism

This brings us to how risk is indispensable to fuelling cosmopolitanism and serving an enlightenment function. To Beck, ongoing debates over global risks from ecological change or avian influenza have highlighted the cosmopolitan significance of fear as humans in distant parts of the world share the same worries and anxieties. War and terror too has acquired a cosmopolitan angle as millions shared in the same sense of shock by the images of 9/11, a truly global event.[60] The previously localised spaces of our emotional imagination have expanded in a transnational sense, generating cosmopolitan empathy. Beck observes that 'involuntary enlightenment' results because such global risks create a global public sympathy with victims of risk *and* a desire to avoid becoming a future victim. Indeed, much modern global debate now revolves around avoiding undesirable consequences such as infectious diseases, global climate change and terrorism.[61] This is not so much about normative universal value-based integration but rather enforced integration.[62] One might call this enforced 'real' cosmopolitanism in a rather negative sort of way: global risks connect actors across borders, who otherwise don't have anything to do with one another. But cosmopolitan empathy is not replacing national empathy. Instead, they permeate and transform each other.[63] Beck claims 'the global perception of global risk represents perhaps the last – and ambivalent – source of new commonalities and interaction networks'.[64] Risk is therefore acting as a negative medium of communication: it forces people to communicate with one another, allocates duties and costs to those who decline them.[65] Beck further distinguishes between 'banal' or 'deformed' cosmopolitanism as something that happens unknowingly as a side effect; it occurs passively through the proliferation of symbols, films, fashion, food etc. across borders to merge with local identities. A non-deformed risk-cosmopolitanism, on the other hand, results from the sense of partaking in global attempts to counter global risks, contributing to world culture.[66]

Perhaps the most interesting of Beck's ideas, risk-cosmopolitanism not only indicates how cosmopolitanism in the traditional sense can be redefined and to some extent rejuvenated by risk, but also raises questions of how a risk-based form of global governance can emerge. A particular shared concern over consequences is however not new. John Dewey's 1927 book *The Public and its Problems* claimed that it was not actions, but consequences that form the heart of politics. The notion of a 'public' does not exist until people share a common interest and perceive how consequences of indirect actions or negative externalities affect them collectively as a whole. What is interesting is how a global risk society with a long list of shared undesirable consequences might perhaps help create just such a 'global public'. In our case studies, therefore, we pay close attention to the possibility that the diverse actors involved in global governance today adopt risk-based guidelines as a starting platform for discussions on measures needed to manage global risks. However, the downside of using risk as a common denominator for global governance is it compels scholars to ask who sets the agenda. Indeed, while risk is often presented as 'scientific' and apparently neutral language, the deployment of risk concepts often tends to mask underlying power relationships where powerful actors push weaker actors to adopt their own particular set of risk-based guidelines.[67] How might one overcome differences in regulatory risk cultures where for instance European standards differ from those in the US? What are the compliance costs for actors implementing new risk-based guidelines and at what point do they decide the costs outweigh the benefits of risk management? These are the sorts of questions that preoccupy our case studies.

Institutionalised cosmopolitanism

Building upon Beck's 'risk-cosmopolitanism', the self-awareness that risks are global generates a shared global horizon of expectation and experience. The crucial question then is how to create or adapt political forms to solve global problems that people become more aware of.[68] With the recognition of these global threats, a shared space of responsibility and agency can promote political action among strangers. Beck suggests that 'institutionalized cosmopolitanism' emerges under certain circumstances leading to global discussion forums and regimes concerned with transnational risks.[69] This was less a result of idealistic enthusiasm than rational calculations of enlightened self-interest. In the wake of the collapse of investment bank Lehman Brothers, a consortium of ten global commercial and investment banks announced plans to provide $70 billion to offset a credit squeeze. Former UK Chancellor Norman Lamont described this move as not just self-interest, but 'enlightened self-interest'.[70] Institutionalised cosmopolitanism seeks to open up the structure of the global system beyond the state alone, redrawing boundaries between state, nation and politics in cosmopolitan terms. All actors – states, international organisations, NGOs, private sector – have to redefine goals, reallocate costs and find appropriate ways to manage new challenges.[71] While Beck's earlier works, such as *The Reinvention of Politics*, did appear to emphasise the role of citizen activism in what he called 'sub-politics',[72] his latest works on cosmopolitanism stress the increasingly diverse range of actors involved in a new global politics, besides citizens alone. Basic rules and norms are being renegotiated not only between the national and international, but also between global businesses and the state, transnational NGOs, civil society and supranational organisations.

Beck's notion of institutionalised cosmopolitanism does lead us to enquire under what conditions and with what actors are certain 'cosmopolitan' principles translated into practice and institutionalised. The world needs to consider altern-ative forms of governance as World Risk Society brings a new historic logic to the fore: no nation can control risks on its own. This peculiar reflexive self-awareness of the shared global nature of risks and the need to cooperate for 'enlightened self-interest' it would seem, according to Beck, is what makes global governance arrangements 'cosmopolitan', as opposed to simply narrow interest politics.

Beck's notion of 'institutionalised cosmopolitanism' is interesting, and it is here that his thoughts seem to gel with our earlier discussions about a more inclusive global governance with Strobe Talbott's understanding of the concept in Chapter 1. One might infer that Beck is hinting at how global governance might develop in response to global risks, without again explicitly stating it in these terms. However, Beck remains vague on just how 'cosmopolitan' govern-ance might operate in practice, only hinting at the International Criminal Court (ICC) and NGO-led anti-globalisation movements as possible examples. What is even more intriguing is the suggestion that pre-existing international mecha-nisms have to be reorganised and rejuvenated to manage global risks, or that new more inclusive and flexible counter-terrorism arrangements have to be arrived at. In this way, risk is to serve as a platform for global negotiations and forums, establishing new global mechanisms for managing risk. But this raises the crucial question: what makes multilateral governance arrangements cosmo-politan, as opposed to simply explainable, by interest politics? Do the entities involved really share a 'cosmopolitan outlook' as Beck claims? With such ideas in mind, we seek in our case studies to examine how global cooperative counter-terrorism arrangements have developed and adapted, and to what extent shared global risk has indeed provided a useful baseline for negotiations. At the same time, Beck's analysis does not seem to touch on how risk might affect, or is affected by, fundamental issues of power and dominance in the international system, which shape how international mechanisms are set up. Beck does admit that the biggest stumbling block remains how to make the difficult transition from mere recognition of scale of the challenge to what form the required response should take.[73] To that end, he notes the beginning of struggles over what shape and form institutionalised cosmopolitanism should take. For instance, would the new range of actors involved, such as NGO coalitions and global civil society, and global business consortiums themselves bring about a new configu-ration of power relations and calculations? Issues of inclusion/exclusion too need to be addressed: who are left out and excluded from such governance arrangements and what are the reasons? Indeed, 'these hidden centres of power are nothing new'.[74]

Cosmopolitan realism

While Beck emphasises that a more inclusive range of actors need to be involved in global cooperation, states remain crucial. Nation-based realpolitik – that national interests must necessarily be pursued by national means – must now be replaced by the maxims of *cosmopolitan realpolitik*.[75] The more cosmopolitan in rationale and design our political structures and activities, the more successful they will be in promoting national interests and individual power of states in this global age.[76] Realistic cosmopolitanism asks how societies deal with 'borders' and 'difference' under the impact of global crises? To consolidate their power, states must cooperate, negotiate international rules and reform corresponding international organisations. Rather than altruism, they act in a purely rational calculative manner, recognising that they can only realise their interests by cooperating with each other.[77] In recognition of how states remain substantial global actors with their surveillance capabilities and regulatory enforcement capacities, his 'cosmopolitan outlook' envisages a central role for 'cosmopolitan realism'.

Risk, security and global governance

Upon closer reading, the combined claims of Beck's 'risk-cosmopolitanism', 'institutionalised cosmopolitanism' and 'cosmopolitan realism' is not that utopian or far-fetched. Indeed, at times he seems more realistic than cosmopolitan in his insistence that states remain relevant and must cooperate to consolidate their power, that they provide the indispensable framework for action, that existing international organisations need to be reformed. New global norms on managing risk are to be renegotiated not only between states, but also between global business, transnational NGOs, civil society and supranational organisations. Beck, however, is not alone in his musings about global cooperation in the age of global terrorism. Consider the following lengthy passage from a recent book on global governance.

> There is a greater need for global governance because globalised challenges require cooperative international approaches ... pollution respects no boundaries ... terrorism, drugs are trans-national problems that dominate not only domestic agenda but international cooperation too. These often demand multi-lateral approaches ... states must cooperate with each other more as well as with non-state actors. The features of shared global problems are that they are often trans-national, with direct domestic impact. No one state can successfully control them ... solutions require a multilateral approach.... Multilateral institutions must adapt to accommodate these emerging, new challenges.... States must work to strengthen and create processes and institutions needed for effective global governance.[78]

It could very easily be Beck who penned this passage. Instead we have two IR scholars writing about global governance, highlighting to us at least the degree of overlap between global governance, counter-terrorism and risk studies.

Take the war on terror and cooperation for instance, where UN Secretary-General Ban Ki Moon stressed for the international community to 'take multilateral counter-terrorism cooperation even further ... and in an integrated manner'.

Arguing that since military force alone rarely brings an end to terrorist groups, 'multilateral counter-terrorism efforts must be done in partnership with regional and subregional organizations and with civil society'.[79] Indeed, the theme of global counter-terrorism cooperation as a more effective means to regulate global terrorism does seem to be developing into a mini-cottage industry. With an emphasis on the UN, Peter Romaniuk has embarked on an effort using regime theory to examine the conditions conducive for state cooperation on the full range of counter-terrorism policies from the use of intelligence and military force to criminal law measures, financial controls and diplomacy.[80] Nesi *et al.* have looked at how the UN and various regional organisations have cooperatively responded to terrorism.[81] However, this particular volume does not engage with the literature on risk and is more concerned with international legal implications. As for trans-Atlantic cooperation between the US and Europe since 9/11, Rees has looked at areas from use of force to intelligence sharing, investigating and prosecuting terrorism, to border and homeland security.[82] Significant milestone agreements reached despite difficult negotiations include the transfer of Passenger Name Records (PNR) to the US, as well as personal data in the investigation of terrorism. While EU–US cooperation is certainly a good example of cooperative approaches to shared security interests, a global governance perspective contends that the nature of the global terrorism risk is more global than bilateral. It also encapsulates far more than formalised institutionalised cooperative arrangements between sovereign state and supra-state actors. After all, students of global governance focus on investigating governance arrangements beyond the state.[83] The problems revealed during EU–US negotiations are also indicative of obstacles to deepening cooperation, such as differences on data protection, which are covered by the EU Data Privacy Directive (Council Directive 95/46/EC), standards of privacy and even whether the 'war' on terror is a war or law enforcement matter. Considering that even amongst close allies such problems emerged at the bilateral level, it is sobering to consider how such problems would intensify at the global level where the governance playing field would broaden to involve a wide array of less sympathetic actors. The British government too recognises the importance of partnership:

> Developing and delivering this counter-terrorism strategy involves all parts of Government acting together and taking a joined-up approach to dealing with this complex and wide-ranging threat. Delivery also depends upon partnerships with the police and emergency services, local authorities, and devolved administrations, as well as with the private sector and the voluntary and charitable sector.[84]

The Bush administration echoes the same line:

> During the Cold War we created an array of domestic and international institutions and enduring partnerships to defeat the threat of communism. Today, we require similar transformational structures to carry forward the fight against terror and to help ensure our ultimate success.[85]

Such discussions, however, bear little explicit reference to Beck's own peculiar understanding of global systemic risks, although quite clearly they share similar premises and assumptions about confronting global risks in the absence of a world government. They all hint at global governance, rather than global government.

Given Beck's conviction that more cooperation would assuage global risks, as well as works by scholars on multilateral counter-terrorism cooperation referred to earlier, what are the links, if any, between global governance and risk studies? Indeed, within risk studies, one often finds references to 'governing by risk' and 'governing terrorism through risk'.[86] Clearly, the implication is that risk can bring about new forms of governance, oriented towards reducing vulnerabilities and averting an uncertain future. What about the other side of the coin: global governance? States have long cooperated on common interests in the absence of a global Leviathan to enforce rules and regulations. Global governance put simply and loosely, refers to the long history of attempts to shape and regulate an otherwise anarchic international system.[87] While this definition has benefits of simplicity, it belies the myriad different understandings of what exactly global governance means. There is no single model of global governance, nor is there a single structure. Covering the study of international organisations and regimes to global civil society actors, it has come to mean 'virtually everything'.[88] Some scholars, such as Craig Murphy's usage of global governance, emphasise the activities of world organisations like the UN. Others see global governance as simply regime theory going global, beyond its previous narrow focus on specific issues.[89] Furthermore, it is not just states alone or international organisations that 'do' global governance nowadays. It is not just about the reinvigoration of global organisations like the UN to help in 'managing risk and change in the international system' as suggested by Mihaly Simai, although this is a significant part of the debate. We suggest that such definitions are too narrow and restrictive, failing to take into account more multifaceted and myriad dimensions of global governance. Indeed, this is precisely why we adopt a broadly inclusive yet loosely defined understanding of what global governance means. Thakur and Weiss define 'global governance' simply as collective efforts to identify, understand or address worldwide problems that go beyond the capacity of individual states to solve (Thakur and Weiss forthcoming).[90] The fundamental question asked of global governance in the global risk society is how to manage risks without formal world government.

Global governance attempts to find patterns of governance in the absence of a formal system of authoritative government. Such arrangements may be formal, in the form of laws or institutions to manage collective affairs by a variety of actors, including state authorities, NGOs, private sector entities, other civil society actors and individuals. But these may also be informal such as best practices or benchmarking guidelines. Global governance then is not just the realm of the UN system but has to include a much more extensive set of interlocking relationships.[91] Using the term 'global' is significant as it indicates a move beyond the scope of solely international (interstate) relations, towards incorporating a broader range of non-state actors.[92] Beck too argues the state is only one element of global governance. It would be fatal to exclude transnational NGO coalitions or global businesses. In this sense, global governance is a perspective on global life, a vantage point to foster regard for complexity and diversity of global life.[93]

There are ample reasons for enquiring into global governance in the twenty-first century, not least the problem of global terrorism risks. As laid out by Wilkinson, these include questions over the capacity of territorial nation states alone to manage security in light of transnational terror networks, the intensification of global interdependence and its downsides, and a range of new non-state actors increasingly active in the governance of global affairs.[94] Wilkinson identifies four major themes that have developed; of which two directly mirror our analytical concerns in this book. The first involves enhancing global governance to manage global problems better and drawing in other actors. The second examines how structures of power and authority are changing and exercised by a wider range of actors beyond states.

While the contours of global governance are indistinct, one can make a useful conceptual distinction between 'governance' and 'government'. Governments are actors accorded formal authority and jurisdiction over defined territorial spaces to enforce policy implementation using police powers. Governance is a broader concept that may not be territorial in scope and may employ only informal influence to achieve compliance without necessarily relying on coercion to overcome defiance.[95] Rosenau suggests thinking of global governance in terms of a continuum of arrangements: between the transnational and the subnational, the macro and micro, the informal and the institutionalised, the state-centric and the multi-centric.[96] Global governance thus ranges from informal practices and processes at regional, national, local levels, to the formal rules and regulations negotiated in grand global-level forums. Karns and Mingst refer to the collection of governance-related activities, rules and mechanisms, formal and informal existing at a variety of levels in the world today as the 'pieces of global governance'.[97] Latham argues that Rosenau's more open, fluid sense of global governance allows us on one end to understand the formal conscious efforts of states and international organisations to regulate aspects of global life. On other end, there are 'less formalized and less meta-conscious forms of governance that emerge in various broad and narrow arrangements arrived at locally, regionally, or nationally through patterns of practice'. Governance involves 'a pervasive tendency ... in which major shifts in the location of authority and site of control mechanisms are under way on every continent'. The combined effect is about steering, or shaping, relations and practices. Underlying that operation must be some consensus on operation and existence of the governing system, rather than the legitimation of top-down authoritative formal government.[98] Latham further distinguishes between 'big governance' that shapes the big financial and political relations of the world order, and 'small governance' that is shaping everyday life in local and national contexts often in response to actions of big governance. More recent interpretations of 'governance' claim it must be understood more precisely than simply any kind of regulation. It refers to new modes of governing, of 'shaping the market and society into a desired direction', which differ from classical-modernist government. Governance must be understood here in a more precise sense than the currently fashionable, casual use of the term for designating any kind of social regulation.[99]

The range of works discussed above suggest that it is useful to think of the governance/government distinction in terms of a sliding scale: at one end we have anarchy with no central authority, and on the other hand we have the classic formalistic Hobbesian state exercising control and sovereignty. In the middle we would have governance arrangements involving a range of actors to mitigate anarchy and manage collective problems in the absence of an overarching world government. The sliding scale would look something as follows:

government, hierarchy, Hobbesian state ↔ governance arrangements ↔ anarchy, no central authority

This sliding conceptual scale allows us to grasp better the shifting balance between actors taking the initiative in various issue areas. States could reassert themselves as the loci of power and authority, for instance through the creation of the Transport Security Administration in the US to oversee airport security. At other times, non-state actors might take the lead, for instance private intelligence firms.

In understanding global governance, it is also useful to focus on actors: one needs to be explicit about what kinds of entities and forces are pertinent to affecting changes and what are the most salient features of the international system at any one time.[100] We need to be conscious of the fact that global governance is no longer simply about states and state regulations: 'today's chains of causation follow crazy-quilt patterns that cannot be adequately discerned if one clings to an ontology that presumes primacy of states and governments'.[100] While works on global governance examine the roles of international organisations and states, global governance has become more inclusive of non-state sub-political actors such as NGOs, civil society, the private sector, right down to individual citizens.[102] In this respect, we 'should recast the relevance of territoriality, shift authority to subnational, transnational and non-governmental levels, and highlight porosity of boundaries at all levels of governance.'[103] Above all, 'global governance hinges on three inter-related elements: the changing nature of the actors and their relationships; the increasingly complex context within which they operate; and the nature of the interdependent trends that make up globalization today'.[104] Actors in global governance today would be as follows:

1 multilateral institutions and global organisations (UN, ICJ, ICC, WTO);
2 supra-state/regional arrangements (EU, AU, NAFTA);
3 states;
4 civil society (individuals, NGOs, interest groups);
5 private sector (small firms to global business consortiums and MNCs).

Such a variety of actors has meant that a recent edited collection on global environmental governance found it necessary to include separate sections on states, civil society and the role of multinational corporations.[105]

At first glance then, the strands of global governance theory outlined above might help to provide a more established theoretical framework in IR within which to locate Beck's thoughts on global cooperation. Many of Beck's claims about the features of World Risk Society, sits rather well with assumptions that underpin the basic premises of global governance. For instance, the UN Commission on Global Governance defined

> governance as the sum of the many ways in which individuals and institutions, private and public, manage their common affairs. It includes formal ... as well as informal arrangements that people and institutions either have agreed to or perceive to be in their interest.[106]

The 'enemy' or 'opponent' of global governance is often defined by the UN Commission as the set of shared global problems – environmental, economic and security – that are in need of collective management. It also counts on achieving consensus as essential to creation of governance.[107] The key concern here is more about management than definitive resolution of the many global challenges today that, as Karns and Mingst point out, 'require cooperation of some sort among governments and the increasing number of non-state actors in the world; some demand the establishment of new international mechanisms'.[108] Clearly, there are echoes of Beck's 'institutionalised cosmopolitanism' and 'risk-cosmopolitanism', which suggest that risk might bring about new opportunities for consensus on governance and that 'cosmopolitan' political arrangements for managing risk might develop.

The only problem is that the vision of global governance set out by the UN Commission seems to be post-political: it takes place only after goals are set and arguments, struggles and deliberation have been played out.[109] To the contrary, Beck advocates precisely the need for political arguments and negotiations to be played out on global forums as part of the process of managing global risks. There is also a danger that a focus on global governance risks empowering and legitimising those actors leading existing international institutions because they seem the most capable and well-placed governors.[110] Such issues will not go away even with a newfound awareness of risk supposedly bringing consensus, as we show in our case studies.

Global security governance and global risk governance

Beyond the basic shared premises that we have already highlighted, contemporary developments in global governance seem to imply a closer alignment with Beck's ideas for managing new security challenges. More specifically, the notion of 'security governance' proposed by Krahmann posits the emergence of a complex system of functionally differentiated overlapping networks in managing international security. Involving a variety of public and private, state and non-state actors at multiple levels, this emerging structure departs radically from the state-dominated bias of security organisations such as military alliances of the past.[111] This theme of changing approaches to tackle new global security challenges has been mirrored by Emil Kirchner and James Sperling in their analysis of the EU's role in 'security governance'.[112] They link governing Europe's security to the changing nature of the state, expansion of the security agenda and the obsolescence of traditional forms of security cooperation. Their earlier analysis of Great Power security cooperation in their book *Global Security Governance* focused on how major states such as the US, UK and Russia are redefining their security agendas accordingly through their own idiosyncratic brand of 'exceptionalism'.[113] The predominant focus on Great Power cooperation and states however does restrict its analytical reach.

What is more relevant to us is what Renn and Walker call 'global risk governance'.[114] Risk governance is defined as 'the complex web of actors, rules, processes, conventions and mechanisms concerned with how relevant risk information is collected, analysis and how management decisions are taken'. This is particularly important where the nature of the risk requires collaboration between different stakeholders, and there is no single authority to take a binding management decision.[115] Translating this to the global level, Renn *et al.* argue that global risks are not confined to national borders; they cannot be managed through the actions of a single sector. Global risks therefore present global risk governance challenges.[116] The governance of global systemic risks therefore requires an integrative approach involving governments, intergovernmental organisations, industry, academia and civil society. However, rather than Beck's understanding of risk, Renn *et al.* apply frameworks for risk governance developed by the independent organisation, the International Risk Governance Council.

The preceding discussion suggests two key interrelated developments. While Krahmann's security governance initially focused on the overlapping trans-Atlantic security architecture that emerged after the Cold War, others such as Kirchner and Sperling have addressed similar themes around 'global security governance'. Simultaneously, in the field of risk studies, Renn and Walker have focused on 'global risk governance' although this was unrelated to Beck's thesis. We contend that these theoretical strands emerging concurrently can be extended and modified both spatially and ideationally. Spatially, such a 'security governance' framework can be seen to be going global in the war on terror as numerous cross-cutting multilevel initiatives are being discussed and put in place to manage global terrorism, hence 'global security governance'. Ideationally, we extend the level of analysis beyond the sort of regional trans-Atlantic security issues that initially motivated Krahmann, to comprise a more global orientation examining the global counter-terrorist architecture concerned with risk governance. Risk governance too is going global. The need for multilevel overlapping partnership between the public and private sectors has already been highlighted by the UN Secretary General's initiative to create a 'Global Compact' in order to foster collaborative policy-making processes involving states, corporations,

NGOs etc. Furthermore, 'in the war on terrorism, it is important to understand how power is exercised through a complex policy constellation including regulatory state bodies, international institutions, industry self-regulating bodies and private risk assessment firms'.[117] The twin related notions of 'security governance' and 'global risk governance' provide us with useful guidelines in thinking about the intersections between risk, global governance and security.

Private authority as global governance

Not only has the literature on governance expanded to encompass new ideas like 'global risk governance' discussed above, another interesting dimension in recent years involves the role of private actors in global governance, which we shall now consider. Examples include international accounting standards and benchmark practices and private bond ratings agencies such as Moody's.[118] These developments hint at the possibility of overlap with Beck's 'institutional cosmopolitanism', which implies an expansion in the width and range of actors involved in global governance activities. We seek to extend our level of analysis to private non-state actors in global governance, and how they too have a role to play in managing risk. As Hall and Biersteker put it:

> Private locations of authority have begun to influence a growing number of issues in our contemporary world. Authoritative private actors are not only important players in the international political economy; they are increasingly beginning to play a critical role in the governance of other important spheres of social and political life. They are engaged in the establishment of standards, the provision of social welfare, the enforcement of contracts, and the maintenance of security.[119]

This rise of private authority implies the transformation of state powers and roles, rather than the imminent replacement of state sovereignty. To the contrary, the sovereign state is actually actively taking part in its own transformation, as it accommodates and even encourages the growing role of market authority to cope with the greater burdens of global governance.[120] Rather than a Hobbesian state of nature, they point to emerging patterns of governance in the international system, which arise and function without formal state or interstate institutions. A growing number of private actors are taking on authoritative roles, ranging from global market forces, private international standards-setting such as the International Organisation for Standardisation (ISO), right to the mafia and mercenaries, human rights and environmental NGOs. Although these are non-state actors, they are accorded or convey some form of legitimacy. Crucially, they perform the role of authorship over some important issue domains such as policy advocacy, setting standards, rules and norms.[121] Lipschultz argues that private actors with expertise acquired through global networks of knowledge and practice are creating a 'very diffused' system of globalising governance (ranging from private to mixed public–private ventures).[122]

Hall and Biersteker suggest there are three types of private authority operating within global governance today: 'market', 'moral' and 'illicit' authority. The first two are of direct relevance to us, while the third is less applicable. To begin with, 'market' authority refers to the ability of private actors to set standards and best practices that are then recognised and adhered to by others, such as the benchmark ISO standards on quality assurance. In terms of countering terrorist financing, an example that comes to mind is the Wolfsberg Group of Banks formed in 2000. This group brings together 12 private financial sector regulators/institutions for informal but regular consultations on best practices in combating terrorist financing. Private market forces should have a role to play in decision making and global governance processes.[123] Similarly, Beck too has stressed the importance of getting global business and private sector actors more actively involved in negotiating new global norms and global cooperative initiatives.

As for private moral authority, such actors can claim 'expertise'. When NGOs or other private actors are seen as credible providers of information that is hard to acquire, analyse or disseminate, they can acquire legitimate authority. For instance private intelligence companies are increasingly recognised for the part they quietly play in the shadows of the war on terror. SITE Institute for instance searches extremist web content to find unreleased material. Hoffman suggests that SITE and other private intelligence companies serve valuable functions. 'The government has its own intelligence sources, and one would hope it's comparing and contrasting, using this as supplements, to round out government intelligence.'[124] Private data mining companies, including British firms Mantas and World-Check, also develop specialised software for financial institutions to single out suspicious transactions.

Having surveyed the contours both of Beck's ideas and various aspects of global governance, we are now in a position to draw together the overlapping strands and threads in two key areas. First, in terms of actors, both agree that addressing states and formal international organisations alone does not provide sufficient analytical traction in understanding the multilevel forms of global governance arrangements emerging. Both the notion of 'risk governance' and Beck's 'instutionalised cosmopolitanism' seem to embody the new spirit of inclusiveness required. Second, in terms of founding rationales, they agree on a pressing need for consensus to manage collectively global problems. Beck's 'cosmopolitan outlook' and 'risk-cosmopolitanism' in particular hint that risk might provide new coherence and renewed consensus for governance. It is worth pointing out that the cases of global governance we have selected are simply those that we would like to examine in some detail. It is by no means saying that these subjects are the *only* ones that need to be dealt with. Other issues such as migration control or infectious diseases could easily be on the list of issues.[125] What remains for us to do is to examine how global governance can fulfil the expectations and principles of risk management. We have argued these arrangements are designed to reduce the risk of global terrorism, but how precisely would they *do* so in practice and what problems might be confronted?

Risk management and counter-terrorism after 9/11

At first glance, 'most people unfamiliar with risk management principles might not recognise how the same risk management techniques that have been commonplace in industry and insurance applications are now being employed in attempts to identify, classify and prevent terrorist attacks in the war on terror'.[126] The centrality of risk management today is summed up by Michael Power:

> Risk management and risk 'talk' are all around us. The risk-based description of organisational life is conspicuous. Not only private sector companies, but hospitals, schools, universities and many other public organisations, including the very highest levels of central government, have all been invaded to varying degrees by ideas about risk and its management.[127]

The purpose of this final part of the chapter is to sketch out some of these risk management techniques and how they might inform our understanding of global governance as a counter-terrorism strategy. Risk society after all alerts us to the centrality of insecurity, risks and their management, the optimum means to pre-empt any adverse outcomes.[128] Risk management is a complex subject with differing approaches and techniques, covering diverse areas from health and safety, business and finance, to terrorism and crime. There is no single generic widely accepted definition or model of risk management. Put very simply, it can refer to any policy or strategy designed to reduce risk, or mitigate it. The core focus is *preventing* the unwanted activity from materialising. When thinking of terrorism risk, it is useful to break down the various features that often define it: threat, vulnerability, probability and consequences. Threat refers to the intentions and capabilities of terrorist actors. Where threats are suspected, then the vulnerability of infrastructure or facilities must be considered. Probability implies dealing with the likelihood of terrorist attack. Consequence means that when a terrorist attack occurs, systems must be able to mitigate that impact. Following on from this, the aims of risk management strategies can vary quite considerably, depending on which of these three aspects are considered. If one targets the nature of threat, this can mean altering the capabilities and intentions of terrorist actors posing a risk. This then reduces the probability of attack happening, 'some efforts to manage terrorism risk are intent on changing terrorist intentions to attack'.[129] A common technique is surveillance efforts to deter illicit activities such as smuggling of goods, people or WMD-related materials. Other strategies seek to reduce risk by reducing vulnerability. For example, concrete blast barriers help to reduce vulnerability of government buildings to terrorist acts. Increased coordination for global governance to eliminate weak chinks in air travel infrastructures through public–private partnerships can also work this way. This can also be seen in the reform of global financial regulations to reduce vulnerabilities of the global banking infrastructure to terrorist financing. Such measures can also work to undermine the capabilities of terrorist financial networks. It is important to bear in mind that the various methods of managing risk, whether altering intentions/capabilities or reducing vulnerabilities are not mutually exclusive: they can in fact be highly complementary.

A risk management approach assumes that if we are able to identify the factors that predict unwanted outcomes, we might then be able to manipulate and alter them so the risk does not materialise. It typically uses methods that reduce the likelihood of the loss occurring. A global governance perspective kicks in when actors recognise that a risk management perspective has to operate cooperatively across borders because of the global nature of the risk. If risk is a probabilistic scenario based on uncertainty, risk management then means reducing likelihoods of that scenario happening. Beck helpfully makes a crucial distinction between risk and catastrophe: risk is not catastrophe but rather the anticipation of it.[130] The implication therefore is that if we are always in anticipation of risks, societies and governments will be perennially concerned with reducing the probabilities of that contingent risk occurring. Indeed, 'the terrorist power of uncertainty is especially strong precisely because we live in a society dominated by the desire to tame change and by institutions increasingly organised around risk management'.[131]

The events of 9/11 only served to drive home how crucial it was to properly manage risk:

> in the immediate months following September 11, the dilemmas of the war on terror were being framed as problems of risk management, clearing the path for a burgeoning homeland security market that was to have implications far beyond the US 'homeland'.[132]

Risk is becoming a crucial tool of governing in the war on terror. US Secretary of Homeland Security Michael Chertoff has installed risk management as a core organising principle for his department:

> we need to adopt a risk-based approach in both our operations and philosophy.... Risk management must guide our decision-making as we examine how we can best organize to prevent, respond and recover from an attack ... what we can do is use intelligent risk-based analysis, advanced technology and enhanced resources to manage risk.[133]

The US 2007 *National Strategy for Homeland Security* reiterated 'applying a comprehensive approach to risk management. We must apply a risk-based framework in order to identify and assess potential hazards, determine what levels of relative risk are acceptable, and prioritize and allocate resources.'[134] Indeed, the recent 'phenomenal expansion of the risk industry reflects a number of different but convergent pressures for change in organisational practices for dealing with *uncertainty*'.[135] 'From the protection of borders to international financial flows, from airport security to daily financial transactions, risk assessment is emerging as the most important way in which terrorist danger is made measurable and manageable.'[136]

The concern with risk management in the war on terror has spawned a variety of approaches and techniques. For instance, 'what is new about contemporary terrorist risk management, is its increasing reliance on technology and computerised data-mining'.[137] A crucial risk management technology is known as *dataveillance*, or 'the proactive surveillance of suspect populations, to identify "risky groups of people" for the purposes of "targeted governance"'.[138] The demand for risk management is a big boost to surveillance.[139] According to the Royal Society, 'monitoring is the tool for investigating how things stand and might evolve, serving as a contributor to precautionary action in the face of uncertainty or ignorance'.[140] Surveillance here means not simply spying but systematic bureaucratised gathering of information for management of populations. The aim is not only to watch every actual event but also to 'plan for every eventuality'.[141] Not only is surveillance touted as useful in managing risks from cancer to food safety and food animal production, it is now put forward as an essential tool in the war on terror. The post-9/11 surveillance environment is indicative of the increasing prevalence of risk management ideas and lucrative surveillance infrastructures developing.[142] The war on terror has already witnessed considerable controversy over attempts to profile airline passengers as well as global financial transactions for the risks they pose, generating concerns over a 'new politics of surveillance'.[143] Even our 'ordinary' mundane day-to-day transactions are scrutinised to identify risky patterns in order to 'connect the dots': 'the transaction has become a specific preemptive means of securing in the face of an uncertain future'.[144] Amoore and de Goede conclude that a system of 'risk governing' has emerged, aimed at the pre-emption of potential terrorist schemes or attacks. The downside is they rewrite the norms of privacy, create new forms of inclusion and exclusion, and alter processes of democratic accountability.[145] Biometric technology has also been deployed for 'risk profiling as a means of governing mobility within the war on terror, segregating "legitimate" mobilities such as leisure and business, from "illegitimate" mobilities such as terrorism and illegal immigration'.[146] The underlying assumption is that had better surveillance and profiling techniques been in place, the events of 9/11 'could have been predicted and averted'. Biometric data thus serves as a means of risk management because it is able to identify the factors – i.e. possible terrorist behaviour, intentions or capabilities – that might lead to harm and we can then alter them.

While the dataveillance literature has emphasised profiling of individuals and populations, surveillance and data collection carry global implications as well. David Lyon suggests that collecting information quickly at great distances is the best way to pre-empt risks by indicating where a potential offender may strike in a global risk society. Globalised, transnational policing now aimed to reduce risks through 'knowledge-based risk management'.[147] It also emerged that the US was monitoring and collecting transaction details and wire transfers processed by SWIFT (Society for Worldwide Interbank Financial Telecommunication), which handles a majority of worldwide transactions. The information gained from sharing surveillance data and cooperation across borders is deemed crucial to managing risks. This can be seen in airline security where the sharing of passenger data allow law enforcement agencies to use 'advanced data mining techniques to reveal patterns of criminal behaviour and detain suspected terrorists before they act'.[148] For similar reasons, there has been a move to machine-readable passports containing biometric information, and advance passenger information systems. Controlling who and what actually gets on a plane in a globalised world is increasingly a matter for multilateral cooperation to reduce the risks at a distance so that, as the Homeland Security Department suggests, 'extend our zone of security outward so that American borders are the last line of defence, not the first'. The same can be said for container port security as America enlists the help of partners to examine 'high-risk maritime containerized cargo at foreign seaports before they depart for the US'. The Secure Freight Initiative scans containers for radiation and information risk factors before departure. As the Homeland Security Department stressed in risk speak, 'this data will be combined with other available risk assessment information such as currently required manifest submissions, to improve risk analysis, targeting and scrutiny of high-risk containers overseas'.[149] Private actors too have been active in this field: CommerceGuardAB Joint Venture, involving Siemens, GE and Mitsubishi, is presently building infrastructure to establish a network of 'secure cargo corridors' between key ports and terminals. The primary purpose is to reduce vulnerabilities of the sea lane-based global trading system through collaborative efforts, data collection and sharing of pre-arrival information through a risk-based approach.

Another risk management technique dissuades terrorists by making them perceive the likelihood of success as slim or that the costs of their efforts are too high. In practical terms, this means making it 'increasingly difficult for terrorists to achieve their objectives'.[150] Various options exist: one can simply detain terrorists to prevent them carrying out their activities. Chairman of the Joint Chiefs Admiral Mike Mullen referred to this when suggesting that Guantanamo Bay 'helps mitigate that global risk'.[151] In fields such as critical infrastructure protection, bridge engineers have recommended incorporating risk management techniques into structural design of key transport nodes such as bridges by making it more difficult for attacks to succeed.[152] Similar concerns now also shape the urban landscapes of cities. London, concerned with reducing the physical risks of terrorist attacks, has launched a series of place-specific security initiatives and informal and formal risk management policies, which led to fortification and spatial restructuring.[153] Sir Alan West's November 2007 review of security in UK public places, recommended the redesigning of public spaces – specifically airports, major railway stations, shopping centres and sports facilities – to deter future terrorists by raising the barriers to success, or to mitigate their possible impact. In this way, risk management can reduce the probabilities of unwanted outcomes materialising. In situational crime prevention, similar interventionist actions such as Neighbourhood Watch are aimed at 'reshaping the environment' in order to reduce criminal opportunities, making it more difficult for criminals to succeed.[154]

Such thinking is now apparent on a global counter-terrorism level as well. As the US National Intelligence Officer for Transnational Threats Ted Gistaro observed:

we assess that greatly increased worldwide counterterrorism efforts over the past five years have constrained the ability of al-Qaeda to attack the United States and our allies and have led terrorist groups to perceive the homeland in particular as a harder target to strike than on September 11.[155]

Indeed, part of the 'strategic vision' for the US 2006 *National Strategy for Combating Terrorism* is 'the creation of a global environment inhospitable to violent extremists and all who support them'.[156] The *National Strategy to Combat Weapons of Mass Destruction* similarly declares:

> We must enhance traditional measures – diplomacy, arms control, multilateral agreements, threat reduction assistance, and export controls – that seek to dissuade or impede proliferant states and terrorist networks, as well as to slow and make more costly their access to sensitive technologies, material, and expertise.[157]

It concludes that, 'overall, we seek to cultivate an international environment that is more conducive to non-proliferation'.[158] This also implies global governance can create an environment that is less vulnerable to terrorist proliferation risks. The private actors we shall be analysing also have roles to play because 'voluntary public–private partnerships that shape the risk environment through market-based incentives can complement a regulatory approach'.[159] The various cases of global governance examined in this book help contribute to risk management in similar ways through cooperative initiatives in monitoring and gathering information on terrorist activities, reshaping the terrorists' global operating environment and reducing the vulnerabilities of global infrastructure, be it financial or transport. The overall effect is raising the bar to attacks.

Risk management however has numerous downsides. After 9/11, it has 'victimised those who have been wrongly detained, more subtly excluded, and affected many more through invasion of privacy, restriction of liberty and spending on physical security infrastructures at the expense of health, education and welfare'.[160] Any risk management strategy must also recognise that risk is reactive: 'as people act on knowledge of risk, they simultaneously change the risk environment and create new uncertainties'.[161] Risk management technologies can manufacture new uncertainties, some of which pose risks greater than those they were designed initially to control. Beck refers to such problems as 'boomerang effects'. Recent terrorist attacks have shown the adaptability of today's terrorists and their support systems. The international approach to terrorism risk management must be equally adaptable.[162] Furthermore, there are countless sources of risk in the world. Why do only some of these gain the attention of risk management? This question merits critical discussion, for risk selection is a social, cultural, political and economic process. As Ericson suggests:

> a few risks are selected because they are seen to have the greatest potential to adversely affect interests of stakeholders. Risk portfolios are often constituted

in politically charged contexts where the risks selected are used to define values, interests and ways of life.[163]

Any attempt at global governance to manage risks must be sensitive to the implications these issues raise, not least in terms of underlying power relations and subjective perceptions of risk.

Conclusion

This chapter has sought to work its way through the theoretical issues arising from the questions we posed in Chapter 1. In the process, it attempted to clarify the theoretical grounds for analysis within this book. First, risk is a contested concept, yet it is so all-encompassing that it has been adopted for use in a variety of ways, most of which are not necessarily compatible with one another. These include Foucauldian ideas of risk and governmentality, risk as an empirical tool of technical statistical analysis used in econometrics and finance, the bio-political nature of risk, to sociologically inspired notions of World Risk Society that underpin the approach taken in this book. Second, there appears substantial overlap between Beck's analysis of 'cosmopolitan' cooperation, and developments in global governance literature. This was demonstrable not just in the basic underlying assumptions about the nature of global problems we face, but also in more recent theoretical innovations such as 'global security governance' and 'global risk governance'. Beck's notions of risk-cosmopolitanism and institutionalised cosmopolitanism on their part hinted at how global governance mechanisms might develop in response to shared global risks. What emerges from the discussion allows us to refine further and operationalise Beck's ideas for empirical analysis. The basic proposition then is as follows: while the historical core concerns of global governance remain essentially unchanged (a need to cooperate on problems beyond the control of any individual actor), risk is increasingly prominent both in terms of rationale (i.e. risk-cosmopolitanism helps bring about consensus through enforced integration to manage shared global risks) and practice (institionalised cosmopolitanism comprising multilevel initiatives of varying formality and involving an array of actors implementing risk-based guidelines to reduce vulnerabilities). Beck's ideas though are not without his detractors, who have critiqued shortcomings such as a relative neglect of the subjective nature of risk, flawed understanding of what 'cosmopolitan' means, and underemphasising the role of power relations. Such issues would need to be taken into consideration in our case studies for a more balanced critical perspective. In the process, we seek to assess to what extent risk is indeed providing a 'neutral' platform for global governance, and whether other more deep-seated phenomena such as power politics might be at play. Last, we argued that Beck has remained rather vague on just how his 'institutionalised cosmopolitanism' might operate in practice to manage risk. Yet risk management has already become central to the war on terror: a point not lost on scholars working on dataveillance, biometrics and risk profiling of individual data and movement. Cognisant of this, we suggested that global cooperation on counter-terrorism too can involve a variety of techniques to reduce likelihoods and alter risk factors, such as surveillance and reshaping the global risk environment.

To sum up then, Beck argues that his risk-cosmopolitanism provides a theoretical basis for renewed consensus on global governance to reduce global systemic risks. The cosmopolitan outlook has to recognise the pragmatic need for cooperation, while institutionalised cosmopolitanism means that international organisations are adapted to include more non-state actors to manage risk more effectively. Risk also suggests guidelines for assessing how global governance practices might operationally manage risk, for example by implementing global risk-based regulatory standards to reduce vulnerabilities of global infrastructure. Yet a more critical reading of Beck also reveals several issues to be reckoned with, such as the role of power in the subjective selection of risk and the subsequent coercive proliferation of risk-based regulatory standards to include/exclude certain actors. The case studies presented in the following chapters are designed to explore these issues in more detail.

3 The Financial Action Task Force

Introduction

Designed to explore further the intertwined themes of risk, global governance and security outlined previously, the first empirical case study in the 'other' war on terror that we wish to address is the Financial Action Task Force (FATF). This particular choice, we recognise, needs some justification. Speaking of global governance arrangements, it must be said, it is the UN, and not the FATF, that first pops into the minds of most people. The world body has after all provided an indispensable legal *and* legitimate global platform for various counter-terrorism efforts, through its Counter-Terrorism Committee, adoption of the 2006 Global Counter-terrorism Strategy and not forgetting the global scale of financial surveillance practices embodied in powerful counter-terrorism resolutions such as UNSC1373 and UNSC1540.[1] However, our predominant understanding of global governance, as stated earlier, is not one that particularly centres on the role of the UN, 'formal' interstate organisations or even states. Instead, we take a less formalised but broader conception of global governance to encompass the whole range of governance-related activities that might be undertaken by various actors, of which the UN is one part. It is perhaps also useful to stress here that in using the term 'global governance', we are not necessarily claiming that there is 'universal' participation or agreement. Sometimes it is simply like-minded actors getting together to confront collective shared problems, a bit like 'coalitions of the willing' except in the non-military sense of the word.

In particular, this case study is designed to highlight two key strategic aims identified by the 2006 US National Strategy for Combating Terrorism: (1) the development of uniform counter-terrorism standards and best practices and (2) partnership with a myriad array of state and non-state actors to build capacity. We will show how the development of these two goals in the key area of terrorist financing can be understood to some extent using concepts and ideas that we have earlier operationalised from global governance literature and Beck's thoughts on 'cosmopolitan' cooperation. With these strategic goals of standards-setting and capacity-building in mind, we opted for the FATF for various reasons. Not only is it a relatively informal multilevel cooperative arrangement that carries no formal sanction under international law, it is also the premier international body dedicated to the establishment of legal and regulatory standards and policies to combat terrorist financing. It can with some justification be labelled the global counter-terrorism counterpart to the private non-governmental International Organisation for Standardisation (ISO), when it comes to standard-setting. Like the FATF, ISO standards too are voluntary and it has no legal authority to enforce implementation or legislate. Further, reflecting the multi-level nature of governance today, the FATF, as we shall see, also has overlapping partnerships with actors from the UN and regional organisations, to global banks and NGOs on the issues of capacity-building and standard-setting.

With regard to standards-setting, the new global counter-terrorist financing standards developed by the FATF deploy risk-based models as a shared regulatory platform for discussion. Just as internationally recognised ISO standards are based on international consensus among the experts in the field, the FATF standards too, on the surface, seem to be providing a new consensus for governance that global governance theory suggests is crucial: there is a whiff here of Beck's 'risk-cosmopolitanism' and enforced integration to avert shared risks. As for the second strategic aim of broad-based partnership and capacity-building, the increasing roles played by NGOs, global businesses to ordinary citizens, seem to suggest that a form of 'institutionalised cosmopolitanism' might possibly be developing in opening up the international system to more actors, at least when it comes to terrorist financing. Such increased activity of non-state actors has after all been a key theme of recent developments in global governance literature. Additionally, as will be shown, Beck would probably recognise the 'cosmopolitan realism' of transnational cooperative states working in their 'enlightened self-interest' as they drive the evolution and adaptation of the FATF from its anti-money laundering (AML) origins to counter-terrorist finance (CTF).

However, on deeper critical reflection, several issues emerge that undercut the supposed 'cosmopolitan-ness' (in Beck's narrow sense of the word) of global governance arrangements in the case of the FATF. Beck's conceptualisation is insufficient to capture adequately the continuing realities of different risk perceptions and power differentials that shape the 'other' war on terror, incidentally just as it does the conventional war on terror. The 'constructivist' nature of the terrorist financing risk highlights how the governance practices of this 'other' war on terror not only seek to manage risks but in many ways themselves shape the kinds of risks that are believed to be out there, in turn creating the very categories of riskiness that then feed back into the global risk governance system. There is no way one can escape the fundamentally subjective constructed nature of risk. This is compounded by underlying power relationships that influence the creation, propagation and acceptance of risk-based global regulations against terrorist financing: it would be naive to assume that acceptance of 'risk-cosmopolitanism' is either uniform, automatic, voluntary or without cost. Instead, it is deeply political. Many so-called 'partners' do not even agree the risk exists or share the same concern with terrorist financing risks, and yet feel compelled to go along for reasons we shall discuss: most of which are unrelated to the supposed 'cosmopolitan' integrative aspect of risk. If that is the case, it raises real questions about whether it is 'cosmopolitanism' or 'power' that brings agreement. The implementation of these global norms in practice also has the ability to affect not just state legislation but also individual day-to-day activities as well. It highlights several implications for surveillance, privacy, human rights and civil liberties, not least the degree of decision-making power granted to democratically unaccountable mid-level bureaucrats routinely charged with assessing risk profiles. Finally, we assess the practical implications of how the emerging global structure of cooperation might manage risk. The FATF standards work, for instance, by reducing vulnerabilities within the global financial infrastructure, increasing the barriers to success and reshaping terrorists' operating environments in the process. However, terrorists have proven extremely adaptable and agile in tweaking their financial activities in response to regulatory attempts. Very clearly, the terrorist financing risk constantly evolves, just like all risks: the 'boomerang effect' simply means any risk management attempt must bear in mind how it might generate new risks or influence the morphing of that original risk it set out to regulate in the first place.

This chapter therefore first clarifies the relationship between terrorist financing, global governance, risk and security. It then examines the rationale and justifications derived from a risk-based approach that underpins various FATF initiatives to stem global terrorist financing, before turning to a more critical evaluation of whether these can truly be seen as 'cosmopolitan' in nature. It then concludes with a discussion of the ways in which these global cooperative attempts can curtail terrorist financing risks in practice, and the problems that have arisen and in turn have to be managed.

Terrorist financing: a global governance issue in the 'other' war on terror

In tandem with the main arguments presented by this book, one of the reasons why we chose to focus on combating terrorist financing is simple: it seems to be one of the most successful yet less-visible aspects of the Bush administration's 'Long War', which stressed global cooperation. Indeed, the 9/11 Public Discourse Project – successor to the 9/11 Commission – has graded US counter-terrorist financing efforts in general an A–, the highest grade it awarded.[2] But why and how is combating terrorist financing considered an important but less noticed cooperative dimension of the 'other' war on terror? Let us begin with the 'war' imagery. On 24 September 2001, President George W. Bush launched what he called 'a major thrust of our war on terrorism':

> this 'war' would be like no other: fought on a variety of fronts ... the front lines will look different from the wars of the past ... it is a war that will require the United States to use our influence in a variety of areas in order to win it. *And one area is financial.*[3]

To emphasise its importance and to maximise media attention, the president insisted on personally unveiling the terrorist financing initiative in the White House Rose Garden himself, rather than delegating it to an under-secretary or worse still, a written statement.[4] Bush later commented on Executive Order 13224, 'the first shot in the war was when we started cutting off their money, because an al-Qaeda organisation can't function without money'.[5] As John Taylor, the State Department official then responsible for disrupting the financing of terrorists recalled, it quickly became a key part of the war on terror.[6] The US Treasury stressed the importance of countering terrorist financing, 'stopping terrorism starts with stopping the money'.[7] The reasoning behind this is that if it was possible to somehow impede or harm the flow of funds to terrorists, then future attacks can be averted and prevented. Obtaining financial data on terrorist transactions is considered useful because the assumption is that 'money trails don't lie',[8] and they are able to disclose 'blueprints to the architecture of terrorist organisations'.[9] Perhaps reflecting President Bush's rhetoric that the war on terror would assume different forms, the financial battle too has been laden with 'war' terminology: the US Treasury touted its new Foreign Terrorist Asset Tracking Centre as 'a new proactive, preventative strategy for waging financial war'.[10] Martin Navias even claimed that the US was now engaged in 'finance warfare' against terrorists.[11] American officials involved in stemming terrorist financial flows also freely and proudly characterise themselves as 'global financial warriors'.[12] While the 'war' terminology certainly still remains prevalent here, what is interesting is how this particular aspect of the 'war' is actually less visible, non-military and emphasises multilateralism rather than the unilateralism that we have come to associate with the word 'war'.

Invariably, the various bodies involved in the 'war' on terrorist finances stress the importance of global cooperation. The Wolfsberg Group of 12 global banks issued a statement on the suppression of financing of terrorism that recognises, 'successful participation in this fight by the financial sector requires global cooperation by governments with the financial institutions to an unprecedented degree'.[13] The FATF agrees that the fight against terrorist financing 'requires the united effort of countries around the world, including both FATF and non-FATF members'.[14] The underlying premise is straightforward: in an age of global financial flows and instantaneous electronic wire transfers, terrorists could simply move their finances to another country if they were being restricted in one, a point that Beck himself has made in the past repeatedly. This is why the State Department's Taylor claims:

> we were talking to everyone under the sun: there was an extraordinary degree of international cooperation in this area following 9/11, perhaps the best example of international cooperation in the field of finance since the establishment of the Breton Woods institutions at the end of World War II.[15]

One of the main vehicles for facilitating such cooperation was the FATF. Not only does it seem to be a good example of the need for renewed global cooperation, combating terrorist financing also requires multilevel coordination between domestic and international agencies, from diplomacy, intelligence, law enforcement to financial regulation and private banking sectors. The globalised scale of the challenge was highlighted when it emerged that the US was monitoring transaction details on the millions of daily wire transfers worldwide provided by SWIFT (Society for Worldwide Interbank Financial Telecommunication), which allowed access to its records. SWIFT argued that it complied because it carried out some processing in the US, which involved European transactions as well. Brussels however charged it had breached European privacy laws. What this particular case illustrates is how the nature of the global terrorist financing challenge has blurred the inside-outside boundary, particularly between different territorially contained jurisdictions: an ideal candidate for global governance on commonly shared transnational risks.

Terrorist financing as a global risk management issue

If terrorist financing provides a strong case for global governance, then what about its relationship with risk and security concerns? For one, the issue of terrorist financing is often approached in terms of risk management ideas and techniques. Financial data mining for instance is considered to be central in managing terrorist risks because it is 'extremely useful in tracing and investigating mere suspicions so that you might also similarly prevent a calamity that you don't yet have definition on'.[16] Tackling terrorist financing can, so the argument goes, help to enable the pre-emption of what could be terrorist schemes or attacks. Put plainly, to connect the dots before an attack occurs.[17] The FATF, to its credit, recognises the vagueness and conceptual difficulties in the language of risk often employed to describe terrorist financing:

> There are currently no standard definitions used internationally within the AML/CFT context for the terms risk, threat, and vulnerability. This project identifies concepts linked to these terms in order to promote a consistent approach by countries, but does not go so far as to suggest precise definitions for adoption by the international community.[18]

It does however recommend that a 'risk management process for dealing with money laundering and terrorist financing' should encompass (i) recognising the existence of risks, (ii) undertaking an assessment of the risk(s) and (iii) developing strategies to manage and mitigate the identified risks. The issue of terrorist financing can thus be broken into the various features of risk discussed in Chapter 2.

First, the capabilities and intentions of terrorist financing networks can often be complex and multifaceted, especially when linked to globalisation. As the FATF points out, 'globalisation has created potential new risks as criminals and terrorists seek to penetrate the global financial system'.[19] Exemplifying the risk language being used to describe the problem, there exist considerable amounts of uncertainty about terrorist financial capabilities. Terrorists groups can finance themselves in a variety of ways. Levi paints a picture of how funds can be disbursed regularly from a central point: or small decentralised cells can receive some start-up funds; sometimes self-starters fund themselves through petty criminal deeds. All in all, these are web-like structures without a central point.[20] The range of actors involved also complicates the problem, ranging from gemstone dealers (allegedly), grassroots fundraisers, recruiters, donors, to couriers carrying bags stuffed with cash, operatives who use the cash, right up to leaders and operational planners at the top. The institutions involved can be legitimate or illegimate, from formal banks, real estate agents, to the informal *hawala* value transfer system or unwitting charities who remit funds thinking it is for a good cause. Terrorists also have various means of concealing their financial activities, such as sending small amounts of money. Funds may also be raised through perfectly legal means or illegal mechanisms. Add to this the porosity and opportunities accorded by globalisation and you have a very complicated problem indeed. A risk management strategy would therefore identify and seek to chip away at these terrorist financial capabilities and intentions mentioned above.

Besides altering terrorist capabilities and intentions, another component of risk lies in the vulnerability of the global financial infrastructure. It is commonplace in the literature to come across FATF claims about how 'commercial websites and Internet payment systems appear to be subject to a wide range of vulnerabilities that can be exploited by criminal organizations and terrorist financiers'.[21] The implication is that if we are properly to manage terrorist financing risks, the vulnerability issue, amongst others, needs to be addressed. This is why the British Bankers' Association organises a one-day 'Managing the Risk of Terrorist Financing Workshop', which teaches delegates how to identify the risks of terrorist financing and ways to reduce exposure and vulnerability. It warns 'the risk of terrorist financing is a great deal wider than is often perceived'.[22] Echoing the risk management ideas discussed in the previous chapter, 'the strategies to manage and mitigate the identified money laundering and terrorist financing activities are typically aimed at preventing the activity from occurring'.[23] Therefore, Gurule is right to suggest that 'the global effort to stop terrorist financing is fundamentally a preventive strategy'.[24] Indeed, after 9/11, it somehow 'became an indisputable argument that surveillance was the means that could have prevented/protected against the event'.[25] In practice, as we shall see, these include new regulations, surveillance, detection, increased checks and hurdles for terrorist financing to cross, in the process weakening terrorist operating capabilities and intentions, and reducing vulnerabilities of infrastructure. When US Homeland Security czar Michael Chertoff talks of separating terrorists from the endless flows of people entering the US, he is referring to similar risk management principles, 'we have to have a way to manage the risk. We have to have a way to know who to focus on.'[26] An identical risk management approach, we shall see, is manifest in the global governance arrangements and risk-based standards that the FATF has put in place to monitor and separate terrorist funds from legitimate financial flows in the global financial infrastructure.

The FATF: 'institutionalised cosmopolitanism' and global governance?

So far, we have already established that combating terrorist financing ideally requires global cooperation on managing the risk. Such cooperation is coming in different forms and one interesting example of how a pre-existing international body has been reformed and rededicated to the war on terror is the FATF. Established by the then-G7 summit in 1989 originally to tackle money laundering, here we have, in its own words, 'an inter-governmental policy-making body whose purpose is to establish international standards, and develop and promote policies, both at national and international levels, to combat money laundering and terrorist financing'.[27] Its four core objectives are to:

1 revise and clarify the global standards and measures for combating money laundering and terrorist financing,
2 promote global implementation of the standards,
3 identify and respond to new money laundering and terrorist financing threats,
4 engage with stakeholders and partners throughout the world.

These four objectives shall be assessed as we go along in this chapter. Originally with 16 members, the FATF now has 33 members.[28] Rather than a formal treaty mandate that is binding under international law, it functions through its so-called '40 Recommendations' originally designed to counter money laundering. After 9/11, the FATF mandate was extended to the financing of terrorism, and another nine anti-terrorist financing (ATF) recommendations were added such as implementing UN instruments, criminalising the financing of terrorism, freezing assets or reporting suspicious transactions. Now known as the '40+9 Recommendations', these were to serve as 'new international standards for combating terrorist financing'.[29] Whether it is appropriate simply to adapt anti-money laundering standards to counter terrorist financing is a legitimate question that raises issues about the differences and similarities in the nature both of criminals and terrorists. However, we leave it to specialists who have more to say on this subject.[30] Our present concern is more to do with the reasoning behind adapting the FATF for the war on terror, and the drivers behind how the FATF 40+9 Recommendations have today become a model framework for governments and private actors alike.

The adaptation of the FATF to combat terrorist financing was an attempt to build on existing capacity within the international financial regulatory framework to overcome new challenges, as part of the 'post-September 11 international trend of merging AML and ATF regimes'.[31] In particular, there seemed to be some built-in flexibility within its organisational structure that could accommodate changing demands. The FATF has no permanent formal treaty mandate laying down legal rules and regulations that are legally binding under international law. Nor does it have a sizeable permanent bureaucracy. The term 'Task Force' itself implies it has a somewhat finite purpose. The FATF's evolution also reflected the Bush administration's preference for less bureaucratic measures that can be moulded, over rigid treaty-based formalised agreements. As the US 2006 *National Strategy for Combating Terrorism* stated, 'we will collaborate with our partners to update and tailor international obligations to meet the evolving nature of the terrorist enemies and threats we face'.[32] The FATF seems to fit the bill.

The FATF was also to some extent the outgrowth of domestic American regulatory initiatives such as the Patriot Act that required US financial institutions to curb terrorist financing. It soon became clear with the global nature of the risk that a global answer had to be found. It is not surprising therefore that powerful states like the US arguably continue to set the agenda in reforming the FATF after 9/11 and, in his defence, Beck has stressed that his notion of 'institutional cosmopolitanism' does not simply mean universal altruism or high-sounding idealism. Rather it is driven by 'cosmopolitan realism' and the enlightened self-interest of transnational cooperative states working together for mutually beneficial aims. This is all well and good, yet, in practice, critics contend the FATF represents Washington's attempt to align international standards with its own domestic regime and pressure others into keeping records that would be accessible to US law enforcement.[33] 'Resentments have arisen over Washington's attempt to set the pace in the finance war.'[34] The US reliance on the informal nature of the FATF to manage risk does appear to be causing problems as Clunan observes: 'while there has been substantial and important movement through informal international bodies such as the Financial Action Task Force and the Egmont Group, the United States has been unwilling to underwrite a formal global counter-terrorist-financing regime'.[35] What initially seemed to be a plus point in terms of flexibility and adaptability to new challenges might now be turning into an obstacle to longer-term deeper cooperation. The US also seems to prefer high-profile designations, targeted technical assistance and freezing of terrorist assets, over the Europeans' broader interest in a 'global multilateral approach to anti-money-laundering/counter-terrorist financing standard setting and technical assistance to implement such standards'.[36] Clunan thus concludes that US efforts in driving FATF reform are more self-centred and nationally focused, than truly 'global' or in Beck's case, 'cosmopolitan'.

Clunan is of course right to suggest that states remain key actors driving the reform of global governance arrangements to manage collective risks, and Beck even more so is acutely aware of the continued relevance of states. One downside of this is an underlying assumption behind terrorist financing, as Biersteker suggests, that states remain ultimately responsible for regulating terrorist financing activities within their borders although they do recognise the risk is cross-boundary. 'The problem is that, while the threat is trans-national, the practical response thus far remains largely contained within individual nation-states, while Al Qaeda on the other hand has creatively taken advantage of globalisation.'[37] The exact role that states play in driving Beck's 'institutionalised cosmopolitanism' is an unresolved tension. Can one for example clearly desegregate FATF activities as a whole, from the state actors that drive it? Although they remain key actors, how much or how little should states do? Certainly it is a difficult balancing act. At what point do certain states start dominating and other actors begin pushing back or, worse still, abandon the whole process altogether?

In spite of the many limitations, there have been some achievements in opening up the state-centric international system to manage risk better, perhaps even as a form of 'instutionalised cosmopolitanism' in action. A new counter-terrorist financing architecture has emerged, built upon on a complex web of horizontal and vertical arrangements and networks of governments, international organisations and private sector institutions.[38] Adapting the FATF to combat terrorist financing does suggest that states like America recognise that to protect their own national interests, individual action is insufficient and that reformed international fora can help develop global norms to manage terrorist financing risks more effectively. This is particularly so in partnership and joint activities with a wide range of actors. We shall now outline these FATF-driven initiatives in some detail, tracing their relationship to risk and global governance.

Governance by risk: 'risk-cosmopolitanism' and global standards-setting

As we have suggested, a crucial dimension of US counter-terrorism strategy is global cooperation on the clarification and adoption of common international standards/best practices, and engagement with partners to build partner capacity. These aims are also to be found in the FATF's core objectives outlined earlier as well. First, it would appear that a negative shared concern with terrorist financing risks is fostering negotiations between actors that might not have wanted anything to do with each other, on common risk management standards as a baseline for global coordinated action. One might even detect in this a hint of Beck's 'risk-cosmopolitanism'. A 'cosmopolitan' (in Beck's sense of the word) opening up of the global governance system beyond nation states alone, might well seem to be in the offing. Second, these risk-based standards can identify vulnerabilities in partner (state and non-state) capacity and infrastructure that can then be addressed. Here, we will outline the various initiatives taken towards achieving these goals, before critically evaluating them.

In countering terrorist financing, the central importance of developing best practices is recognised in the UN's 2006 *Global Counterterrorism Strategy*, which commits 'to encourage States to implement the comprehensive international standards embodied in the Financial Action Task Force's Forty Recommendations on Money Laundering and Nine Special Recommendations on Terrorist Financing, recognizing that States may require assistance in implementing them'.[39] The logic behind global cooperation on benchmarking is that since the risk is global, the world cannot afford national loopholes or vulnerabilities to be exploited, and all actors have to follow the same rules to manage that risk. In this way, a shared concern with a concern with risk is serving not only as a common denominator to bring people together in the first place but is touted as a solution as well. This particularly illustrates the various dimensions and uses of risk that we discussed in Chapter 2. Risk is used here as a descriptive term to highlight a perilous or undesirable outcome to be averted (terrorist financing), while also simultaneously employed as a policy proposal in the broader sense of a focus on probabilities and vulnerabilities that need to be addressed in order to avert that unwanted outcome (risk-based approach). The policy solution touted is not just international cooperation but cooperation on a global scale: 'a global strategy is needed if the fight against money-laundering is to succeed',[40] and 'counter-measures must be universally applied'.[41] What the FATF standards aim to provide are such universal counter-measures in the form of common risk-based evaluation criteria for the 'susceptibility of any firm, agency or national financial system to money laundering activities'.[42] Crucially, the FATF sees these standards applying beyond just its member states as well. In other words, as a risk management technique, it recommends ways in which to identify and manage vulnerabilities in the global financial infrastructure such as loopholes in regulations. 'Our approach to regulation is risk-based', declared US Treasury Financial Crime Centre director William J. Fox:

> We believe effective implementation must be predicated upon a financial institution's careful assessment of its own vulnerabilities to money launder-ing and other financial crime.... It is not a 'rule-based' approach, where the regulator gives the regulated a laundry list to be checked.[43]

Such risk-based standards are, according to Michael Power, becoming common-place in all sectors of society: 'The self-control activities of organisations have become an essential component of regulatory agendas which are developing in the direction of "risk-based regulation". This is a blueprint for the risk management state.'[44]

The fingerprints of a risk manager's mindset can be seen all too clearly in the 'gold standard' FATF 40+9 Recommendations, which are characterised above all by its emphasis on risk; 'customer risk profiles', 'risk management systems', 'operating on a risk-sensitive basis', 'lower risk categories', are concepts liberally peppered throughout.[45] Among others, it recommends legislating to make terrorist financing a crime, allowing freezing of terrorist assets, implementing due dili-gence and 'know your customer' (KYC) requirements for banks and other finan-cial institutions, establishing a suspicious transactions reporting process, and sharing financial intelligence with foreign partners by setting up Financial Intelli-gence Units in countries worldwide. Indeed, 'the risk-based approach is either incorporated into the Recommendations in specific and limited ways, or it is inherently part of or linked to those Recommendations'.[46] Under Recommenda-tion 5, for instance, a country's financial institutions must perform enhanced due diligence for higher-risk customers. A risk-based approach also means 'a risk analysis must be performed to determine where the money laundering and terror-ist financing risks are the greatest. Countries will need to identify the main vulnerabilities and address them accordingly.'[47]

Indicative of an emerging global consensus on these risk-based approaches as a shared governance platform, these Recommendations have been endorsed by the World Bank and the International Monetary Fund (IMF) as benchmark global standards. UN Security Council Resolution 1617 in 2005 too 'strongly urges all member states to implement the comprehensive international standards' contained in FATF recommendations. Judging from the numerous documents it has published on the topic, risk-based global norms are now seen by the FATF to provide a framework for negotiations with a range of partners in its attempts to proliferate and implement these common standards worldwide as a system of risk governance. The FATF's self-defined core activities revolve around a need to engage with stakeholders and partners on terrorist financing risk, and to promote global implementation of its risk-based standards. Somewhat reminiscent of Beck's 'cosmopolitan' opening up of the states-system, the FATF actively facilitates cooperation at supra-state, regional, interstate and substate levels. Even from the early stages, 'the review process for revising the Forty Recommendations was an extensive one, open to FATF members, non-members, observers, financial and other affected sectors and interested parties'.[48] Zagaris cites 'the recent change at the FATF to allow for a comment period open to all persons ... [which] have shown promise of a regime increasingly interested in working with all nations'.[49] The annual FATF 'typologies' exercise also brings together experts from the law enforcement and regulatory authorities of FATF member countries to exchange information on significant money laundering cases and operations. It provides a vital opportunity for operational experts to identify and describe current money laundering trends and effective countermeasures. In this sense, the global governance approach taken by the FATF appears distinctly global in rationale and outlook, perhaps even 'cosmopolitan' in Beck's sense of the term.

A number of outreach mechanisms have been launched at different levels, the rationale being that 'working more closely, for example, with the various FATF-style regional bodies (FSRBs), the Egmont group[50] and other international partners is likely to prove a valuable source of information as well as a key forum for dialogue on emerging trends'.[51] To begin with the regional level, there are now nine FSRBs spanning the globe, such as the Asia-Pacific Group on Money-Laundering, all committed to diffusing the same 40+9 Recommendations.[52] Through these FSRBs, the FATF hopes to 'leverage global efforts and ensure effective implementation of FATF recommendations in all regions of the world'.[53] FATF also grants access to FSRB delegates at meetings, 'thereby increasing ownership of FATF strategies to fight money laundering and terrorist financing by these non-FATF member countries'.[54] The FSRB initiative is interesting in that, to use an analogy coined by Mark Pieth, the resulting global governance structure is one of concentric circles where the FATF members are in the innermost centre, surrounded by the network of FSRBs and other associate organisations.[55] Consequently, many states are not FATF members but might be members of their FSRBs, thus bringing them in line with FATF-style standards.

Through partnerships with international organisations, especially the IMF, World Bank and the UN, the ultimate goal of global governance here is to create a global interlocking network of organisations to manage terrorist financing risks. Employing the same operational risk-based guidelines, these global bodies coordinate their activities closely. FATF works on harmonising joint training packages for assessors from FATF/FSRB/IMF/UN so they have the same common risk-based standards to evaluate. The UN's powerful Counter-Terrorism Committee (CTC) has also been providing technical assistance to help build capacity of UN member states that have been unable to meet requirements of the FATF standards. APEC has also adopted its Counter-Terrorism Action Plan, encouraging its members to identify needs and offer assistance. The G8's Counter-Terrorism Action Group too provides assistance to donors with a forum to identify needs and coordinate capacity-building. It also works closely with the UN's CTC, and FATF. These overlapping and complex multilevel relationships on global standard-setting and capacity-building might be beginning to vindicate Beck's claims about the ability of a 'risk-cosmopolitanism' to bring about a form of 'institutional cosmopolitanism' to manage shared global risks. Global governance theorists too would applaud these attempts to recognise and regulate collective problems, inviting more actors to participate.

The FATF has declared its intention to be more inclusive, and hence more effective, in the governance of global terrorist financing risk, or as Beck might have it, a 'cosmopolitan opening up of the system'. For this reason, the FATF recognises that 'the private sector is at the front line of the international battle against money laundering, terrorist financing and other illicit financing threats'.[56] The FATF president stressed in his 2007/08 Annual Report:

> one of my key priorities has been to develop a more open and constructive working partnership with the private sector in order to raise awareness of the FATF's work, to inform FATF policymaking and to encourage more effective implementation of AML/CFT measures.[57]

In October 2007, the FATF launched a new online forum – the Private Sector Consultative Forum – to strengthen existing dialogue with key private sector bodies from around the world and promote implementation of risk-based standards. The first such meeting to exchange information on terrorist financing with the private sector was held in London in December 2007.

The FATF has clearly identified a need to engage closely with the global business community not only on the collective risks of global terrorist financing but also the best way to manage it. In June 2007, in close consultation with members of the international banking and securities sector, such as the Japanese Bankers Association, European Association of Public Banks and JPMorgan Chase, the FATF jointly published *Guidance on the Risk-Based Approach to combating Money Laundering and Terrorist Financing*. The overarching aim was to 'support the development of a common understanding of what the risk-based approach involves and to indicate good practice in the design and implementation of effective risk-based approaches'.[58] This document essentially advocates the benefits of adopting a broad risk-based framework as a shared global governance platform while recognising the most appropriate format remains dependent on individual country risks. Being the first occasion that the FATF has used a public–private sector partnership approach in developing guidelines, the document concludes that a key element of success against terrorist financing is the 'emphasis on cooperative arrangements among the policy makers, law enforcement, regulators, and the private sector'.[59]

The FATF also has a joint working arrangement with the Wolfsberg Group of 12 global banks including Citigroup, Barclays, Bank of Tokyo-Mitsubishi, Goldman Sachs, Deutsche Bank. In 2006, the Wolfsberg Group issued 'Guidance on a Risk-Based Approach for Managing Money Laundering Risks'. By fostering the industry standard, which is now 'risk-based rather than a rule-based voluntary code', the Wolfsberg Group has helped to bridge the gap in attitudes to banking practice, especially between American and European banks.[60] As a medium of communication, shared global risk has ostensibly brought different sides of the debate closer together in this case. The Group aims to develop financial services industry standards for Counter-Terrorist Financing policies, working with NGOs such as Transparency International, and academics from the University of Basel. After 9/11 the Group published a 'Statement on the Financing of Terrorism' in January 2002.[61] Overall, this Wolfsberg process is often cited as an example of the private sector getting active on their own initiative and cost, recognising a need for standardised risk-based norms against global terrorist financing. Previously banks would have left the issue in the hands of national regulators.[62] The role that the private banking sector plays today in global governance is highlighted by the British Bankers' Association, in promoting its one-day 'Managing the Risk of Terrorist Financing Workshop'. It reminds us that 'in the current political climate financial institutions as well as corporate citizens must play their full part in mitigating the risk'.[63]

At a meeting in Berne in December 2007, the FATF decided to extend further global negotiations on terrorist financing, this time to key non-financial businesses that have been designated as handling large amounts of money, and hence posing a risk. In September 2007, FATF met with organisations that represent lawyers, notaries, accountants, trust and company service providers, jewellers, casinos, real estate agents and dealers in precious metals and precious stones. This private sector group expressed an interest in contributing to FATF guidance on implementing a risk-based approach for their sectors. Further meetings culminated with the release in June 2008 of a slew of documents on RBA (risk-based approach) Guidance developed in close consultations with representatives of Trust and Companies Services Providers. Other RBA guidance notes were negotiated with the accountants industry, dealers in precious metals and stones, and the real estate industry. Using language strikingly similar to earlier guidelines for global banks, the purpose of the guidance notes was likewise to:

> support the development of a common understanding of what the risk-based approach involves, outlines the high-level principles involved in applying

the risk-based approach, and indicates good public and private sector practice in the design and implementation of an effective risk-based approach.[64]

Playing a part in the governance of terrorist financing risk, the private sector also redeploys commercial risk techniques first pioneered in private financial markets in novel ways. Private data mining companies, including the British data mining companies Mantas and World-Check, have developed specialised software tools for financial institutions to single out suspicious transactions. Data are then analysed through risk-based calculative models that aim to identify suspicious transaction, populations and unusual activity, producing new spaces for governance.[65] A 'complex assemblage' composed of government officials, security experts, risk analysts and IT technology consultants working on risk models and indicators has emerged. The result is a more complex space of governing by risk where commerce and security become mutually implicated in a myriad of ways.[66]

One consequence of applying this risk-based approach is that, 'in order for financial institutions to have effective risk-based approaches, the risk-based process must be imbedded within the internal controls of the institutions ... a culture of compliance'.[67] FATF Recommendation 15 prescribes that financial institutions provide all employees with training on terrorist financing. In other words, the goal in this case is to have best practices integrated into daily routines of financial institutions such that it becomes a normal accepted activity. As risk management manuals suggest, 'good risk management will be a routine activity and therefore integrated into everyday management activity'.[68] The ultimate goal, as US Homeland Security czar Chertoff observed,

> is a time when security measures are a comfortable, convenient part of our routine; a time when people go about their daily lives mindful of risks but not encumbered by fear, unwavering in their resolve and full participants in their own protection.[69]

Indeed, scholars working in IPE are now suggesting that we should adopt a bottom-up perspective as 'our everyday actions shape and transform the world economy', not just powerful states and multinational corporations. Seemingly ordinary or subordinate small-scale local actors and everyday people too have agency in shaping their political and economic environments.[70] In a similar vein, we suggest that the goal of cooperatively managing terrorist financing risks is becoming integrated into daily routines of people working in banks, financial institutions as well as their customers. Indeed, bank customers come into contact with this new risk-based surveillance regime whenever they are asked for various forms of identification. This has become 'standard, normal, unremarkable behaviour'.[71] The seemingly routine surveillance of financial data interrogates 'the "normal" financial transactions of citizens and non-citizens in an attempt to identify the future terrorist'.[72] Governance by risk is becoming a daily reality as shared terrorist financing risk not only helps engender new global regulatory standards, it also filters down to individual levels of society.

Power, the social construction of risk, exclusion and alienation: not so 'cosmopolitan' after all?

So far, we have discussed how risk-based norms are being negotiated and implemented in the global governance of terrorist financing. 'Risk-cosmopolitanism' on the surface then might be able to explain how a wide range of actors is coming together in a form of 'institutionalised cosmopolitanism' set up against a shared global risk. But if such risk-based norms are touted as a solution to the problem, we have not yet touched on another crucial question: how do actors become aware of that risk in the first place and what are the factors shaping risk-cosmopolitanism? After all, Beck himself is quite clear that the new awareness of risk has the potential to unleash new debates and conflicts on how best to manage risks. It is by no means a post-political process. To the contrary, it is the very 'political' nature of this new awareness of global risk and the reconfiguration of politics and political structures that concerns him most. Furthermore, on the face of it, there is nothing 'cosmopolitan' about the enforced sharing and transfer of private details and data. One might therefore legitimately question the underlying processes behind the identification of terrorist financing as a risk and the subsequent development of regulations to control them. Indeed, as Hulsse observed, the global governance literature is usually more concerned with how global governance works, especially how rules are set, how compliance is achieved and whether a specific set of global rules is effective. It is comparatively silent regarding the nature of the risks that these global rules seek to regulate.[73]

The oft-neglected question is how a problem is cast as a global phenomenon, in order to create demand for global cooperative solutions.[74] In other words, if 'cosmopolitan' in Beck's understanding of the word is a world view or horizon based on shared global risk beyond the nation state, how does this horizon arise in the first place? By employing a narrative that emphasised that the global financial system was only as strong as the weakest link in the chain, the FATF created pressure for change and a need for global governance.[75] In this sense, the FATF appears to be 'socially constructing' into existence a shared consensus about the risk, where none might have existed before. This awareness apparently has to be created and disseminated, as risk on its own does not automatically generate risk-cosmopolitanism. Here, not only is the FATF 'constructing' *consensus* about the global risk, it is also constructing the problem itself. As Power points out, 'the risk management of everything involves the creation of new risk categories for managerial and political attention'.[76]

One such category, according to Warde, was the 'prevailing fantasy of a buzzing trans-national network of seamless electronic transfers'. In truth, terrorist networks operated more often than not on shoestring budgets and envelopes of cash.[77] The way in which this fantasy was spun serves to highlight how risk is seldom objective but socially constructed and 'problematised'. As Hulsse suggests, global problems should not be taken as a given because, in fact, states have to be persuaded a problem exists in the first place and then accept the solutions offered to them. Therefore those seeking to regulate a problem have to 'construct the issue as a global problem requiring global rules in order to be solved'. The same actors that create rules are also often the creators of problems.[78] This seems to be the case with anti-terrorist financing regulations because just ten or 15 years ago, none existed. Now almost every country in the world has such systems.[79] Consequently, 'the demand for global governance is not given, but has to be created'.[80] Similarly other global risks such as global warming 'needs to be defined as a problem that requires action by key actors in the system'.[81] Hulsse demonstrates that the FATF has constructed money laundering as a risk that requires global governance by talking the problem into existence and 'creating globalness'.[82] As the FATF notes, 'action to eradicate the problem in a single country is likely to lead to its rapid re-emergence in another, probably nearby country'. This creates the need for global cooperation.[83] Through making statements about the 'worldwide nature of the problem' and how 'no country is immune', the FATF depicts the global risk as a consequence of the globalisation of the financial system.[84] Through its annual reports, organising conferences for 'teaching' non-member states that depend heavily on FATF financial support, 'FATF constructs money-laundering as a global phenomenon, and into an international problem necessitating an international solution.'[85]

In its attempts to convince the world of the terrorist financing risk, the FATF often banks on its 'expert knowledge and can thus present its description as an objective description based on expertise'.[86] How 'objective' such expertise really is, is another question altogether. In truth the FATF sought to raise 'awareness of the nature and scope of the problem', in order to make others see the world in the particular way that it does. By deploying 'awareness' rhetoric, 'the use of a certain vocabulary is by no means innocent, but constructs reality in a certain way – in this case it objectifies the problem of money-laundering'.[87] Hulsse concludes that 'this brief history of the changing explanations for why there is a money laundering *problem* sustains our central claim that, rather than being objective facts, policy problems are the result of social constructions'.[88] There was really no shared consensus on terrorist financing, until it was 'problematised' into a global security risk that required a global solution.

While deploying the language of risk in the various FATF risk-based guidance notes, hints at a 'scienticised', 'objective' and ostensibly neutral approach to depoliticise problems, in fact, the use of risk concepts is deeply political and belies underlying power relations. We do need to pose the legitimate question of who sets what kinds of rules.[89] Real questions have to be asked of Beck's brand of 'cosmopolitan realist' states: are they actually more realist and power-based than cosmopolitan? For instance, 'much of today's innovation in surveillance practice and technology is driven by state apparatuses – like that of the United States – gathering information about populations and firms, collecting data on legal and illegal activities'.[90] Indeed, the common 'notion of a cold, analytic, actuarial risk assessment is largely a myth. Risk is a social construct that incorporates value judgments about context and cause.'[91] Simply painting terrorist financing as a global risk makes people pay attention, as the FATF occupies a powerful 'dominant discourse position,[92] composed mainly of rich powerful countries. State Department official Taylor in his memoirs too implies that the US Treasury essentially created the 'Special Recommendations on Terrorist Financing' and then had the FATF rubber stamp them.[93] This does seem to hint or at least imply at the dominant role of the US in developing and promoting practices to suit its own needs and preferences. However, 'little of this occurred over the opposition of other rich countries, most of whom supported these moves ... one should not forgot the key role that international organisations and private firms have played in spreading these standards'.[94] On the other side of the Atlantic, de Goede contends that the EU was being equally aggressive in this regulatory area as the US. Rather than a reluctant subordinate follower of what is usually seen as US unilateral practices, the EU has in fact taken a very strong lead, including asset freezing and data retention.[95] Sharman concludes that 'although power has been central to policy diffusion in this instance, it has not been hegemonic power'.[96] Power in any form is still power though.

Therefore, instead of any presumed 'cosmopolitan' solidarity on shared risks, the diffusion of anti-terrorist financing norms, particularly in the developing world, 'seems more power-based than voluntary' and on a 'coercive basis'. The mechanisms behind such diffusion are seen to be discursively mediated exercises of power rather than rational learning.[97] One example is the FATF's Non-Cooperating Countries and Territories (NCCT) initiative to 'secure the adoption by all financial centres of international standards to prevent, detect, and punish money-laundering, and thereby effectively co-operate internationally in the global fight against money laundering'.[98] Of the 23 states blacklisted as lacking in their counter-terrorist financing efforts, many were outside FATF membership and had no legal formal obligation to comply; yet these eventually gave in. This raises questions about compliance costs for these entities. At what point will they conclude that the costs of compliance outweigh the benefits of intransigence? The reasons were varied. Generally, countries recognised that adopting such standards enhanced protection of their financial systems. Also there were 'reputation costs'.[99] This is a more fundamental concern, as 'blacklisting questions the legitimacy of the country's right to conduct financial business in the global environment'.[100] Above all, the reasons why 'blacklisted' states respond seem to be largely self-interested and nationally defined; it had less to do with the supposed integrative effects of a shared global risk. Rather, as a form of mimicry, it is 'driven by fear of losing social acceptance'.[101] Adopting FATF standards is 'not so much because they are actually effective at lowering the risk ... but rather it serves as an indicator of membership of an "in-group"'.[102] The NCCT initiative did pressure target states to change tack but rather than creating a shared reflexive self-awareness of global risks, simply 'set in train self-reinforcing but largely unintended processes of socialisation and competition that have now made AML policy a near-universal standard'.[103] Furthermore, the reputational argument, rather than risk-cosmopolitanism, gives insight into how power is playing out in discourse: 'it is due to the FATF's power of definition that some states' financial systems may lose credibility and, resulting from that, its customers may lose their confidence'.[104]

Rational learning and replicating successful initiatives on how to combat common problems of global risk has in fact played little role. As Hulsse suggests, actors will comply with rules set by others only if they agree there is a problem that the rules address. 'Input legitimacy' implies that rules are seen as legitimate because the rule making has followed a representative participative process of inclusion and consultation. However, to many, the FATF standards are 'characterised by precisely a severe lack of input legitimacy ... exclusive rules set up by a small group of states but intended for global application'.[105] They adhere more closely to the 'Club' model where rules are made by a few members with a common interest. The perceived 'exclusivity' of these rules can mark them out as not particularly legitimate to non-members, regardless of whether there is consensus on the need for global governance in the first place.

Legitimate or not, direct coercion in the form of the NCCT process was a 'deliberate and calculated use of power by the FATF to impose policies that elicited instrumental compliance by states'.[106] There was 'nothing subtle' about the NCCT blacklist.[107] Sharman suggests the NCCT initiative was a result of the FATF losing patience with its efforts to lead by example and getting everybody else to agree on risk-based practices. Having no formal legal existence itself, it cannot make international law, and formal trade sanctions would have required a total legal revamp of the organisation, which not all members wanted.[108] Material penalties arose for states blacklisted, as they became perceived to pose increased risks. Especially in developing countries, the 'primary audience for AML authorities to satisfy has not been the local financial services industry or government but rather international organisations and foreign firms'.[109] Rather than 'risk-cosmopolitanism', policy makers in these countries were more worried about the demonstrative effects of being blacklisted and damage done to their economies: the 'heads on sticks' effect.[110] As the Malawi Minister of Economics and Planning put it, 'We did as we were told.'[111] The NCCT raise the costs of business by recommending all financial institutions impose a higher level of scrutiny on transactions going through a blacklisted state: a de facto financial blockade.[112] Additionally, taking advantage of its position as an authoritative international organisation accorded legitimacy, the FATF through its NCCT initiative has 'been able to confer a new negative status on certain jurisdictions and affect the way they are treated by others'.[113] As Sharman concludes, power in this instance was exercised not in an explicitly brute material force kind of way, but in a more implicit, and discursively mediated form.

There are other instances of disparities in power and thinking, which in some ways makes a mockery of the ability of risk-cosmopolitanism to bring all actors to the table of 'institutionalised cosmopolitanism' on an equal, rather than hierarchical, basis. This is reflected in how risk-based counter-terrorist financing initiatives are often 'created and employed in the developed states with little regard for the differing dynamics and market penetration of the banking and financial service sectors in a developing economy'.[114] This also neglects the significant differences between terrorism concerns of Europe/America and the rather more pressing development/human security problems that developing states confront.[115] Vlcek concludes that there exist different national priorities such that the global terrorism risk is not equally shared or perceived by all: officials in Europe/ North America must recognise that 'trans-national terrorism is not as much a problem for human security in the Global South, as is the lack of local economic development, clean water and a cure for HIV/AIDS (to list but a few specific problems).'[116] So, while global risk-based standards that seek uniformity in global governance approaches to manage shared risk are driven by developed states, the rest of the world does not quite share the same consensus on risk perceptions: a major blow both to the premises of 'risk-cosmopolitanism' and global governance.

The development of global regulatory practices based on risk has also unfortunately encouraged the practice of risk profiling with consequences for legality as well as democratic accountability. There is hardly anything 'cosmopolitan' about such practices arising from a concern with managing collective global risks. Risk is not serving a positive 'enlightenment' function here. Who has the power to decide which risk is worth regulating and are they democratically accountable? Essentially it is that banks are now expected to make value risk judgements about their customers: 'this is a subjective and time-consuming strategy that can also lead to discrimination on the basis of ethnic background and create biases linked to personal characteristics'.[117] As De Goede argues, this has created a 'legal space of exception where everyday and perfectly legal financial transactions of particular groups can become subject to monitoring and freezing, without juridical remedy'.[118] These practices produce 'unaccountable spaces of decision-making' as bureaucrats and mid-level officials who lack legal and democratic accountability, are newly authorised and empowered to make security decisions on the basis of their professional judgement of risk.[119] What Butler called 'petty sovereigns'[120] are to be found not just in government bureaucracies but also in airline companies and banks as they decide, according to risk profiles, who to allow to board a plane or to transfer money between bank accounts.

Governing by risk has also created exclusion and inclusion rather than the 'cosmopolitan' integrative effects Beck had in mind. In particular, there have been discursive associations forged between terrorism financing, *hawala*, wire-transfers and Islamic charitable groups.[121] The targeting of 'risky' financial transactions has also engendered new forms of alienation and resentment. Ericson observes that 'in its exceptional efforts to criminalise in response to uncertainty, the state helps manufacture malicious demons ... selected populations are criminalised in ways that create terror, insecurity, injustice ... uncertainty ends up proving itself'.[122] Data retention and mining are most often critiqued in terms of the politics of surveillance and the implications for individual privacy.[123] Sceptics have warned the global banking network was being turned a 'global espionage apparatus'.[124] These problems are indicative of how fundamental questions over risk can lead to a fierce politics of disagreement and dissension, rather than the 'cosmopolitan' solidarity that Beck suggests. Who will be included and excluded in this risk management system? These types of political questions do need to be at the forefront, beyond purely 'technical' discussions about the means of risk management.[125]

Not only do these measures have negative impacts on civil liberties of individual citizens as data might be transferred to countries that are not as rigorous about privacy, they also have knock-on effects on the ability of migrants to remit much-needed funds back to their home countries. Already on the fringes of society, as Vleck argues, these people are marginalised even further and have to resort to informal value transfer systems. Attempts to regulate such informal systems further have the 'potential of a far more detrimental impact upon developing states than it has for any likelihood to identify and isolate terrorists'.[126] People without a permanent address or regular financial transactions might also be segregated as well: 'it increases financial exclusion by limiting access to financial services based on possession of approved identity documents'.[127] Overall, Vlcek is sceptical whether the financial surveillance measures themselves even work to impair terrorist financing, and the costs seems to outweigh any perceived benefits.[128]

Evaluating the FATF as a global risk management exercise

We have so far examined both the stated rationale and unstated shortcomings of an emerging risk-based framework of global cooperation against terrorist financing. Power, more than 'cosmopolitan' solidarity, appears to be the main driver in generating a shaky global consensus (if one might even call it that) on the need for global governance to manage shared global risks. The implementation of risk-based standards incurs compliance costs such as infringement of civil liberties, discrimination and exclusion; these might not warrant any risk-reduction benefit accrued. But casting aside these stumbling blocks for a moment, assuming it did secure global uniformity and implementation, how could these FATF initiatives have functioned to reduce risks? If the core focus of risk management is preventing the unwanted activity from materialising, then likewise for the FATF, its 'strategies to manage and mitigate the identified money laundering and terrorist financing risks in financial institutions are typically aimed at preventing the activity from occurring'.[129] The 40+9 standards do precisely this: first identifying the risk factors (vulnerabilities of infrastructure, terrorist financial capabilities and intentions) and then altering them to avoid undesirable outcomes. This mirrored wider developments towards preventive approaches in criminology. As Castel has noted, 'what the new preventive policies primarily address is no longer individuals but factors, statistical correlations of heterogeneous elements. They deconstruct the concrete subject of intervention, and reconstruct a combination of factors liable to produce risk.'[130]

In evaluating the global measures adopted so far, they have clearly had an impact on legislation and institutions, including criminalisation of the activity, regulation of financial services and establishing Financial Intelligence Units. But the actual effect on terrorist capacity to store and move funds remains open to question.[131] This vagueness raises difficulties in gauging the progress of coopera-tive attempts at global risk management. Most evaluations have focused on process (e.g. coordination between different departments) or dissemination of regulatory standards worldwide. As of June 2008, the FATF claims its 'stand-ards have now been endorsed directly by 180 jurisdictions, representing more than 85% of the world'.[132] But it is important also to evaluate impact. Yet it is extremely difficult to reach any quantitative measure of flows of terrorist finance with any degree of accuracy. Furthermore, it is hard to distinguish funds obtained from legal means that are then used to finance terrorist activities, such as donations to charities and madrassas. How can one have an adequate perform-ance evaluation baseline? Yet as Levi points out, there is not much desire in the US for scientific proof of impact. Positive progress is difficult to demon-strate except in purely organisational terms such as increased seizures and 'disruptions', a term increasingly popular in the UK and Europe.[133]

In its attempts to rationalise its global counter-terrorist financing campaign, the White House makes a rather useful before-and-after comparison,

> Before 9/11, financiers of terrorism and terrorist financing networks went untouched and largely ignored by the international community. Today, we continue the aggressive worldwide campaign to disrupt terrorism financing, making it harder, costlier, and riskier for al-Qaida and other terrorist groups to raise and move money around the world'[134]

The key words here, from a risk management perspective, are *'making it harder, costlier and risker'*. In a recent Hearing before the US House of Representatives, Fox similarly argued that 'financial intelligence is actionable intelligence. It can ... lead to effective strategic action that stops or disrupts the flow of money to terrorist and their networks, which, in turn, serves to *halt or impede terrorist operations'*.[135] One key risk management aim through coordinated global gov-ernance arrangements and risk-based best practices is to 'keep the financial system clean by *increasing the difficulties and costs* of money laundering'.[136] Through global coordination making the global financial environment less hos-pitable to Al Qaeda operations and creating more hurdles to cross, the greater the likelihood of disruption. Each disruption in turn weakens the operational capa-bility and alters the intentions of terrorists: a key goal of risk management. But this does not translate into 'perfect security'. Risk management is not tantamount to risk elimination.

The 9/11 Commission's Monograph on Terrorist Financing makes a similar point:

> While a perfect end state – the total elimination of money flowing to Al Qaeda – is virtually impossible, current government efforts to *raise the costs and risks* of gathering and moving money are necessary to limit Al Qaeda's ability to plan and mount significant mass casualty attacks. We should understand, however, that success in these efforts will not of itself

immunize us from future terrorist attacks; completely choking off money to Al Qaeda is 'essentially impossible'.[137]

The FATF too recognises that 'authorities should publicly recognize that the risk-based approach will not eradicate all elements of risk'.[138] It continues that 'any reasonably applied controls, including controls implemented as a result of a reasonably implemented risk-based approach will not identify and detect all instances of money laundering or terrorist financing'. Nonetheless, it maintains that a 'risk-based approach is designed to make it more *difficult* for these criminal elements to make use of financial institutions due to the increased focus on the identified higher risk activities that are being undertaken by these criminal elements'.[139] Similar lessons can be drawn from other attempts to regulate global problems:

> The Kimberley process has made blood diamonds more difficult to get to market. It will not ultimately cut off the supply of illicit diamonds. What the process does is add *layers of difficulty* for those wishing to abuse the system and install some accountability mechanisms to punish those who do not play by the rules. All are useful pieces of a much larger puzzle but are not a silver bullet.[140]

While exaggerated statements about 'starving the terrorists of funding' raise unfounded expectations, an intercepted letter between Al Zawahiri and Abu Musab al Zarqawi dated 9 July 2005 indicates that 'many of lines of financial support have been cut off, Because of this, we need a new payment while new lines are opened.'[141] There is evidence to suggest that it is indeed becoming 'more difficult' for terrorists and their key supporters to use the formal financial sector to support their operations today than in 2001. But we do need to consider whether the costs of hindering flows across international networks is actually worth the benefits of constraining terrorist financing.[142] As Reuter and Truman conclude:

> little systematic evidence has been advanced that ... extensions of the anti-money laundering regime, with the costs they impose on legitimate businesses and their customers, will do more than marginally inconvenience those who need to launder the proceeds of their crimes.[143]

One might also add so far there is little concrete evidence that these new measures have made life significantly more difficult for criminals or terrorists seeking to launder money.[144]

Al Qaeda funding has also evolved and global governance arrangements like the FATF have to keep up to manage the risks better. Movement of funds in the formal sector has apparently diminished compared to 2001.[145] But the tightened controls on formal banking sectors may only have displaced terrorist finances into informal illegal channels such as *hawala* or crime. These 'ultimately reshape rather than resolve the issues'.[146] The 2004 Madrid bombing suggests that funding is increasingly coming from criminal activities within a single state. The 2005 London bombers were radicalised British residents using locally obtained funds to commit terrorism: surveillance of SWIFT transactions or FATF regulations would have had great difficulty uncovering these internal financial transactions.[147] The scale of transnational movements of funds thus has apparently diminished but this cannot be seen as an unmitigated success for the regulation of formal international financial sectors since 9/11.[148] It only reminds us that risks constantly morph and evolve; there is no realistic hope for complete elimination. Counter-terrorist financing strategies must identify and respond to developing trends, a core self-defined goal of the FATF. It has a dedicated 'Methods and Trends' working group to monitor changes in techniques and methods. It also recognises that 'efforts to combat money laundering and terrorist financing should also be flexible in order to adapt as risks evolve'.[149] To support the goal of producing a global threat assessment and identify priority global concerns, the February 2008 FATF plenary initiated the Strategic Surveillance Initiative (SSI). The SSI process includes aggregating existing national money laundering/terrorist financing risk assessments, surveying FATF and FSRBs regarding emerging trends and high priority money laundering/terrorist financing risks.

One particularly worrying trend today, as Phil Williams points out, is how the jihadi movement is increasingly reliant on self-funded petty criminal activities or organised crime methods. For instance the Islamic Movement of Uzbekistan relies on kidnapping and drug smuggling, notoriously holding for ransom some Japanese geologists. The Group for Salafist Preaching and Combat in Algeria too is becoming profit-motivated by kidnapping, drug and human trafficking. This increasing terrorist use of organised crime will render existing attempts on curtailing terrorist finances ineffective, premised as they are on money laundering assumptions.[150] The FATF's use of sophisticated technologies and risk-based analysis may also be easily overcome by 'mundane tactics using the large pool of supporters attracted to the declared goals of a radical organisation'. If Bin Laden can 'recruit 20 people willing to die on his behalf, he will have no problem getting 100 to open bank accounts'.[151]

Formal financial controls and global risk-based FATF standards are thus in danger of becoming obsolete. As Biersteker observes, more attention is needed for global governance to shift against criminal activities, as the funding risk from Al Qaeda is increasingly becoming a criminal one. Indeed, risk is reactive: 'as people act on knowledge of risk, they simultaneously change the risk environment and create new uncertainties'.[152] 'Tactics that make criminal conduct difficult are also making legitimate actions more difficult. The increased difficulty experienced by migrants may unintentionally further encourage the use of informal or underground methods by them to send money home.'[153] What Beck calls 'boomerang effects' clearly abound. Levi observes that one lesson from the war on crime that might be applied to controlling terrorist financing is that 'any strategy runs the risk of unintended consequences'. He rattles off a long list of such consequences. Global cooperation to curb remittances both in official or informal sectors might harm recipient countries reliant on such remittances. Those at the receiving end would hardly perceive these initiatives as 'cosmopolitan' in origin. The conventional wisdom that disruption or arresting leaders will reduce overall risk is also not self-evident. Terrorist financing may simply become more streamlined and efficient in response, making the risk harder to monitor. Targeting the dominant group may only generate opportunities for competitors, spawning a larger number of smaller hard to track groups.[154]

A global governance apparatus premised on risk-based approaches has emerged nonetheless, adding layers of difficulty to reduce the risk. Disrupting funding flows can create a hostile environment for terrorism, constraining the overall capabilities of terrorists and helping frustrate their intentions to execute attacks. Weak vulnerable spots in the financial infrastructure need to be targeted where interventions can 'reduce the opportunities for offenders and increase the risks they face'.[155] By making it harder for terrorists and reducing vulnerabilities, a truly 'global counter-terrorist financing infrastructure could change the operating environment of terrorists, forcing them into criminal activities that are easier to trace and prosecute than is pre-criminal terrorist financing'.[156] In Britain for example, the 'Fighting Crime and Terrorism: We Need Your Help' campaign launched in mid-2003, requires high-street banks to step up security checks not just of new retail customers, but also of existing ones. The campaign leaflets operate under a banner that sums up the risk management mantra we have outlined so far: 'You can make life harder for terrorists.'

Many experts agree that:

> the combination of routing the Taliban, taking away training camps, policing financial networks, killing many al-Qaeda lieutenants, and maintaining electronic and aerial surveillance has put bin Laden and al-Zawahiri in a situation in which they can survive and inspire but not do much more.[157]

In essence, it has become harder to perform basic organisational functions:

> Because of increased intelligence efforts by the United States and its allies transactions of any type – communications, travel, money transfers – have become more dangerous for the jihadists. Where bin Laden's central leadership team could once wire money around the world using normal bank networks, it now relies on couriers with money vests ... Where bin Laden's network could once use satellite phones and the Internet for communication, it now has to avoid most forms of electronic communication, which leave an electronic trail back to the user.[158]

Electronic funds transfers are now more difficult but have by no means eliminated the risk of attacks. It has however made it 'significantly harder for terrorists of any provenance to achieve a "second 9/11"'.[159] Even increased public scrutiny of anyone who 'looks Muslim ... a terrible, racist reaction but it has made it harder for them to operate'.[160]

Besides reshaping the environment by adding layers of difficulty and reducing vulnerabilities, a key aim of the global campaign against terrorist financing has been getting as high a participation rate as possible. This was not just a question of idealistic cosmopolitan solidarity. Rather, as Taylor emphasised, getting more countries on board also reduced the chances of terrorist funds slipping through since it is fundamentally a global problem.[161] Another private sector body that the FATF engages with, the Basel Committee on Banking Supervision (comprising representatives from the central banks of G10 countries) issued 'Consolidated KYC [know your customer] Risk Management', to provide banks with guidance on managing risks. The guidelines 'protect the integrity of the banking system by reducing the likelihood of banks becoming vehicles for money laundering, terrorist financing and other unlawful activities'.[162] This notion of reducing likelihood is anchored in US thinking about the war on terror from the start. As then Secretary of State Colin Powell suggested in September 2001, we can 'reduce the likelihood of these incidents if we go after those terrorist organisations'.[163] Through global governance, it is in truth more realistic to hope for reducing probabilities, rather than completely choking terrorist financing.

But in the narrower tactical sphere, not much can be done against determined suicide bombers who have relatively few funding needs. Restricting terrorist financing can help reduce the scale of damage but since their scale is quite small, it would be very hard to limit them sufficiently (just ten average credit card frauds would be enough to finance the Madrid bombings). But, forcing terrorists into committing crime would also increase their risks of discovery.[164] In reality, the best that can be achieved by 'follow the money' methods is obtaining intelligence allowing for arrests, surveillance and preventing particular groups from obtaining funds for particular attacks – or simply make them run higher risks in the search for funding.[165]

Conclusion

The campaign against terrorist financing, we suggest, is an interesting case study that illuminates the intersecting roles of risk, global governance and security. Risk here serves not only as a description of an unwanted outcome, but also suggests targeted risk-based policy proposals to reduce probabilities and vulnerabilities to avert that outcome. Global governance here manifests in the reform of the FATF to combat terrorist financing. The 'cosmopolitan realist' states driving the FATF's rededication to the war on terror appear cognisant of shared risks and the need for global cooperation, on the one hand, to protect their own national interests, but Beck's 'institutionalised cosmopolitanism' has not quite developed to the degree he would have hoped for. Although there is movement towards what Beck might suggest is the 'cosmopolitan opening up' of the international system, critics such as Biersteker contend that much of the response is still nationally centred and premised. The desire to include more non-state actors is reflected in active engagement with business organisations such as the

Wolfsberg Group of global banks, as well as NGOs like Transparency International, in the drafting of common guidelines against terrorist financing based on risk. There is also engagement with regional organisations such as the Asia-Pacific Group, as a form of 'enforced integration' to manage more effectively a common shared risk. However, the net has been drawn so wide that law enforcement agencies face overload.[166] As the Wolfsberg Group itself acknowledges, 'it is difficult (at times impossible) for an institution to distinguish between legal and illegal transactions, not withstanding the development and implementation of a reasonable designed risk-based approach'.[167] There are further problems in terms of burden sharing. Much of the implementation falls on the private sector: 'it is private financial firms following FATF-mandated rules legislated by national governments that have borne most of the burden of fighting money laundering' and to report 'suspicious transactions'.[168] Smaller banks complain about competitive disadvantages compared to larger banks, faced with higher administrative costs. Indeed, the issue of terrorist financing demonstrates how global governance straddles the various levels of analysis in IR, from individual private citizens to international organisations. In practice, the successful implementation of global standards against suspicious transactions hinges on the vetting integrity of individual financial services professionals and bank tellers, as well as those further down the line.[169] It is imperative that these individuals working in the financial and banking sector recognise that they are actually on the front lines of this 'other' war on terror, and by applying a risk-based approach they too can play roles in counter-terrorism. As Carol Sergeant, head of anti-money laundering at Britain's Financial Services Authority stressed, 'anybody, whether you are a financial institution or a fish-and-chip shop, is obliged to report any suspicion of terrorist activity'.[170]

While the FATF does demonstrate an attempt to reinvigorate international organisations to tackle global terrorism, states, especially in the Third World, still view the risk through a national lens rather than 'cosmopolitan' ones. Many countries do not perceive themselves at the same risk of terrorism as the West. Divergent interests and local sensitivities remain.[171] These divergences needed to be papered and smoothed over by the FATF's attempts to construct terrorist financing as a shared global phenomenon afflicting all and sundry alike. In this sense, the 'cosmopolitan' outlook itself still needed to be created; there is less evidence of 'risk-cosmopolitanism' uniformly emerging as yet.

However, recognising the shared global risk of terrorist financing, at least among some quarters if not uniformly around the world, has served as a negative form of integration. At the very least, it has certainly compelled more global negotiations on new benchmarks and norms to regulate the risk. The US 2006 *National Strategy for Combating Terrorism* notes that 'the Group of Eight [G8] along with other multilateral and regional bodies also have been instrumental in developing landmark counterterrorism standards and best practices that have been adopted by international standard-setting organizations'.[172] This is particularly seen in the FATF 40+9 Recommendations and the Wolfsberg Principles: both of which derive from a set of risk-based procedures. From the viewpoint of global governance, a significant part of the rationale behind the NCCT initiative was that costs would have to be allocated to those risky blacklisted states that decline to meet new global risk-based norms.

But here, the propagation and eventual acceptance of these risk-based procedures seemed to be dependent more on coercion and power relationships than any reflexive self-awareness of 'cosmopolitan' solidarity on shared global risks that Beck seemed to have in mind. Instead powerful actors such as the FATF, US and EU continue to set the agenda and rules, using the language of risk to foster awareness and compelling others to toe the line. In this sense then, deploying concepts of risk are deeply related to underlying power differentials between those who 'problematise' the risk and recommend risk-based regulatory standards, and those who have to follow suit. There is not so much 'cosmopolitan' as 'realist' there.

While Beck may have been optimistic about the potential of global cooperation to regulate shared risks, he has remained somewhat silent on the practical implications that might result. The evidence so far from combating terrorist financing suggests we need a reality check. There will not be perfect security or 100 per cent success in completely eliminating terrorist financing. In reality, the best anyone can hope for is to raise the difficulties for terrorists obtaining funds by strengthening global cooperation and tightening global norms. Risk management gurus term this 'reshaping' the environment, to reduce the opportunities for risks materialising by altering the operating context. The effect of this can be seen at various levels. From restructuring the global financial infrastructure to reduce vulnerabilities and impair terrorist capabilities, down to 'everyday' activities carried out in banks and real estate agents, various actors of all stripes and colours have the potential agency to shape the terrorist financial environment in different ways. In effect, any individual can at some point be, unwittingly or not, positioned in the front lines of this 'other' war on terror, not just soldiers or intelligence agents. Given the elusive nature of transnational terrorist financing, positive progress is difficult to quantify. It is usually assumed that disrupting terrorist finances will reduce overall activity but the groups concerned may simply adapt, paradoxically becoming more streamlined and efficient.[173] Indeed, experience with CCTV cameras hint at similar problems: 'the presence of cameras will not *prevent* the determined attack, and in some circumstances serves only to displace criminal activity to unsurveilled locales, or to force behaviour changes such as wearing hooded coats as a means of concealment'.[174] A clampdown on the formal financial sector seems to have only displaced terrorist financing elsewhere into other sectors such as criminal activity or informal value transfer systems. This has the paradoxical 'boomerang effect' of making the original risk evolve into something even harder to monitor and regulate. It is unsurprising therefore that Levi concludes there is a need for more precise terminology that allows determination of the goals of anti-terrorist financing measures.

The FATF's activities, being dedicated to standards-setting and capacity-building, are essentially non-military, low-key, multilateral and adapted to managing shared global risks, in both rationale and implementation. These features, we suggest, are crucial to building a better understanding of the hitherto unrec-ognised convergences between global governance, risk and security studies. As such it has served as a less-visible alternative to military force in the 'other' war on terror. While we have no doubt identified serious and possibly fatal questions about the 'cosmopolitan' nature of its governance activities and negative impact on civil liberties and democratic accountability, it is a leading example of how the language and techniques of risk have been installed and institutionalised as a cornerstone of global counter-terrorist financing standards. In the next chapter, we shall explore further these convergences between risk, global governance and security in another case study of informal governance arrangements: the Proliferation Security Initiative.

4 The Proliferation Security Initiative

Every senior leader, when you're asked what keeps you awake at night, it's the thought of a terrorist ending up with a weapon of mass destruction, especially nuclear.

US Secretary of Defense Robert Gates, *World at Risk* report, December 2008

In this chapter, we assess a rather different case of cooperative attempts at managing global security risks: the Proliferation Security Initiative (PSI). As with the FATF, the PSI has no formal treaty mandate, but it goes one step further and represents a somewhat different and even looser variant of an informal multilateral effort in the 'other' war on terror. The PSI adds a further layer of global governance that intersects and overlaps with a variety of other multilateral and universal anti-proliferation regimes in order to control proliferation risks. More specifically, as a global risk management strategy, the PSI works to reduce the likelihood of terrorists obtaining WMD materials, through increasing layers of difficulty for terrorists to succeed, identifying vulnerabilities and reshaping terrorist operating environments by constraining their freedom of movement. The PSI policing the oceans is in some ways an ideal case for examining the development of global security governance structures. The global maritime transportation infrastructure by its very nature presents problems for traditional territorially defined and hierarchically structured forms of government, and at the same time is identified as posing vulnerabilities to terrorist exploitation. Outside territorial waters, the reality of maritime affairs has always more reflected a state of anarchy than hierarchy. Hence it is a prime case for global governance. As we shall see in the discussion of the evolution of the law of the sea, earlier attempts to regulate and govern sea traffic have relied on national responsibility, denoted by the flag of the vessel in question, or in certain limited circumstances to bilateral or multilateral agreements. Resistance to a more comprehensive global treaty arrangement has been strong on the basis that state (and non-state) actors have been reluctant to accept any potential infringement on the right of 'innocent passage'. The ideas of Beck and recent developments in global governance literature again help us in our assessment of the PSI as a global governance mechanism in the World Risk Society. It represents an innovative attempt by what Beck would call a 'cosmopolitan realist' state in the form of America as it responds to new global risks and creating a global governance structure that preserves existing rights while addressing the very real risk of weapons trafficking to terrorists, but at the same time avoids the rigidity of treaty-based solutions. In touting proliferation as a global risk, it is banking on 'risk-cosmopolitanism' to generate a new consensus on new informal forms of governance and cooperation, particularly in arriving at agreed best practices as well as capacity-building of partners. As a form of 'institutionalised cosmopolitanism', it has tried in its outreach attempts to be as inclusive as possible, working to build capacity with its partners, consulting with the private sector and also engaging with dissenting parties. Once again, it repeats a common theme in global governance literature: the role of private actors. However, whereas the PSI exhibits similar rationales with the FATF in its creation, it also shares the short-comings we have identified in Chapter 2. Despite it being touted as a flexible cooperative arrangement for new times and new concerns with non-state proliferation risks, once again it cannot escape the subjective nature of risk and the divergent perceptions that result. The role of power in the social construction of WMD proliferation risk and the development of practices to regulate that risk further undermines the 'cosmopolitan' (again, in Beck's sense of the word) nature of the endeavour. Indeed, many partners such as Russia and Japan are lukewarm at best towards the PSI for their own particular 'national' reasons. As we shall show, 'WMD' as a concept itself is also constructed and states need to be convinced of the problem as well as the solution touted. Much of the difficulty it faces stems from its image as a vehicle of American hegemony in the service of narrow American self-interests, rather than 'cosmopolitan solidarity' on a global shared risk. As if the list of litanies were not enough, there are also concerns over the PSI's legality and the discriminatory nature of its focus as well.

WMD proliferation risks: a global governance issue

The relationship between the concepts of proliferation, WMD, global governance and risk requires some clarification and, in the case of WMD in particular, the concept itself requires some justification for questions have been raised about its usefulness as a security concept.[1] This part of the chapter begins by discussing the variety of historical attempts on the global level to deal with the threats of chemical, biological and nuclear weapons before moving on to a discussion of WMD as a concept. The underlying thread of the argument is that there occurred a shift through the twentieth century from an almost exclusive focus on states and formalised legal treaties in the control of the spread of WMD, to a more nuanced, informal and flexible approach that sought to manage the risk of WMD proliferation as non-state actors, terrorists and criminal gangs came to be seen as agents of proliferation concern. It wasn't until the events of 9/11 that this emerging pattern crystallised into a clear form that demanded a change in both the theory and practice of cooperative attempts at counter-proliferation. Indeed the shift in nomenclature from 'non-' or 'counter'-proliferation, as in the Non-

Proliferation Treaty (NPT) or the Defense Counter-proliferation Initiative (DCI), to the PSI, reflects in some ways this shift from a logic of deterrence to one of management and risk.

Once again, the reason why we chose to address the PSI roughly parallels our choice of the FATF in Chapter 2: it is a less-noticed aspect of the 'long war' that emphasised the need for multilateral cooperation on a shared common risk of WMD proliferation to terrorist networks. 'PSI appears to be a new channel for interdiction cooperation outside of treaties and multilateral export control regimes.'[2] As Winner suggests, 'President George W. Bush and other world leaders regularly cite the initiative as an example of a new form of multilateral cooperation in the post-September 11 world.'[3]

Like the justifications that we have heard before from the FATF on global terrorist financing risks, the oft-repeated official mantra in WMD proliferation is that 'proliferation is truly a global threat; no region is immune'.[4] Other similarities in approach abound with the FATF. In signing Executive Order 13382 in 2005, President Bush authorised targeted financial sanctions against non-state proliferation networks, modelled on those we have come across in Chapter 2 implemented against terrorist networks that had earlier been signed into law in 2001 with Executive Order 13224. At the same time, 'much PSI activity is very quiet; successful interdictions are usually not publicized'.[5] The complex global nature of proliferation shipments is illustrated by Squassoni:

> the October 2003 interdiction of a shipment of uranium centrifuge enrichment parts from Malaysia to Libya illustrates the need for multilateral cooperation. The Malaysian-produced equipment was transported on a German-owned ship, *BBC China*, leaving Dubai, passing through the Suez Canal. The ship was diverted into the Italian port of Taranto, where it was searched.[6]

There is clearly a case for intensified global cooperation and John Bolton contends that the PSI is 'foremost among President Bush's efforts to stop WMD proliferation'.[7] The issue of non-state proliferation networks also gained global prominence with United Nations Security Council Resolution 1540 that required all member states to criminalise proliferation by non-state actors and to adopt and enforce effective export controls, as well as focus on international financial transactions that support WMD proliferation.

But as we will now show, global cooperation against WMD has a long chequered history that is constantly evolving. Chemical weapons were probably the first of the WMD triumvirate to receive concerted international attention in terms of attempts either ro reduce or remove their use. As early as 1675 a Franco-German treaty prohibited the use of poisoned bullets.[8] In 1874 and 1899, attempts were made to outlaw the use of such technologies. Article 23 of The Hague Convention outlaws the use of 'poison or poisoned arms' in time of war.[9] These were reiterated in the 1907 convention.[10] The 1928 Geneva Protocol sought to outlaw the use of gas and biological weapons. The language of the text of the protocol is in itself revealing:

> Whereas the use in war of asphyxiating, poisonous or other gases, and of all analogous liquids, materials or devices, has been justly condemned by the general opinion of the civilised world ... this prohibition shall be universally accepted as a part of International Law, binding alike the conscience and the practice of nations.[11]

The normative, even 'cosmopolitan' language captures the global nature of the problem. Yet research continued apace and chemicals were used in contravention of The Hague Conventions in subsequent wars.[12] From the problems of gas clouds blowing back on attacking forces in the First World War, protecting one's own soldiers from chemical weaponry has been the main hindrance to the use of chemical weapons in warfare. Indeed, non-lethal chemicals have found much more productive roles in domestic crowd control than in the battlefield.[13]

As with chemical weapons, biological weapons have a relatively long history in warfare. Early crude forms of biological warfare are in evidence in medieval sieges where rotting carcasses of animals (and humans) were hurled over battlements or placed in the water supply to spread disease among the inhabitants. Biological weapons were also explicitly outlawed by the Geneva Protocols in 1928 and this ban has been reinforced by a number of subsequent treaties outlawing not just the use of active biological agents but also the tainting of water supplies or food chains. One of the key problems for biological weapons is the indiscriminate nature of their effectiveness, protecting one's own troops and, indeed, civilians is next to or near impossible. The potential for superbugs targeted at particular population strains remains a part of science fiction rather than security fact and, as such, the strategic uselessness of biological weapons has rendered them almost irrelevant to conventional battlefields. However, the ability of such agents to cause panic in civilian populations suggest that where this is the aim, as in acts of terrorism, both biological and chemical weapons are very useful indeed. This is where the post-9/11 concern with WMD kicks in.

Furthermore, besides biological and chemical weapons, nuclear weapons are arguably more useful, or at least effective, strategic weapons. As such the regimes governing nuclear technologies are much more focused and, indeed, much more rigorously policed. Although it must be noted that the relative, albeit debated, success of non-proliferation efforts is as much a reflection of the technical difficulty of developing nuclear weapons covertly as it is of the robustness of the regime itself. As Goldstein observed: 'From the beginning of the atomic age there has been an awareness that, because of the unprecedented destructiveness of the newly invented weapons, their spread to additional countries would increase the danger to world security.'[14] Although there are some disputes about the effects of proliferation, few disagree that controlling the spread of nuclear technology is in the interests of international security.[15] In 1953, President Eisenhower warned:

> the dread secret and the fearful engines of atomic might are not ours alone. In the first place, the secret is possessed by our friends and allies, the United Kingdom and Canada, whose scientific genius made a tremendous contribution

to our original discoveries and the designs of atomic bombs. The secret is also known by the Soviet Union.... To pause there would be to confirm the hopeless finality of a belief that two atomic colossi are doomed malevolently to eye each other indefinitely across a trembling world. To stop there would be to accept helplessly the probability of civilization destroyed, the annihilation of the irreplaceable heritage of mankind handed down to us from generation to generation, and the condemnation of mankind to begin all over again the age-old struggle upward from savagery towards decency, and right, and justice. Surely no sane member of the human race could discover victory in such desolation.[16]

Eisenhower went on to call for global governance: the creation of a global atomic energy agency that would manage nuclear capabilities for peaceful ends: the International Atomic Energy Agency (IAEA) was born. However, after France and China joined the small group of nuclear weapons states (NWS), concerns about further proliferation led to the Non-Proliferation Treaty (NPT) in 1970. This limited the number of NWS to five and called on all other countries to renounce nuclear weapons and to channel any nuclear resources into civilian use. The NPT also included obligations on existing nuclear powers to reduce their arsenals and to ensure that non-NWS suffered no commercial disadvantage due to limits on nuclear research.[17] Thus a clear state – and formalised treaty-based logic – was at work in designing the counter-proliferation architecture. A series of bilateral and multilateral treaties followed aimed at limiting the numbers of nuclear weapons (SALT I and II), testing nuclear weapons (CTBT) and in START I and II, the actual reduction of weapons stockpiles. Throughout the period from the NPT to the present, four other states have developed nuclear weapons. Of these, South Africa disarmed and joined the NPT. India, Israel and Pakistan maintain their arsenal. North Korea is believed to have tested a nuclear warhead; Iran and Syria are viewed as being of proliferation concern. A further group of countries has either stopped their nuclear weapons programmes – Iraq, Libya, Argentina, Brazil, South Korea and Taiwan – or have handed over stockpiles to an existing NWS, as in the cases of the Soviet Successor states – Belarus, Kazakhstan and Ukraine.[18] Whether the above should be judged a success or failure of the non-proliferation regime is debatable. Certainly things could have been much worse. For present purposes though what is significant is that for the Cold War period, counter-proliferation efforts focused on hierarchical, treaty-based efforts that assumed that the threat of proliferation came from state actors. Furthermore, chemical and biological weapons were treated separately from nuclear weapons as a category of security concern. This set of assumptions was to change dramatically in the post-Cold War era as globalisation and the obsolescence of formalised state-centric treaties to regulate proliferation by non-state actors such as terrorist networks became key drivers for change.

Risk and WMD proliferation

Especially after 9/11, the Bush administration has repeatedly voiced its concern that 'terrorism and the proliferation of weapons of mass destruction, including the danger that terrorists may succeed in their effort to acquire these incredibly lethal weapons, represents the defining threat of our age'.[19] There seems little doubt in its mind that the 'greatest risk' facing the world today is 'weapons of mass destruction in the hands of terrorists'.[20] By disrupting WMD proliferation to terrorists, the goal is clearly preventive: deny access to and using weapons of mass destruction. To paraphrase, using the language of risk, that is the unwanted scenario that policy initiatives such as the PSI are designed to avert in the first place. More precisely, with the PSI, the aim is to interdict proliferation shipments *before* they reach their intended destination. Indeed, words associated with avoiding and denial is often used to describe PSI activity: interception, disruption, interdiction, detection, reduction. As Senator Dick Lugar put it, 'the minimum standard for victory in this kind of war is the prevention of any of the individual terrorists or terrorist cells from obtaining WMD'.[21]

The issue of proliferation risk can thus be broken down into core components: intentions and capabilities of actors, and vulnerabilities in the system. The US *National Strategy to Combat Weapons of Mass Destruction* states categorically and without doubt its assessment of terrorist intentions: 'terrorist groups are seeking to acquire WMD with the stated purpose of killing large numbers of our people and those of friends and allies – without compunction and without warning'.[22] Not only does Al Qaeda have the intention, it is developing capabilities to acquire WMD. According to then Deputy Defence Secretary Wolfowitz:

> Al Qaeda leader Osama bin Laden said in the past that the acquisition of weapons of mass destruction by his terrorist gang is a religious duty. U.S. and coalition troops in Afghanistan found evidence that al Qaeda was aggressively pursuing chemical, biological, radiological and nuclear information and material.[23]

Indeed one of the most chilling Al Qaeda tapes recovered from Afghanistan shows the terror network experimenting with chemicals and poison gas on goats, and documents with information about nuclear weapons designs. Couched in terms of probabilistic language, there exists clearly a risk scenario here, as the Institute for Science and International Security concluded, 'if al Qaeda obtained enough plutonium or highly enriched uranium, we believe it is capable of building a crude nuclear explosive, despite several difficult steps'.[24] Stephen Younger, Director of the Defence Threat Reduction Agency commented:

> al Qaeda leaders may have connections in other countries that already have the technological base for building nuclear weapons. They have the money to make such links ... and they may have ... access to people in countries with advanced technological capability.[25]

Numerous religious *fatwa*s have also been issued to justify possible terrorist use of WMD. To sum up, then-CIA Director George Tenet warned there is 'a significant risk within the next few years that we could confront an adversary – either terrorists or a rogue state – who possess them [chemical or biological weapons]'.[26]

In addition to Al Qaeda's intentions to use WMD, there is the question of how the organisation would choose to deliver such a weapon. Not only do they have the desire but there is also some evidence to suggest that Al Qaeda may have been looking to develop naval capacity, not least as evidenced by the attack againsts the USS *Cole*.[27] More recently a jihadist website, Al-ikhlas, is reported as calling on militants to engage in attacks at sea:

> As we draw near to the [crucial] hour when the leadership of the Zionist-Crusader campaign will be dragged to the [negotiation] table to accept the [mujahideen's] terms ... it is necessary to [extend] the battle to the seas. The mujahideen have successfully established units of martyrdom-seekers on land; the sea is the next strategic step towards controlling the world and restoring the Islamic caliphate.[28]

More generally there have been questions over Al Qaeda's logistical operations and some suggestion that the organisation has access to or owns larger ships. As the *Christian Science Monitor* noted in 2003:

> AL QAEDA may have already amassed a navy, of sorts ... Rep. Chris Bell (D) of Texas asked administration officials about intelligence reports that indicate Al Qaeda could own as many as 15 cargo ships.... Most of these ships may be coastal vessels that operate in the area of the Red Sea or the Horn of Africa... 'There were ships associated with bin Laden's organization [that moved] weapons, and also people,' a Defense official knowledgeable in the area also notes. Other officials confirm that US intelligence believes Al Qaeda controls at least 15 ships.[29]

This capability is significant not just in logistical terms, there also exists the distinct possibility that a large ship itself could be turned into a weapon, as Al Qaeda has done with other forms of transportation. Such a possibility needs to and has been taken seriously in defence planning as evidenced by the security exercise 'Impending Storm' carried out by the National Defense University in Washington in 2003.[30]

Despite the immense difficulties of actually employing these weapons, the risk has attracted significant policy attention. As we have seen, one way of reducing risk is to alter the perceptions and intentions of enemies about WMD proliferation, hence 'the preferred approach is to convince our adversaries that they cannot achieve their goals with WMD, and thus deter and dissuade them from attempting to use or even acquire these weapons in the first place'.[31] In other words, the idea is to make it more difficult and dangerous for would-be nuclear terrorist proliferators in their activities. It is also common to encounter discussions on identifying and reducing vulnerabilities to WMD proliferation. 'The events of September 11 and the subsequent public discovery of al-Qaeda's methods, capabilities, and intentions has finally brought our vulnerability to the forefront.' Dick Lugar goes on to conclude, 'We must anticipate that they will use weapons of mass destruction if allowed the opportunity.'[32] As we shall see, cooperative attempts to manage risk such as the PSI are focused on denying terrorists that very opportunity. Simply put, the 'PSI aims to deter, impede and stop shipments of WMD, their delivery systems and related materials by any state or non-state actor engaged in or supporting WMD proliferation programs'.[33] The PSI operates with a 'Statement of Interdiction Principles', which are essentially dedicated to interdiction activities. These were:

1   Undertake effective measures, either alone or in concert with other states, for interdicting the transfer or transport of WMD, their delivery systems, and related materials to and from states and non-state actors of proliferation concern.

2   Adopt streamlined procedures for rapid exchange of relevant information concerning suspected proliferation activity, protecting the confidential character of classified information provided by other states as part of this initiative, dedicate appropriate resources and efforts to interdiction operations and capabilities, and maximize coordination among participants in interdiction efforts.

3   Review and work to strengthen their relevant national legal authorities where necessary to accomplish these objectives, and work to strengthen when necessary relevant international laws and frameworks in appropriate ways to support these commitments.

4   Take specific actions in support of interdiction efforts regarding cargoes of WMD, their delivery systems, or related materials, to the extent their national legal authorities permit and consistent with their obligations under international law and frameworks, to include:

    a   Not to transport or assist in the transport of any such cargoes to or from states or non-state actors of proliferation concern [...]

    b   At their own initiative, or at the request and good cause shown by another state, to take action to board and search any vessel flying their flag in their internal waters or territorial seas [...]

    c   To seriously consider providing consent under the appropriate circumstances to the boarding and searching of its own flag vessels by other states [...]

    d   To take appropriate actions to (1) stop and/or search in their internal waters, territorial seas, or contiguous zones (when declared) vessels that are reasonably suspected of carrying such cargoes to or from states or non-state actors of proliferation concern and to seize such cargoes that are identified; and (2) enforce conditions on vessels entering or leaving their ports, internal waters, or territorial seas that are reasonably suspected of carrying such cargoes, such as requiring that such vessels be subject to boarding, search, and seizure of such cargoes prior to entry.

e   At their own initiative or upon the request and good cause shown by another state, to (a) require aircraft that are reasonably suspected of carrying such cargoes to or from states or non-state actors of proliferation concern and that are transiting their airspace to land for inspection and seize any such cargoes that are identified; and/or (b) deny aircraft reasonably suspected of carrying such cargoes transit rights through their airspace in advance of such flights.

f   If their ports, airfields, or other facilities are used as transshipment points for shipment of such cargoes to or from states or non-state actors of proliferation concern, to inspect vessels, aircraft, or other modes of transport reasonably suspected of carrying such cargoes, and to seize such cargoes that are identified.[34]

A need for 'institutionalised cosmopolitanism'?

The United Nations Conference on the Law of the Sea

But why did the PSI need to issue this statement of principles in the first place? As we have suggested in earlier chapters, a case for 'institutionalised cosmopolitanism' arises when 'cosmopolitan realist' states recognise first the magnitude of shared global risk and second, that existing international forums and international law are no longer adequate. New cooperative mechanisms and legal norms then have to be developed, as Beck argued, in the process bringing on board a wider variety of actors affected by and interested in managing these global risks. This situation has particular bearings on the PSI in light of the inadequacies of the pre-existing international legal treaty framework based around the United Nations Conference on the Law of the Sea (UNCLOS) to address issues of WMD proliferation, which this this part of the chapter shall now consider. The oceans represent a peculiar problem for traditional models of government. On land, the issue of jurisdiction is clearer – there is normally a recognised government with a clearly defined territory, although there are exceptions to this rule.[35] An ICJ judge put it as follows:

A distinction must be made between prescriptive jurisdiction and enforcement jurisdiction. The above mentioned dictum concerns prescriptive jurisdiction: it is about what a state may do on its own territory when investigating and prosecuting crimes committed abroad, not about what a state may do on the territory of other states when prosecuting such crimes. Obviously, a state has no enforcement jurisdiction outside its territory: a state may, failing permission to the contrary, not exercise its power on the territory of another state.... In other words, the permissive rule only applies to prescriptive jurisdiction, not to enforcement jurisdiction: failing a prohibition, state A may, on its own territory, prosecute offences committed in state

B (permissive rule); failing a permission, state A may not act on the territory of state B.[36]

The issue here then relates to the distinction between prescription and enforcement. A state may pass laws that make certain acts illegal even if committed outside its territory; however it may not act on another state's territory in order to enforce such a law without the other state's permission. So how does this relate to the law of the sea?

The peculiarity of the sea in terms of law enforcement rests on the lack of sovereign jurisdiction over large swathes of water. Historically, the relative lawlessness of the sea has been exploited by state and non-state actors alike, from the use of privateers or pirates by states from the thirteenth up to the nineteenth centuries[37] to the use of international waters by private cruise liners to allow gambling just outside territorial waters where it is otherwise prohibited.[38] However, in both cases chains of sovereign authority can be traced back through vessel flagging. Formal commissions were given to privateers to capture enemy vessels (although in the case of outright piracy the lines were somewhat blurred between commissioned and freelance activity). Gambling laws also applied to the vessel that reflected the laws of the state whose flag the vessel was carrying.[39] The practice in maritime affairs has been that although prescriptive jurisdiction allowed states to prohibit the carriage of certain goods across its own or indeed any waters, enforcement jurisdiction remains with the 'flag state' of the vessel. The only exceptions are where a vessel is not displaying a flag or is suspected of displaying a false flag, or the vessel is engaged in piracy (real or radio).[40] Although a state's sovereignty does extend up to 12 nautical miles from its shoreline, and with limited rights in the contiguous zone and exclusive economic zone that border this extending outwards, these powers are tempered by established rules under the UNCLOS. A state only has enforcement jurisdiction over its own flagged vessels, and those either bound for or leaving its territorial waters. Otherwise commercial vessels retain a right of 'innocent passage' although there are some question marks over the strength of the prohibition under the UNCLOS.[41] A state then interested in pursuing enforcement rights over vessels not flagged by itself and not acting directly in its territorial waters has in the past had to seek bilateral or multilateral agreements with other flag states in order to exercise such authority.

In other words formal treaties can be signed between participating states or else permission can be sought on a case by case basis. The practice dates at least as far back as British attempts to bring the international slave trade to an end and continues to the present in the areas of drug trafficking and counter-proliferation.[42] Thus counter-proliferation efforts are hampered by the relatively restricted nature of jurisdiction in the oceans (and indeed air transportation as well). Only in limited cases such as self-defence can flag-state jurisdiction be overruled and as such the logic of both the existing law of the sea and enforcement operates on a limited and patchwork basis of overlapping and discrete zones of enforcement responsibility depending on a number of factors – the location of the vessel relative to the various territorial waters of a state, its flag-state identity, the port of destination and the imminence of the threat from any cargo. As far as traditional counter- or non-proliferation regimes are concerned, this was acceptable as the main suspected proliferants were states. The rise of non-state actors as security concerns in relation to WMD proliferation has altered the equation considerably.

The nexus of rogue states, WMD and terrorists cooperating has loomed large in the strategic calculations of the Bush administration. This has already been prominently featured in the build up to war in Iraq but it also had far reaching implications for the US approach to maritime security more generally. As James Cotton noted:

> Since 11 September 2001, non-proliferation has become perhaps the most important global concern. If the struggle against terrorism is to be protracted, the acquisition by terrorists of weapons of mass destruction represents, in the new climate, the greatest potential threat to world order.[43]

This linking of previously separate dangers under the umbrella of the war on terror is key to understanding the new conceptualisation of proliferation as an area of security concern by the Bush administration. Indeed it also should be noted that this conceptualisation highlights the important ways in which the construction of risks through political discourse shapes the way in which those risks are prioritised and responded to. This is an issue we return to later. The linkages between maritime security and proliferation issues were crystallised in the *So San* incident in December 2002, although concern over North Korea's proliferation activities were not new.[44] The *So San* incident is thus worth unpacking in order to highlight gaps in the existing UNCLOS-based legal regime of maritime security governance that the PSI was aimed at plugging.

Following a request from the United States, a Spanish naval vessel intercepted the *So San* in the Arabian Sea where 15 Scud missiles were discovered hidden in the hold. Clearly here was a case of concern to international counter-proliferation efforts. However, as mentioned above, although prescriptive jurisdiction would allow any state to make proliferation activities illegal, enforcement jurisdiction is limited to the port of origin, port of destination and flagged nationality of the vessel. In this case the initial interdiction was justified as the vessel was not flying a flag. The Spanish were only entitled to establish its status; once its Cambodian flagging had been established, further action was prohibited.[45] As the missiles were bound for the port of Aden in Yemen and had been bought by the Yemenese government from North Korea, there was little under existing maritime law or non-proliferation regimes that the US or anyone else could legally do. There is no legal authority to interdict vessels on the high seas on suspicion of WMD proliferation. As White House spokesman, Ari Fleischer noted: 'We have looked at this matter thoroughly, and there is no provision under international law prohibiting Yemen from accepting delivery of missiles from North Korea.'[46] Neither North Korea nor Yemen were bound by the terms of the voluntary Missile Technology Control Regime and therefore no legal basis existed to impound the cargo or prevent the delivery.[47] In the post 9/11 security environment, where the risk of a nexus of rogue states, terrorists and weapons of mass destruction had been placed at the forefront of the US' *National Security Strategy 2002* and indeed, in the public rhetoric of the Bush administration, such a state of affairs was unacceptable. The question was how best to respond to these new challenges of proliferation. In December 2008 the Report of the Commission on the Prevention of WMD Proliferation and Terrorism touted the PSI as a solution, denying both terrorists and rogue states access to WMD materials.

It should be noted that the *So San* incident was not the first time that North Korean proliferation activities motivated attempts to reform international legal frameworks. In 1992, Washington expressed concern about Pyongyang's shipments of missile technology to the Gulf on the *Dae Hung Ho*. Like the *So San*, little could be done. Recognition of this growing legal loophole led to the Defense Counter-proliferation Initiative (DCI) in 1993.[48] Unlike the later PSI, the DCI focused mainly on reorganisation and training within US defence and intelligence institutions and the strengthening of international law in counter-proliferation.[49] The 1990s proliferation environment was furthermore predominantly focused on managing existing nuclear powers – particularly post-Soviet states such as Belarus, Ukraine and post-apartheid South Africa.[50] The post-9/11 security environment however was recognised as being very different. The difficulties of combating proliferation in this transformed security environment demanded a new approach, of which the PSI, as we shall see, embodies almost completely. Writing of the challenges of the new environment Ellis argues:

> U.S. and international success in this fundamentally transformed security landscape is likely to be measured more by an actor's ability to cope effectively with the persistent threat posed by potential adversaries in a post-proliferated world than its ability to defeat these adversaries unambiguously or even to roll back extant capabilities.[51]

As we have seen in the discussion so far, from the 1990s, we have established that existing international legal frameworks predicated on UNCLOS and state actors were insufficient in tackling non-state proliferation concerns from terrorist groups. Particularly after 9/11, there seemed to be a real need to adapt pre-existing approaches or develop new ones to cope with the global challenge. We next explore the PSI in more detail outlining the possibility of a 'cosmopolitan' rationale behind its creation and its attempts to manage proliferation risks in a post-9/11 world.

The PSI and 'institutionalised cosmopolitanism': 'cosmopolitan' opening up?

If not before, then after the *So San* incident the need more actively and flexibly to manage new types of proliferation risks was intensely felt by the Bush administration. 'We're living in fast-moving times'[52] was the common official refrain.

The question was how a new multilateral form of governance to manage a new global awareness of the risk of proliferation to terrorists could arise. As US officials repeatedly observe:

> the terrorist attacks on September 11th underscored the new threats we face and that the institutions of the Cold War were not sufficient to provide security. Nowhere is that more evident than in meeting the threat posed by proliferation of WMD and terrorism.[53]

As the notion of 'institutionalised cosmopolitanism' suggests, the implication is that either existing global governance arrangements were updated, like the FATF was, or entirely new initiatives launched. The international climate in the aftermath of the *So San* incident didn't lend itself to the creation of new global institutions. The US had little political capital to spend; this was the era of the 'Freedom Fry' after all.[54] Therefore it is remarkable that in the roughly six months that followed, a new initiative took shape that went far beyond the scope and credibility of the 'Coalition of the Willing' that joined the US in Iraq. As Donald Rumsfeld put it:

> we will see revolving coalitions that will evolve and change over time depending on the activity and the circumstance of the country. The mission needs to define the coalition, and we ought not to think that a coalition should define the mission.[55]

One such coalition was the PSI. Its emergence bears at least some of the hallmarks of a new 'institutionalised cosmopolitanism' in Beck's sense, in that it was aimed at actively managing what it recognised as a global risk but doing so in a voluntary and cooperative manner. It is an informal flexible arrangement and 'at its core, the PSI is a coalition of the willing with the potential for participants to vary the degrees of their commitment and participation'.[56] This does not entirely escape the constructed nature of the risks in question or the limited nature of the emergent coalition or indeed the role of power in constructing the PSI as an 'activity' and proliferation as a problem, but it does arguably represent a significant departure in the governance of the sea that offers a potentially fruitful framework for future cooperation and development. The set-up of the PSI structure:

> reflects the Bush administration's preference for less formal, multilateral partnerships. By working within such an informal structure and with like-minded governments, Washington was able to produce the strongest possible language and political commitment to interdiction in a relatively short period of time.[57]

The PSI, rather than replacing, seeks to harness the existing framework international law and adapt it in order to manage better the global risk of weapons proliferation, 'the initiative builds on decades of multilateral efforts to stymie proliferation and, in fact, relies on previous measures as a principal component of its potential effectiveness'.[58] The State Department maintains that 'PSI activities, of course, take place consistent with national and international law'.[59] So what exactly was it? Somewhat similar to the FATF reviewed in the previous chapter, the PSI is not a conventional formal international institution. It does not have a secretariat or permanent base or budget; it doesn't even have 'members' in a traditional sense, reaffirming the administration's favourite catchphrase that the PSI is 'an activity not an organisation'.[60] 'Partners' were called upon to pool resources and cooperate but not to submit to external legal formal authority in relation to proliferation concerns. More crucially, 'it is a regime, designed for a new era, recognizing that proliferation threats today are different'.[61] As the Chairman's statement at the meeting marking the first anniversary of the PSI put it:

> An emphasis was made that the PSI is a global endeavour with an inclusive nature. It relies on the widest possible cooperation between states around the world.... States participating were welcomed to engage in such cooperation [to counter-proliferation] as well as to undertake national action to identify law enforcement authorities and other tools or assets that could be brought to bear against efforts to stop proliferation facilitators.[62]

Here then was an apparent example of global cosmopolitanism writ large, a risk of global shared concern that should be managed by 'cosmopolitan realist' states acting in a cooperative, inclusive and evidence-based manner in their 'enlightened self-interests'. Although this overstates the case for the PSI as a purely 'cosmopolitan' initiative, a question we will return to later in this chapter, looking at the detail of the initiative and its attempts at a 'cosmopolitan opening up of the system' to involve non-state actors, it does appear to fulfil the theoretical image of what a 'cosmopolitan' initiative to manage global risk might look like.

Speaking at a Maritime Industry Workshop in London, the British Minister for the Armed Services Adam Ingram said:

> Every country and *shipping company* in the world has a key part to play in preventing proliferation of Weapons of Mass Destruction. This meeting is an important step towards ensuring that ship-based proliferation of chemical, biological and nuclear weaponry continues to be prevented while ensuring the needs of the global shipping industry are understood by governments around the world.[63]

Just as in the case of ATF, an effective proliferation regime was not only reliant on the cooperation of states but also on commitments on the part of private actors such as shipping companies. Since the private sector covers almost all the various forms of global transportation – air, sea, land – it is essential and entirely indispensable to involve the private sector. The PSI works to help ensure they do not inadvertently become involved in the shipment of illegal cargo and materials. There are ongoing attempts to:

> harness the capabilities and willingness of the private sector to minimize the risk of proliferation and WMD terrorism. Many WMD terrorist attack scenarios will touch some element of the private sector, whether those elements are ports, financial institutions, or logistics providers. Public–private partnerships can play a key role in sensitizing the private sector to these risks and in encouraging them to take steps to cooperate to support our international security.[64]

The two-day London workshop focused on improving the operational capabilities of the PSI among participating states and industry partners. As such, it was a clear recognition of the need for public–private cooperation for effective governance in the realm of maritime affairs.[65] The meeting was the third such government–industry workshop organised through the PSI. It dealt with a number of practical issues related to the conduct of interdiction and other aspects of maritime governance and security.[66] What the meetings highlight is the interaction between private interests and public action and the multilevel and multi-actor nature of the PSI. To that end, various annual meetings since 2004 have been held in Los Angeles, Copenhagen and London on various issues such as container security, air cargo security, the roles of freight forwarders and shipping line owners and operators. Although there are no formal roles for the private sector within the structures, such as they are, of the PSI, there is a clear recognition of the common interests between states seeking to manage proliferation risks and companies seeking to carry out business as usual on the high seas. As the PSI celebrated its fifth anniversary in May 2008, it began to:

> look at some ways to deepen the initiative through things like greater usage of customs and border authorities, through usage of financial tools, because after all, most of the people involved in the proliferation game around the world, whether it's front companies or middlemen or others, are in it for financial gain.[67]

It is seeking to broaden its base as a platform for 'institutionalised cosmopolitanism' and bringing in as many relevant actors as possible.

Two aspects of the interaction of public and private security are worth exploring here in order to assess their relationship to the PSI. These are the resurgence of piracy in certain areas of the globe and the issue of port security. Piracy appears to be a lacuna in the PSI global security governance web, its re-emergence in the headlines over the last number of years raises questions about the security of dangerous materials being transported across the world's oceans. Unlike proliferation however there are robust powers under existing customary and formal international law to act against piracy. Most recently, French troops stormed a yacht that had been taken over by pirates in the Gulf of Aden.

French President Nicholas Sarkozy called for greater international efforts to control international piracy, particularly around the Somali coast: 'The world cannot accept this. Today, these are no longer isolated cases but a genuine industry of crime. This industry casts doubt on a fundamental freedom: that of movement and of international commerce.'[68] In response, the EU has established a special task force to organise and coordinate patrols off the Somali coast. But does this have anything to do with proliferation? On Thursday 25 September 2008, a ship operated by a Ukrainian arms supplier was hijacked by Somali pirates. The ship was carrying 33 tanks and a large supply of grenade launchers and ammunition. The cargo was officially intended for Kenya although Western diplomats suspect that Kenya may have merely been acting as a transit point for Sudan. American warships engaged the vessel and a Russian frigate was also despatched.[69] Although in this case the weapons in question were conventional, the potential for WMD to fall into the wrong hands, state or non-state, in this way demands recognition and represents a serious challenge for any attempt to govern proliferation on a global scale. UNSC Resolution 1851 of December 2008 now permits states to take 'all necessary measures in Somalia, including its airspace, for the purpose of interdicting those who are using Somali territory to plan, facilitate or undertake acts of piracy and armed robbery at sea'.

The other challenge for the effectiveness of the PSI is how it interacts with the more mundane 'everyday' aspects of global shipping, particularly how it seeks to manage the enormous flow of material through the world's ports. One initiative designed to tackle just that problem is the Container Security Initiative (CSI). The CSI announced in January 2002 allows US Customs and Borders Protection officials to pre-inspect container cargo bound for the United States. Its aim is to prevent the use of container shipping by terrorist groups to launch attacks on US ports or to smuggle WMD into the US. Over 58 ports are participating as of October 2007, representing a wide range of geographical locations in Africa, South America, Asia and Europe.[70] The CSI operates by identifying high-risk cargo based on intelligence information and subjecting them to further screening using technology such as X-rays, gamma ray machines and radiation detection devices. It operates on a bilateral basis between the US and the port country involved, with US officials operating in the port country. The CSI claims to cover 86 per cent of all container traffic bound for the United States.[71] There are however some limitations to the CSI report: as Haveman *et al.* have noted, the US continues to receive a large proportion of imports from non-CSI ports (although this proportion is decreasing) and it's also unclear whether the CSI is giving sufficient focus to the highest risk shipments: 'Although US officials are able to inspect up to two thirds of U.S. containerised imports before they leave their final foreign port, officials are able to inspect less than one-third of imports from the riskiest countries.'[72] Thus there are some questions as to the scope of the gaps in the CSI as a risk management regime where some of the riskiest targets escape the gaze of the governance mechanism. Domestic institutions do pick up some of this slack; the National Targeting Centre using intelligence-based profiling targets specific suspicious cargo for inspection in US ports.[73]

As highlighted above, the proliferation issue overlaps with broader security concerns in global governance of the sea. A variety of risks, not just proliferation, exist in the maritime transportation industry of which the PSI is a link in the chain. The *National Strategy for Maritime Security* (2005) lists a number of multilevel threats to maritime security – state, terrorism, criminal and piracy threats, environmental destruction and illegal immigration.[74] Such a broad range of risks – from the individual to the non-state group to the state to the ecosystem – requires the kind of 'cosmopolitan' response called for by Beck. The question we shall address later in this chapter however is, to what extent does the PSI reflect a step towards such a response or is it a case of the powerful shaping the environment and coercing others to follow?

Governance by risk: 'risk-cosmopolitanism', standards-setting and capacity-building

As we have pointed out previously, the US strategy for combating terrorism outlines two key priorities: bringing all actors together for standards-setting, and capacity-building of partners. In the previous chapter, we observed how the FATF helped to fulfil these goals. These twin aims can now be seen in the PSI as well, which defines itself as 'a global initiative with an inclusive mission. Successful interdiction of trafficking in WMD, their delivery systems and related materials requires the widest possible co-operation between states.... WMD is a global threat which calls for a global response.'[75] In justifying the need for global cooperation to prevent 'ruthless terrorists' gaining access to WMD-related materials, the then British Foreign Secretary Jack Straw employed language that verged on what Beck might appreciate as 'risk-cosmopolitanism', 'this is not a matter of concern to just a few countries or regions of the world but to the entire international community. A global menace requires a collective global response'.[76] What brings PSI partners together is how they 'share a common objective: to prevent the proliferation of WMD, their delivery systems and related materials in order to enhance international security'.[77] Here, the PSI is assuming that recognition of this shared global challenge will help trigger what Beck termed 'risk-cosmopolitanism' in forcing more state and non-state actors together, including those in the crucial global transportation sector. There is some evidence of a 'cosmopolitan' concern with shared global risk here. US officials stress the need to:

> make clear to the private sector the common interest we share in ensuring that their assets and infrastructure are protected from either direct attack or from exploitation by terrorist actors seeking to acquire or use nuclear or radiological materials. We must develop voluntary public–private partnerships that offer a low-cost means to reduce the risk of nuclear smuggling and nuclear terrorism.[78]

Using the PSI as a basis for negotiation on how best to manage the shared global WMD proliferation risk, this is also triggering discussions between state actors, such as China, the US and India, that might not have wanted to speak with each other in the first place. However, India and China have refused to sign on despite considerable US efforts. India for its part was miffed, as it was 'not involved or asked' when some countries got together to 'trigger off this initiative'.[79] Especially amongst the hold-out countries, China has particularly 'national' concerns about external interference in its own sphere of maritime influence, American leadership in the PSI and how its own relationship with North Korea might be affected. India takes a more subjective 'national', as opposed to cosmo-politan, perception of the matter. It will join only 'provided the Government decides that it is in consonance with our national interest'.[80] Despite obvious common shared interests in curbing proliferation, India and China have both refused to join due to a combination of issues including 'domestic politics, dis-parate geographical and strategic worldviews, and cultural traditions'.[81] Questions about its legality and the desire of some states to bring it within the formal UN fold also obstruct further integration and 'cosmopolitan' expansion of the initiative. Even more fatally for the idea of 'risk-cosmopolitanism', the supposed 'global' risk is just not perceived as such. Just as in the case of terrorist financ-ing, 'for many countries, the threat of WMD falls low on national agendas. Other more immediate challenges such as political stability, poverty, mortality rates and infrastructure gain more attention and resources.'[82] Once again, the supposed 'cosmopolitanness' of a global risk falls short of being universally shared or perceived.

However, in seeking to establish a common baseline for discussions on best practices, the initial 11 countries that joined the PSI[83] did agree on a 'Statement of Interdiction Principles' that would form the framework of cooperation for participation. The principles simply represented a network of initiatives that, although they did not represent the creation of any new legal powers, aimed at harnessing the best out of the existing framework of international law and intelligence and naval resources. It focused on establishing agreement among partners to share information, engage in joint actions and allow other partici-pating states 'enforcement rights' on their national flagged vessels where such rights were deemed necessary and appropriate by both the flag state of the vessel and the state acting on proliferation concerns. It also included suspect air cargo in its proliferation model, with air transportation presenting similar challenges to sea transportation in terms of jurisdictional authority. Land cargo is also subject to the agreement. Although the PSI is often seen as being more concerned with action, the PSI's 'Statement of Interdiction Principles' does attempt at the very least to 'codify a set of internationally-agreed-upon standards for interdiction'.[84] The State Department describes it as a 'global initiative', that 'does not create formal "obligations" for participating states, but does represent a political com-mitment to establish "best practices" to stop proliferation-related shipments'.[85] Since its inception, participants have expanded to over 90 countries, including Russia, and further attempts have been made to bring China into the fold.[86] With the 'support' of 90 countries giving effect to PSI-endorsed norms, the State Department declared, 'we're very pleased PSI is going to be recognized as one of the standards for non-proliferation behaviour around the world'.[87] In 2006, London hosted the Maritime Industry Workshop, which addressed cooperation with the shipping industry, aiming 'to bring governments and industry together to share best practice'.[88]

In developing global best practices to counter proliferation, the PSI is not alone. The Australia Group is another informal forum of countries, which aims to help exporting or trans-shipping countries minimise the risk of assisting chemical and biological weapon (CBW) proliferation. To do this, its participants explore the scope for increasing the effectiveness of existing export controls, through information exchange and harmonisation of national measures and standards. Like the PSI, participants do not undertake any legally binding obligations.

Compared to the FATF's intensive concern with global standards-setting, however, the PSI appears relatively more preoccupied with capacity-building of partners to manage better the shared global risks. As then US Under-Secretary of State for Non-Proliferation and International Security Robert Joseph argued, 'The PSI must focus on activity, rather than on creating organizational structures.'[89] It is above all, an 'activity' focused upon issues of practical cooperation such as intelligence sharing, interdiction exercises and related efforts to address the proliferation threat. Capacity-building has occurred with more than 35 interdiction exercises carried out, involving more than 70 countries.[90] As the State Department suggests:

> one of the things that PSI does is that it gives countries the ability to have capacity-building. They can improve their own capabilities through this confederation of states acting together. You get a synergy of countries operating together. It creates a focus, and then a means by which countries can cooperate.[91]

What we have then is a broad, multilateral 'coalition of the willing', that appears to be engaged in global risk governance practices shaped by the kinds of collective cooperative and fluid principles envisaged by Beck earlier in this book. Two further key questions then need to be addressed. The first is whether it fully reflects a 'cosmopolitan' vision or whether, as with the FATF, the role of power and subjective 'national' interests cannot be overlooked. Second, there is a need to consider whether the initiative is effective in achieving its goals as a global risk management exercise.

Power and the social construction of WMD proliferation risks

The new awareness of this global risk did not arise automatically; indeed as in the case of terrorist financing, it had to be 'constructed' to a certain degree by those actors such as the United States with the greatest stake in managing it. Beck has after all reiterated that this new reflexive awareness of risk can potentially trigger fierce debates on how best to manage that risk. Before turning to discuss the linking of these concerns through the re-emergence of the concept of WMD, some comments should be made on the transformation of the proliferation environment in the aftermath of the Cold War and how it was the case that WMD proliferation by non-state actors now became perceived as such a major global risk. As Sopko put it:

> Technological advances and new adversaries have reduced the relevance and effectiveness of American non-proliferation strategy.... The familiar balance of nuclear terror that linked the superpowers and their client states for nearly 50 years ... has given way to a much less predictable situation, where weapons of unthinkable power appear within the grasp of those more willing to use them. Rogue nations and 'clientless' states, terrorist groups, religious cults, ethnic minorities, disaffected political groups, and even individuals appear to have joined a new arms race toward mass destruction.[92]

Ten examples from 1994 and 1995 alone exist where chemical, biological or radiological arms were either used or threatened or caught in transit. The groups involved were as diverse as Chechen rebels, Iraq, white supremacists, a Japanese cult, a US militia and Islamist terrorists.[93] Two aspects of the changed environment are key. One is the broadening of proliferation concerns to include biological and chemical weapons, besides nuclear and radiological ones. The latter distinction reflects the difference between conventional nuclear weapons, and radiological dispersion devices or 'dirty bombs' where radiological material is mixed with conventional explosives. The latter are easier to build, but also are much less effective in that the conventional explosives would be much more dangerous than any radiation risk, hence the term coined for such bombs as 'weapons of mass disruption'.[94] Instead, the effectiveness of 'dirty bombs' lay in the panic and public chaos that would magnify the disruption of the original explosion, hence its linkage to terrorism.

This brings us to the second key change in the proliferation environment, which is the heightened degree of uncertainty as to who or what the next proliferation risk would be. Non-state actors are not subject to treaty obligations or conventional deterrence nor are they prone to engaging in diplomatic efforts. Thus uncertainty replaced predictability in assessments of the proliferation risk. This uncertainty was even constructed in popular culture. Films such as *Broken Arrow* (1996), *Golden Eye* (1995) and *The Rock* (1996) all deal with the theme of WMD falling into the hands of unpredictable non-state actors. Other films reflected the new sense of uncertainty about where threats would emerge such as *Outbreak* (1995), which dealt with renewed fears of plague-like disease threatening mankind, foreshadowing panics caused by the SARS outbreak in 2003.[95] The point being that during the 1990s a void existed where once, for the West at least, had stood a clear and present danger (to keep the movie theme going). The lack of clarity about the future was reflected both in policy and popular culture; one of the ways in which shape was given to that void was the re-emergence of WMD as a security concept.

The usefulness of the term 'WMD' has been questioned in the literature, and though it may seem remarkable given the prevalence of the term today its emergence as shorthand for nuclear, biological and chemical weapons really only occurred in the last decade or so. For example the 1996 annual report of the Department of Defense does not include WMD in its glossary, it refers to nuclear, biological and chemical as 'NBC's' instead.[96] Oren and Solomon give a detailed account of the conceptual history of WMD. The term was coined by the Archbishop of Canterbury with reference to the civil wars in China and Spain in the 1930s and therefore almost certainly referred to effective but conventional modern weaponry, particularly aerial bombardment, and retained that meaning throughout World War Two. In 1945 the concept was linked to but not limited to atomic weapons and from there was included in several arms control treaties. By and large, by the 1980s it had fallen out of the public mind until it was revived somewhat by its inclusion in UN resolutions detailing the inspection of Iraq after the first Gulf War.[97] WMD as a proliferation concept then conflates nuclear, radiological, chemical and biological weapons and thereby broadens the scope of any proliferation regime constructed with WMD, as opposed to a specific weapon system. The definition of WMD is a political act rather than a neutral term. This construction of the evolving WMD threat in turn necessitated the creation of the PSI. Prior to the 9/11 attacks, the Cold War's state-centric counter-proliferation regime was under pressure. The new Bush administration had signalled its intention to withdraw from the Anti-Ballistic Missile Treaty and the Republican congress had rejected ratification of the Comprehensive Test Ban Treaty in 1999. The administration had also proposed constructing a missile defence shield. Non-state groups were increasingly viewed as significant threats to international peace and security,[98] and as such the rigid treaty-based state-centric counter-proliferation was ill suited to tackling contemporary proliferation risks. Slowly but surely, like the FATF's construction of terrorist financing as a global problem, the US had prepared the ground by 'talking' its way to a more proactive approach focused on interdiction, particularly in its 2002 *National Strategy to Combat Weapons of Mass Destruction*, which aimed to 'enhance the capabilities of our military, intelligence, technical, and law enforcement communities to prevent the movement of WMD materials, technology, and expertise to hostile states and terrorist organizations'.[99] The PSI and interdiction had just been 'talked' into existence as a new counter-proliferation option.

The new security practices of the 'other' war on terror thus not only seek to manage risks but in many ways shape the kinds of risks that are believed to be out there and to create the categories of 'riskiness' that then feed back into the system to be managed in turn. Eventually the proliferation risk became presented as a global problem requiring global attention. As the Polish Foreign Minister put it at a PSI meeting in Krakow:

> the proliferation of weapons of mass destruction is a particularly challenging, real and a universal threat. No state is immune to it and protected from its consequences. In the era of globalization no single country alone can fully ensure its own security.[100]

A common argument is to link it to the security implications of globalisation: 'the same development that has fostered globalization and economic growth, opportunity and independence can also be leveraged against us by our enemies – including the terrorists seeking to acquire and use weapons of mass destruction'[101]. Al Qaeda allegedly has a fleet of freighters that is used to transport money, operatives and materials, which might include WMD-related components. Hence, the discussion is always about the 'continued vulnerability of the global maritime transportation system'.[102] By constantly warning of the vulnerabilities in the global transportation system to terrorist WMD proliferation, PSI participants generated a consensus on a need for global governance where none might have existed before.

The PSI focus on WMD as a key area of concern is indicative of the politicised nature of the field of risk. After all, Article 1 of its Statement of Principles suggests that who or what poses a risk is essentially 'constructed' by participants:

> 'States or non-state actors of proliferation concern' generally refers to those countries or entities that the PSI participants involved establish should be subject to interdiction activities because they are engaged in proliferation through: (1) efforts to develop or acquire chemical, biological, or nuclear weapons and associated delivery systems; or (2) transfers (either selling, receiving, or facilitating) of WMD, their delivery systems, or related materials.[103]

There is nothing 'automatic' or 'cosmopolitan' in the subjective designating of such risks. The PSI is far from globally or universally acceptable for various reasons that we have earlier outlined, among which is a concern about US power and leadership. Many other states might also have refrained from participating because of concern about its 'ad hoc, extra-United Nations, U.S-driven nature'.[104]

As already mentioned 'WMD' is in itself a contentious and politicised term, one whose use has implications that go beyond simply a shorthand description for biological, chemical, nuclear and radiological weapons but rather carries with it normative judgements about both the weapons themselves and those who use them.

> The wide discrepancy between 'weapons of mass destruction' qua an existential Iraqi threat to America's security and the simultaneous association of the term with 'two gallon-sized jugs of . . . a corrosive material' powerfully attests to the historically-contingent and contestable meaning of this concept.[105]

Lack of input legitimacy, transparency and exclusion: far from 'cosmopolitan'?

If WMD itself is a contestable concept, then the narrow concerns of the PSI with only *certain* states of concern is an indictment of what Beck might term the 'cosmopolitan' nature of the effort. Then Under Secretary of State for Arms

Control John Bolton, admitted openly that the PSI was not concerned with Israeli nuclear weapons nor even those of India or Pakistan. He did deny that the initiative was a direct attempt to blockade North Korea but it was clear that the states of concern tallied closely with the 'Axis of Evil' earlier outlined by President Bush and a handful of other 'rogue' states such as Syria and Libya.[106] These were driven by strictly American perceptions of the greatest risk rather than a 'cosmopolitan' consensus. As John Bolton, put it:

> We are obviously worried about some places more than others as proliferants or would-be proliferants. In fact in Brisbane, at the meeting there, the 11 PSI participants said that North Korea and Iran were two states of particular concern.[107]

Obviously, the designation of Iran and North Korea (Iraq had already been invaded) as the key states of concern reflects the Western and US led nature of the initiative and as such is evidence that the cosmopolitan nature of the PSI was and is very much linked to questions of both power and construction. Even so, as the PSI has expanded, new states and new concerns have been added to its remit, which complicate a simplistic dismissal of the initiative as merely a tool of Western and particularly US power. It is that but has the potential to be more. Similarly the distinctly Western nature of the original 11 states involved in the PSI gives rise to questions not only about its legitimacy but also the initiative's 'cosmopolitan' or even global claims. Only two non-European countries, Australia and Japan, were involved in the establishment of the PSI. Neither of which could be said to reflect the viewpoints of either the Islamic world or more broadly, the global south. India in particular has complained loudly and bitterly at what it feels is the discrimination inherent in the initial 'two-tiered' exclusive structure of the PSI with a 'core' group of partners who set the rules and standards to be followed by those 'outside' who subscribed later. If, however, India were to join it now, 'we would like to be part of the decision-makers in PSI, not a peripheral participant … India's status in world affairs warrants that we should be one of the core countries.'[108] The 'core' group has since been replaced by an Operational Experts Group. As with the FATF standards, this suggests a real concern about lack of transparency in setting interdiction best practices and hints at lack of 'input legitimacy'. Indeed, rather than bringing countries together to manage the global WMD proliferation risk, the PSI 'has been criticized for insufficient public accountability, stretching if not breaking the limits of existing international law, undermining the UN system, impeding legal trade, being politically divisive, and having limited effectiveness'.[109]

The PSI in action: evaluating global risk management

A risk management strategy seeks to reshape the environment where the risk exists, to add layers of difficulty to inhibit risks emerging and to reduce the likelihood of the risk being realised. In the case of the PSI, strategies are thus designed to alter intentions and capacities of proliferators or to reduce vulnerabilities. Looking at the interdiction principles outlined above the PSI does aim to achieve these goals. The PSI multilateral exercises serve two purposes: deterrence and denial. By deterring would-be proliferators from attempting in the first place, this helps to alter their intentions. By denying WMD materials to proliferators means making it more difficult for them to succeed. By pooling knowledge and cooperating within the existing terms of the law of the sea, cooperating states are clearly shaping the environment within which proliferation risks are perceived to exist. Where previously 'innocent passage' and flag-state rights would protect potential proliferators, as in the case of the *So San*, the existence of the PSI introduced a greater degree of control for those seeking to limit such opportunities as well as elements of uncertainty and difficulty for would-be terrorist proliferators. Overall, 'the initiative is designed to make it more costly and risky for proliferators to acquire the weapons or materials they seek'.[110] As Australia's Foreign Minister pointed out, the aim was to 'make the trafficking of the world's most dangerous weapons as near to impossible as we can'.[111] In evaluating the PSI, it is important to note that it is not a stand-alone initiative.

Together with other counter-proliferation mechanisms like the NPT, CSI and multilateral export control regimes such as the Australia Group and Nuclear Suppliers Group and UNSCR 1540, it forms a 'layered defence system'.[112] US officials call the approach a 'layered non-proliferation defence'.[113] The White House claims that the PSI has 'made significant strides in shaping a new environment to combat trafficking to and from states and non-state actors of proliferation concern of weapons of mass destruction, their delivery systems, and related materials'.[114] As a risk management tool targeted at altering the capabilities and intentions of terrorists, the PSI affects the strategic calculations of terrorists and rogue states to discourage them from acquiring or using weapons of terror. President Bush declared the purpose was 'taking cooperative action to stop the proliferation trade and to deny terrorists, rogue states, and their supplier networks access to weapons of mass destruction (WMD), their delivery systems, and related materials'.[115] The notion of 'denial of access' is key to keeping these weapons out of terrorists' hands. One criticism of the PSI is though that it is distinctly limited in its scope, although it has managed to expand far beyond the original 11 founder states, the states of greatest proliferation concern to the participants are unlikely to cooperate in the foreseeable future.

In addition to reshaping the global transportation environment by creating a bloc of 90+ cooperating countries, how then does the initiative add layers of difficulty to the practice of proliferation? Indeed one of the key questions related to the initiative is how to implement the principles outlined above. In theory, implementation is clear – intelligence-led actions should be carried out by cooperating states against suspected cargoes and proliferants. The problem being, of course, identifying interdiction targets accurately and effectively. In terms of electronic surveillance, satellite systems do exist such as the Naval Ocean Surveillance System; however such systems were built with very different targets in mind. As one analyst put it:

We have a global maritime surveillance capability that was basically designed to keep track of a few hundred big Soviet warships ... Now you've got thousands of little no-name ships all over the world and you have no idea who they belong to and what they're carrying.[116]

So, interdiction is based on a combination of electronic or signal intelligence (SigInt) and human intelligence (HumInt), neither of which is 100 per cent reliable. A second aspect of the additional layer of difficulty added is the extension of the territorial reach of the initiative. Previously a vessel needed only to worry about interdiction by the authorities of its own flag state or those of its destination or port of departure. But the PSI extends the potential for action by any participating state within a range of previously unavailable territories, namely the internal waters, territorial seas and contiguous zone of a participant state, but also in international waters,[117] albeit with limitations both on receiving permissions through bilateral arrangements and legal restrictions on taking action in the seas of non-participating states and/or against vessels flagged in non-participating states. Furthermore the high seas element of the PSI can be overstated: dramatic boardings of ships is always likely to receive more coverage, but the main focus of the initiative maybe elsewhere. As the BASIC report on the PSI notes, 'According to UK officials interviewed, the vast majority of interdictions are expected to take place in key transfer ports, rather than at sea.'[118] Likewise, the success of intelligence-based missions is likely to be kept from the public eye for obvious reasons.[119] So the question must then be raised as to how potentially successful or otherwise is the PSI. In other words following the risk management model, does the PSI reduce the likelihood of proliferation? Albeit with the proviso that the initiative was never intended to halt all proliferation but rather the proliferation activities of specific state and non-state actors,[120] an issue that will be returned to in the conclusion of this chapter.

One of the first claimed successes of the PSI came in October 2003 when centrifuges with potential use in the production of weaponised nuclear fuel bound for Libya were seized aboard the *BBC China*. The subsequent ending of Libya's nuclear programme and cooperation with non-proliferation standards made the case a particularly alluring standard bearer for the then as yet unproven initiative. Initially credit was attributed to the PSI, for example Condoleeza Rice said:

PSI provided the framework for action in the 2003 interdiction of the ship BBC China. That interdiction played a major role in the unraveling of the A.Q. Kahn network and figured in Libya's wise decision to eliminate its WMD and longer range missile programs.[121]

However claims of credit for the PSI were subsequently disputed. Both non-US government officials and the then Assistant Secretary for Non-Proliferation John Wolf, have suggested that the cargo was interdicted as the result of activities that preceded the establishment of the PSI.[122] As the PSI did not establish any new institutions, bureaucracies or laws, the source of the confusion is clear. Certainly from the perspective of those supporting the PSI, any interdiction activity carried out by participants became effectively part of the PSI regime.

It is a major question then as to how to assess the effectiveness of risk management exercises such as the PSI. One of the key features of a risk approach is that it reduces the likelihood of a risk event but at the same time operates on a logic that assumes the event in question is always to some greater or lesser extent possible. As Beck himself argued, part of risk management is the effort to feign control over the uncontrollable.[123] In this light the question of how success on a grand scale should be judged is questionable and the problem is compounded by the degree of secrecy and ambiguity surrounding the activities of the PSI given their intelligence-based nature. Indeed, in May 2008, the State Department official handling the PSI had a hard time from the press, questioning him about the 'metrics' of defining success beyond the numbers of partners.[124] One of the few relatively public acknowledgements of PSI success was a briefing given to foreign government officials attending a PSI conference in 2008 where a list of five examples of successful interdictions were given and later released to some non-governmental organisations. The first in the list was the denial of an export licence to a European company in relation to coolers that could be used in heavy-water reactors to Iran. A second similar example involved a shipment of components with potential use for testing ballistic missiles. The components made by a US company and purchased via an intermediary were bound for Syria when they were seized and returned to the US in a third party port. The three remaining examples involved issues or shipments that fell under UN Security Council resolutions. Chromium-nickel steel plates bound for Iran from an Asian company were interdicted in a port of a third country under the authority of UNSCR 1696, which prevents the sale or transfer of items to Iran that could be used in its ballistic missile programme. A second Iranian-bound shipment, this time of sodium perchlorate, was returned to its port of origin from a third party Asian port. This time UNSCR 1737, again relating to certain missile technologies, provided the relevant authority. Finally, a Syrian plane was denied overflight rights to make a round trip to North Korea due to suspicions, mooted by the US, that the cargo was related to missile technology. Overflight rights were denied on the basis of UNSCR 1718, which obliges states to cooperate to prevent the transfer of missile technologies to North Korea.[125]

Legal problems

The five examples given above give a clear insight into the functioning and logic of the PSI as a relatively loose and flexible coalition of states pooling resources and legal prerogatives in their proliferation control efforts. Although some have raised questions about the legality of aspects of the PSI, Erin Harbaugh, writing in 2004, noted:

> Is the PSI legal? As it stands today, the legality of the policy still hangs in the balance. International customary law, which trumps the caveats of

international statutory law, provides a solid foundation for which a legal framework for counterproliferation strategy can be built. However, without more universal acceptance to increase its legitimacy, the policy will never survive. The PSI has enormous potential to become both a legal and effective policy, however, much more work by American policymakers must be done to ensure this.[126]

Likewise, caveats have been raised about the legality and effectiveness of the initiative by non-participating countries. Under UNCLOS, interdictions are not legally allowed for counter-proliferation purposes. For example a Chinese Foreign Ministry spokesman pointed out that 'Quite some countries have doubts over the legality and effectiveness of the PSI.'[127]

To rectify the legal problem of ship boarding, the US has signed bilateral agreements with major shipping registries Liberia and Panama, but this was not within the aegis of the PSI. With the expansion of the initiative to more than 80 countries since its inception, both legitimacy and capacity of the PSI for managing proliferation risks has increased massively. As can be seen from the examples above, the PSI in action has involved the pooling of existing legal powers rather than creating new ones and the sharing of intelligence has created a more robust proliferation regime possible. In the examples given, we can see the combination of domestic legal instruments with enforcement power transferred to third parties as in the case of the seizure of American made components and the enforcement of international legal instruments such as the various UN Security Council resolutions. Indeed, the statement of principles argues that it is conceived within and 'consistent with national legal authorities and relevant international law and frameworks, including the U.N. Security Council'.[128] The PSI is often presented by its supporters as being in support of UNSCR 1540, which mandates states to take action against non-state proliferation networks. The United Nations' High Level Group on Threats, Challenges and Change has encouraged all states to support the PSI. On 10 March 2005, at a speech to the Madrid Summit, former UN Secretary-General Kofi Annan said 'I applaud the efforts of the Proliferation Security Initiative to fill a gap in our defences.'[129] There does seem to be some endorsement of the PSI's activities although questions about its legality remain. Certainly there has been no explicit formal endorsement from the UN Security Council that would be equivalent to that body's endorsement of FATF counter-terrorist financing standards.

In other words, since the setting up of the PSI more work has indeed been done both to extend the practical reach of the initiative but also to shape global norms about proliferation. It's not insignificant that the publicly known targets of the PSI to date have included Syria, North Korea and Iran. Clearly proliferation in this context is a constructed risk, something we'll return to in the conclusion of this chapter. In the meantime a true assessment of the effectiveness of the PSI remains nearly impossible in the absence of publicly available records. Even with that information it's unclear what metric could be applied. Rather the initiative needs to be judged in the context of shaping the environment for proliferants, and part of a multifaceted campaign that overlaps between public and private and military and non-military aspects to control risks in a global security environment. Indeed it also underlines the way in which ostensibly voluntary arrangements shape the choices of actors in the international environment, by not joining an initiative like the PSI a state is begging the question of how firm its commitment is to managing proliferation and indeed to supporting the US. Again this is a question of the relationship of power to otherwise apparently 'cosmopolitan' institutions.

Conclusion

There are several key parallels that can be drawn between the PSI and the FATF – both lack a permanent institutional structure or base, cooperation (at least in formal terms) is non-coercive and voluntary, each involves practical commitments both by governments and non-state actors. As such they reflect elements of the kind of cosmopolitan institutionalism that Beck argues is the most appropriate response to managing globalised risks such as terrorism, or in this case proliferation. Similarly, the shift away from universal treaty-based solutions towards less formal forms of cooperation reflects a sea change in the manner in which proliferation is viewed as a security issue. Even the change in nomenclature from 'counter-' or 'non-'proliferation to simply proliferation has significance. Counter-proliferation and non-proliferation suggest a definite outcome to efforts to control proliferation – that it can be ultimately deterred and prevented. Dropping the preposition in the case of the Proliferation Security Initiative is significant in that it reflects a shift to a logic of risk management. Proliferation is part of the global security environment; it cannot be removed from that environment completely but rather can be managed or mitigated by a global governance regime. Inherent in any risk-based approach to a problem is the focus on reducing the probabilities of the risk becoming reality, but dealing in probabilities acknowledges the inevitability that the chance always remains that the worst will occur. What has to be questioned is the cosmopolitan nature of the recognition of the risk of proliferation.

The PSI then, it could be argued, is very far from a cosmopolitan institution in Beck's sense of the term. Rather it is another tool of Western and perhaps more specifically US power in the world, established to address distinctly Western security concerns rather than the cosmopolitan recognition of global risks. The lopsided agenda pursued by the PSI is evidence of this, although the growing membership and outreach activities to the private sector, has lent a more cosmopolitan hue to the initiative's activities. However, as with the FATF, despite these caveats the PSI does represent an initiative built on the logic of managing global risk that depends for its effectiveness on the mutual recognition of such collective risks by participants. The PSI's activities seek to shape the environment, add layers of difficulty and ultimately mitigate against the possibility of WMD (however loosely defined) falling into the hands of terrorists or rogue states (however so defined). That the cosmopolitan cannot escape the political is not in itself a fatal criticism of the PSI as an example of the convergence of global governance, risk and security. In the next chapter, we explore further attempts to mitigate global risk in the cases of aviation security and the construction of risky individuals through the application of dataveillance technologies. As highlighted in the previous chapter, the construction of risk is a political question with normative implications; the PSI reflects the application of a particular construction of risk. The question remains whether the PSI can evolve beyond that limited frame to reflect a more cosmopolitan vision of proliferation as a security issue.

5   Aviation security[1]

Introduction

Our last and final case study relates to aviation security risks and global multi-level attempts to manage them. Our understanding of the term 'aviation security' is deployed flexibly to refer to the idea that airports are key sites where global governance regimes interact directly with citizens but that these regimes are not necessarily restricted to the airport or even aeroplanes. Aviation security then is essentially concerned with regulating the people and objects that may gain access to global aviation systems – including airports, aeroplanes and flights – in order to prevent security risks from disrupting either the aviation sector itself, society more generally or both. Like its predecessors, this chapter continues to highlight and reiterate the recurrent themes that have permeated this book so far: risk, global governance, security and the 'other' war on terror. Once again in using the term 'global governance', we are not necessarily claiming that 'universal' participation or formal agreement exists. Instead, as we have laid out in Chapter 2, we take a broad and looser understanding of the term. Sometimes it is simply like-minded actors getting together to confront collective shared problems. Other times, it can also involve a wide variety of private sector actors. In our previous cases of the FATF and PSI, although these were relatively 'informal' versions of global governance that attempted to be as inclusive as possible in Beck's 'cosmopolitan' sense, these were still largely dominated and driven by 'cosmopolitan realist' state actors as they attempted to develop responses to new global risks. Indeed, one of the problems we encountered so far was the unresolved tension between on one hand, serving narrow 'realist' interests based on power and on the other, fulfilling a broader 'cosmopolitan' global agenda. Thus, in this final case study we chose to address closely the role of non-state actors, particularly global trade bodies, at the other end of the broad global governance spectrum and how they in turn have developed alternative responses to common aviation security risks after 9/11.

With regards to the war on terror, as we have suggested earlier, the two overarching strategic goals of US counter-terrorism policy are: global standards-setting and capacity-building/cooperation with state and non-state partners. Here with aviation security, as before, we move to examine to what degree these twin aims can be reconciled through ideas of global governance and those of Beck on 'risk-cosmopolitanism' and 'institutionalised cosmopolitanism'. In the words of Mark Salter:

> unfortunately, contemporary security analysis of aviation takes place within a realist, empiricist frame that simply reinforces the state-centric assumptions of power politics. It ignores the networked nature of threats and the complex web of state and non-state security actors that actually provide security.[2]

Hence we opted for aviation security for a variety of reasons that might be familiar to the reader by now. To begin with, Salter continues, 'aviation security is a vital but under-studied component of contemporary security'.[3] This resonates with our concern over the less-noticed dimensions of the 'other' war on terror. Yet its central importance has been highlighted because on 11 September 2001, 19 individuals using box cutters managed to take control of four passenger jets, turned them into missiles targeted against the commercial and military heart of the United States. Of course, aviation security is not a new concern. With terrorist hijackings and bombings from the past several decades, 9/11 simply amplified and magnified the scale and nature of the risk, particularly in terms of vulnerabilities and catastrophic consequences like the collapse of the Twin Towers. The social construction of risk and the implementation of new risk-based security measures in public–private partnerships is another issue of concern. In terms of its relation to risk, the individuals involved in carrying out the attack were largely unknown even to the security services. As such the attacks came from nowhere. True as the 9/11 Commission report notes, the warning systems, such as they were, were flashing red in the summer of 2001, but these systems and the people that managed them were ill-equipped to pre-empt the looming attacks. Indeed, the US airport security system pre-9/11 was fragmented, with responsibility shared between various actors.[4] Commercial airports were directly responsible for the law enforcement presence on site, controlling access to secure areas and the airport perimeter. These functions were carried out by directly controlled staff, private security firms and in some cases regular police forces. Commercial airlines were responsible for the security of the aircraft that in turn implied responsibility for screening passengers, baggage and other cargo usually with private contractors. Finally the Federal Aviation Authority had regulatory responsibility for setting and enforcing security standards and providing a limited amount of funding.[5]

There certainly has been much criticism of the fragmentation of responsibility, airlines underinvesting in security due to cost–benefit analyses or failures of systemic design or enforcement of regulations. One particular issue highlighted was the very low wages being paid to private baggage screeners. Eventually aviation security in the US was federalised with the government assuming responsibility, with a reduced role for the private sector that was contracted to the authorities rather than previously with commercial airlines. We do not seek to rehash the whole finger-pointing blame exercise again. Instead, this chapter seeks to explore how the vulnerabilities in the aviation sector that 9/11 highlighted has been responded to both by governments and the private sector, particularly in terms of risk and global cooperation. As with terrorist financing and WMD proliferation, there is complex multilevel engagement with global, regional and even private attempts to manage aviation security. We discuss how for instance the private sector such as international airlines have got together to harmonise global norms based on common risk-assessment methodologies, as well as similar overlapping regional and inter-governmental attempts to do so.

While our previous cases dealt more with issues relating to terrorism (such as financing or WMD proliferation), in this chapter we also address the *risky individual* terrorist. What we have witnessed is a reorientation and restructuring of airport security and intelligence operations towards the logic of risk management. Rather than waiting for specific causes, the aim is to reshape the environment and actively to manage individuals so that the 'risky' individual can be sorted from the innocent. Such an approach demands massive amounts of data collection and analysis but also important political decisions about what constitutes risk and what process the sorting should take.

The chapter begins with the definition of the aviation security issue: the stated need and rationale for global governance and the nature of the risk at stake in terms of vulnerabilities. Then we turn to look specifically at the social construction and practices of risk in the airport, both by governments and private actors with the greatest stake defining and managing the risk. This faciliated the emergence of 'dataveillance'[6] as a new security practice. At the same time it reflects the crucial role of non-state actors in contemporary global governance. In terms of standards-setting and capacity-building, we take a multilevel approach, beginning with changes in European and United States airport security and a number of bilateral and multilateral initiatives at standards-setting and 'cosmopolitan' outreach to other partners. We then move to consider the inadequacies and criticisms of a traditional 'formal', state-centric global institution like the International Civil Aviation Organisation (ICAO), the premier UN agency dedicated to civil aviation. Like the FATF, it has its own global benchmark standards known as Standards and Recommended Practices (SARPs). A concern with shared global aviation security risk does appear to be igniting what Beck might recognise as 'risk-cosmopolitanism'. A range of state and non-state actors are compelled cooperatively to develop new frameworks and global norms that seem to be invariably based on risk. But as we have consistently stressed throughout this book, global governance is not just about the UN-centred system like the ICAO, but increasingly involves private actors getting active as an indicator of 'institutionalised cosmopolitanism'. Indeed, airlines who are members in the global trade organisation International Air Transport Association (IATA) have themselves developed best practices to manage new aviation risks, in light of the inadequacies of existing institutions like the ICAO to do so. Furthermore, a significant portion of contemporary airport security practice also involves private actors in the collection and analysis of data to create risk assessments of passengers. Finally, we turn to evaluate how the multilevel, overlapping global aviation security regimes serve risk management goals, bearing in mind the implications and downsides so far. As with the previous two chapters, what is at stake here is the extent to which these new approaches represent a shift towards an 'institutionalised cosmopolitan' form of global governance engendered by Beck's 'risk-cosmopolitanism' and 'enlightened self-interest', or are we merely dealing with a case of power and narrow national interests simply repackaged as old wine in new bottles?

'Faceless individuals': civil aviation as an issue for global governance

Like terrorist financing, many justifications for aviation security are presented in terms of how, as the US *National Strategy for Aviation Security* recognises, 'international cooperation is critical to ensuring that lawful private and public activities in the Air Domain are protected from attack and hostile or unlawful exploitation'.[7] Airliners and airports are symbolic of the cross-boundary flows relating to globalisation: 'cutting across national and international boundaries, as well as economic, political, and social divisions, civil aviation is a vital sector of contemporary global life'.[8] As US Transportation Security Administration (TSA) chief Kip Hawley put it, 'Nowhere is the world more networked than in the aviation system. From producing aircraft, staffing the industry, managing the airspace, and assuring its security and the security of our passengers – we depend on each other every day.'[9] Much like the risks of terrorist financing or WMD proliferation to terrorists, and given its cross-boundary nature, aviation security is a prime case for global governance. National regulations can cover to some degree national carriers but cannot ultimately regulate foreign airliners and their security standards, entering territorial airspace. Indeed, 'airlines and terrorists share one thing in common – a global base of operations.... Global cooperation will enhance safety and security levels.'[10] In October 2007, the American TSA set up its Office of Global Strategies to increase aviation security by working more proactively and intensively with foreign partners. The skies after all, like the high seas we discussed in Chapter 4, do not have sovereign jurisdictions over them, 'the need for a strong and effective coalition is reinforced by the fact that most of the Air Domain is under no single nation's sovereignty or jurisdiction'.[11] A glance at the Preamble to the Chicago Convention on International Civil Aviation, which established the ICAO in 1944, highlights the global nature of the issue and more importantly the need for global consensus,

> WHEREAS the future development of international civil aviation can greatly help to create and preserve friendship and understanding among the nations and peoples of the world, yet its abuse can become a threat to the general security; and
>   WHEREAS it is desirable to avoid friction and to promote that cooperation between nations and peoples upon which the peace of the world depends;

THEREFORE, the undersigned governments having agreed on certain principles and arrangements in order that international civil aviation may be developed in a safe and orderly manner and that international air transport services may be established on the basis of equality of opportunity and operated soundly and economically.[12]

After 9/11, as Salter observed, 'more scholarly attention has been paid to aviation and airport security. However, this kind of public and scholarly attention focuses on the role of government or the private sector in security screening, or on evaluations of various detection technologies.'[13] We suggest that a broader discussion of aviation security based on illuminating the linkages between theories of risk and those of global governance might prove more theoretically enriching. In a similar light, Szyliowicz suggests that a 'systemic' response would be ideal,

widespread changes in all aspects of aviation – in planning, design, implementation, and operation – are required if such a [resilient, flexible] system is to emerge. The goal should be to incorporate security into every element of the system to the extent possible.[14]

This 'systemic' approach, we argue, could also be transplanted to the global governance system to deal with aviation security risks.

Risk and civil aviation

The emphasis on assessing and managing risk is clearly apparent to senior US officials tasked with aviation security, 'we will evaluate risks and consequences, factor in known and unknown terrorism threats, and acknowledge in the design of our programs that terrorism is not predictable'.[15] Concepts and ideas that we first encountered in justifying the need to manage terrorist financing risks are mirrored in aviation security as well, 'we will connect the dots between people and behaviour; and ensure that we develop and nurture relationships and communication structures so that those dots are always connected'.[16] Once again, the assumption here is about risk management. If we are able somehow to reduce the risk, then the future unwanted outcome (i.e. terrorist exploitation of aviation security infrastructure) can be averted. Thinking in terms of risk then leads to a concern with how nefarious actors have both the intention and capacity to exploit weak chinks in the system, as we have seen previously. Indeed, the US understanding of the basic risk is presented in these very terms, 'individuals and groups hostile to the United States have demonstrated the ability, and a continuing desire, to exploit vulnerabilities and to adapt to changes in aviation security measures to attack the nation and its global interests'.[17] As with the case of terrorist financing and WMD proliferation, the risk here is considered a function of threat (intentions and capability of terrorists to exploit civil aviation), vulnerability and consequence. The events of 9/11 were a dramatic and tragic reminder of the vulnerabilities of the global air transport system that could easily be exploited by terrorists. After 9/11, it became 'fashionable' for British media outlets to probe airport security for holes and uncover weaknesses, for instance smuggling weapons on to aircraft or getting on the restricted areas like tarmacs unhindered.[18] The point of this was really to highlight, as with the FATF or PSI, loopholes or gaps in the global infrastructure that could then be exploited by potential terrorists. Therefore, as TSA Administrator Kip Hawley testified, 'I think the key point is there are vulnerabilities in every system of security. And that what we're engaged in is risk management.'[19] Hence, TSA is increasingly concerned with 'exposing vulnerabilities in the system through covert testing'.[20] At the global level too, the ICAO recognises, 'the global air transport system is secure but remains vulnerable'.[21] Risk management in this case, is therefore about addressing vulnerabilities and 'the steady accretion of security screening procedures and the widening list of banned items have occluded the irreducible vulnerability of open societies'.[22] Crucially it also means recognition that perfect security is impossible. The aviation infrastructure is so widespread that it is impossible to do everything. Instead, risk management is thus about 'playing the odds', writes Bruce Schneir, 'it's figuring out which attacks are worth worrying about and which ones can be ignored. It's spending more resources on the serious attacks and less on the frivolous ones.'[23] To manage risks then implies reducing vulnerabilities of the underlying system, in order to alter the strategic calculations or impair the capabilities of terrorists to exploit the system. This then theoretically reduces the likelihood of the undesirable outcome materialising.

The security problem presented by the 9/11 attacks stems from the fact that if this was an act of war then it was very different from any previous act of war. Unlike in Pearl Harbor or when the British burned the Capitol in 1815, there was no clear chain of responsibility leading to a foreign capital. The perpetrators had all been killed, leaving little or no trail of the kind of command and control structure that normally governs conventional military action. Indeed the 19 hijackers had all been based within US jurisdiction, the four flights had taken off from domestic terminals at airports in Boston, Newark and Dulles and were heading for destinations within the United States.[24] On the other hand, it was unlike other acts of terrorism such as the 1993 World Trade Center bombings that were also carried out by Islamic extremists or the Oklahoma bombing in 1995.[25] The scale of the attacks and the visceral emotional effects they invoked[26] called for a very different type of response. As President Bush put it:

Americans have known wars – but for the past 136 years, they have been wars on foreign soil, except for one Sunday in 1941. Americans have known the casualties of war – but not at the center of a great city on a peaceful morning. Americans have known surprise attacks – but never before on thousands of civilians. All of this was brought upon us in a single day – and night fell on a different world, a world where freedom itself is under attack.[27]

As we have already argued the militaristic nature of the wars in Afghanistan and Iraq have captured headlines. In terms of targeting individual terrorists, the military response has had successes such as the assassination of Qaed Al-Harethi, in Yemen, using an unmanned aircraft[28] or killing of Abu Musab Al-Zarqawi in Iraq.[29] Scholars have also suggested these extra-judicial killings might in themselves constitute a form of risk management.[30] However we are more concerned with the risk posed by relatively 'faceless' terrorists dotted around the globe all with the potential to penetrate Western societies using the global transport network.

In the immediate aftermath of 9/11, two further incidents highlighted the need to reduce the risk of attacks by unknown individuals. In the US, attacks using the bacteria anthrax led ultimately to five deaths and the individual responsible is yet to be brought to justice.[31] Even though the death toll remained relatively low the disruption was widespread – Congress and the Supreme Court were temporarily shut down, costs to the US postal system were enormous, estimated at $3 billion, with clean-up costs in Congress estimated at $24 million.[32] A report on the incident calls for risk management strategies to mitigate against future attacks, including information sharing and bio-surveillance:

> The United States faces new challenges in a world shaken by attacks with hijacked planes and biological agents.... No one knows if and when future bio-terrorist attacks might occur, but actions taken to bolster US biodefense today can help mitigate the consequences, improve public health, and strengthen US national security in the future.[33]

The other major incident that highlighted the need for a shift towards managing risks was the 'shoe-bomber' incident in December 2001. Richard Reid, a British national, was prevented from detonating a device hidden in his shoe while onboard a Boeing 767 from Paris to Miami. Remarkably, it was Reid's second attempt at aviation terrorism. On the previous day Reid had attempted to fly to Miami from Paris but his dishevelled appearance, the fact that he paid in cash and carried no luggage set off alarm bells. He was questioned for so long that he missed his flight.[34]

The uncertainty engendered both by the 9/11 terrorist attacks and those hitherto 'unknown' assailants that followed demanded a response. President Bush captured the nature of the problem aptly when he said: 'Freedom itself was attacked this morning by a *faceless* coward, and freedom will be defended.'[35] The emphasis in the above quote is ours, it highlights the degree to which the attackers were unknown and arguably, without a reconfiguration of Western security practices, unknowable. The response to this challenge took shape in two ways, on the one hand visible enemies were identified in the form of Osama bin Laden, Taliban-governed Afghanistan and then Saddam Hussein's Iraq.[36] It is the other response that concerns us here – the harmonising of global standards and reshaping of the global aviation security apparatus to identify 'risky' individuals, sort them from the general public and apply preventive security strategies against them.

The social construction of 'risky' individuals

Whereas the identification of states with some degree of responsibility for providing support to Al Qaeda was relatively straightforward (regardless of the relative merits of the cases), identifying individuals operating within Western societies was very difficult indeed. Often, the need to do so is presented by those who perceive the highest stake in regulating the problem. As noted by Sir David Pepper, then director of Government Communications Headquarters (GCHQ), the main British intelligence eavesdropping agency:

> We had said before July [2005] ... there are probably groups out there that we do not know anything about, and because we do not know anything about them we do not know how many there are. What happened in July [the 2005 London bombings] was a demonstration that there were [material redacted for security reasons] conspiracies going on about which we essentially knew nothing, and that rather sharpens the perception of how big, if I can use [Secretary of Defense Donald] Rumsfeld's term, the unknown unknown was.[37]

Sir David, in speaking on such terms, was basically helping to construct the risk for us. Like the case of terrorist financing, although the risk does exist, it has to be constructed as a problem to be managed. As FBI Director Robert Mueller claimed on separate occasions in 2003 and 2005, 'the greatest threat is from Al Qaeda cells in the US that we have not yet identified' and that 'I remain very concerned about what we are not seeing.'[38] A fundamental part of any effective aviation security system would now have to include a means for identifying individual terrorists that potentially pose 'risks'. De Goede has already suggested how the construction of certain imaginary nightmare scenarios in the public mindset in turn helps to 'foster new conjunctions of governing and expertise that are in urgent need of analysis'.[39] It is a tool used for governing by risk. Salter also points out, 'an important activity of the "managers of unease" in particular security sectors is the construction of the "risk" field itself and the concomitant construction of expert knowledge in that field'.[40] When it comes to questions of Homeland Security, which inevitably covers aviation sectors after 9/11, it seems everyone has an incentive to exaggerate risks and be alarmist.[41] As John Mueller points out:

> politicians are being politicians, and security businesses are being security businesses. It's just like selling insurance – you say, 'Your house could burn down.' You don't have an incentive to say, 'Your house will never burn down.' And you're not lying.[42]

Mueller argues that 'Americans have been regularly regaled with dire predictions of another major al Qaeda attack in the United States.'[43] One consequence of this construction of the risk is a directed concern with aviation security risks that are most closely associated with 9/11. The risk has been talked into exist-ence notably by Department Homeland Security (DHS) chief Michael Chertoff: 'he introduced the idea of risk and it has caught on'.[44] This influence now extends to aviation security, which is under the remit of DHS. As Chertoff himself put it:

> there's no question after 9/11, but even before 9/11, one of the biggest priorities that we have to focus on, in terms of risk, is securing our transpor-tation system. And by this I mean not just aviation security, although that's clearly very important, but all modes of transportation.[45]

Others involved in constructing the risk come from security consultancies and 'security experts' in the media who constantly claim the aviation system is vul-nerable to attack; for instance, the 2006 study of aviation security by DFI Inter-national, a Washington, DC, security consultancy, which suggests that drunken passengers too pose risks as they can kick in reinforced cockpit doors.[46] Here we have both public and private sector actors themselves involved in constructing the risks to aviation and then positioning themselves as in a position to manage those risks. As Anna Leander has noted on private military contractors (PMCs) but with relevance to private security consultancies involved in constructing aviation security risk as well:

> This privatisation of intelligence has direct consequences for the relation between PMC's and security discourses ... firms may have a significant impact on the routine boxing of information which is in itself a way of creating threats and security concerns that might not previously have existed.[47]

Tensions have always been evident in relation to the definition of terrorism and how best to combat it; the crux of the issue being that one man's terrorist is another man's freedom fighter. Arguably by treating terrorism as risk, while the politicised aspect of definition does not disappear, the question can be somewhat transformed into more of a managerial problem. Risk strategies here involve the inductive profiling of individuals using a variety of metrics, thus such a strategy would be able to at least postpone the most politicised aspect of the question by breaking potential riskiness down into more pragmatic and less contested terms of reference – using patterns of behaviour as evidence of riskiness rather than a-priori characteristics such as race, religion or ethnicity (although these are not entirely excluded). One clear area that demanded action was aviation security. But meeting that challenge would be difficult. As Salter has noted:

> Since first becoming a high-profile target for terrorists and hijackers since the late 1960's, aviation security has waxed and waned in the public imagi-nation. Tolerance for security procedures and delays at airports decreases as the memory of attacks fades, while demands for a secure and efficient sector

are made continuously by industry members and the businesses that depend on global mobility.[48]

The challenge was how to create a functioning global system governing aviation security that reduced the risk of further attacks but remained flexible enough to allow the return of business as usual for those both working in and reliant upon the aviation industry. The answer would have to involve developing new tools and practices of security that would allow passengers and goods to flow as quickly as possible through airports but also would allow for the risk of further terrorist attacks to be sufficiently reduced for confidence to remain in the aviation system. TSA Administrator Kip Hawley talks up the problem in terms of risk:

> While it is *necessary*, it is no longer *sufficient* to focus on finding threat devices, like guns and knives. We must also enhance our ability to recognize suspicious patterns and behaviors, so we can identify people who may have devised new means to attack our transportation systems or passengers, or who may have evaded other layers of our security system.[49]

Aviation security and global governance by risk

As discussed earlier, one of the risks highlighted by 9/11 is the relatively faceless nature of the terrorist risk to aviation security. The scope of 'unknown unknowns' is remarkably broad. In practical terms, this means selection and control of who gets on a plane. A central focus of the new global aviation security architecture has been the development of procedures to profile passengers in order to categorise the degree of risk. The US Aviation and Transport Security Act, November 2001, required that all flights provide US authorities with electronic passenger name records (PNR).[50] This allows law enforcement agencies to use 'advanced data-mining techniques to reveal patterns of criminal behaviour and detain suspected terrorists before they act'.[51] For similar reasons, there has been a move to machine readable passports containing biometric information, finger-printing of all individuals entering the US and advance passenger information systems.[52]

These data collection and control techniques are a classic example of risk management to break 'the individual up into a set of measurable risk factors'.[53] In particular, by linking passenger information to other law enforcement and intelligence databases allows the creation and maintenance of risk profiles for all passengers. In the US this has taken the shape of the US-Visit programme that links more than 20 databases with a view to 'weeding out' criminals and terrorists. These include IDENT, the automatic fingerprint ID storing biometric data on all visitors, immigrants and asylum seekers; ADIS, storing entry and exit data; APIS, storing passenger manifest information; SEVIS, storing information on exchange and foreign students; IBIS, a watch list linked to Interpol; CLAIMS 3, holding information on foreign nationals claiming benefits 'and an array of links to local law enforcement, financial systems and educational records'.[54] The goal of linking such information is to be able to categorise and identify people by their degree of 'riskiness'.[55]

Indicative of the roles non-state actors now play in governance by risk, the US-Visit contract was awarded to the 'Smart Border Alliance', a private consortium headed up by management consultants Accenture. Other companies involved include Raytheon, the Titan Corporation, Dell, AT&T, Sprint, SRA International, Global Technology Management, Sandler and Travis Trade Advisory.[56] There is a global governance dimension to this as US-Visit pertains to managing the flows of foreign passengers originating from foreign airports and entering US airspace. The involvement of Titan Corporation is particularly significant as this company is also responsible for supplying interrogators and interpreters at Abu Ghraib. Thus the same company is involved at more than one stage of the dataveillance project – directly gathering intelligence and providing initial analysis while also helping to design the systems that ultimately put that data to use. Louise Amoore has questioned the technocratic nature of private security solutions to public security problems:

> In effect, the expertise becomes the norm, as one immigration lawyer explained 'Since 9/11 the public authorities have turned to the private authorities [*sic*] to design the architecture of the systems, to make "efficient systems" ... so this is only ever treated as a technical problem, and not a question of politics.'[57]

As with the shift of authority to bureaucratic levels in the FATF, we see then in the construction of dataveillance systems a similar shift away from public accountability in terms of the definition and management of aviation security risks, towards private contractors. This is somewhat worrying as the role of private intelligence is expected to become more and more important. As Singer has noted: 'The private intelligence sub-sector is at the initial stage of a huge boom. For many nations and political groups, most of their intelligence analysis and operations are gradually being outsourced to private firms.'[58] Furthermore with the growing importance of open source intelligence, this role of private actors in the intelligence arena is already significant. Former CIA director James Woolsey estimates that 95 per cent of intelligence comes from open sources with a significant proportion from private firms.[59]

US demands for greater access to passenger information was quite contentious and highlights again how a concern with global risk often has legal implications. After intense negotiations the EU and the US signed an agreement on the sharing of PNRs with 34 pieces of data to be shared. However this agreement was struck down by the European Court of Justice in May 2006, and has since been replaced with an interim and further long-term agreement in July 2007. The amended agreement reduces the number of elements to be shared to 19 to comply with EU privacy laws. Even so the data to be transferred contain quite comprehensive information, as the EU FAQ on the topic note that:

The US Department of Homeland Security (DHS) ... will filter out and not use sensitive information, save in exceptional cases where life is at risk. Sensitive information means data revealing racial or ethnic origin, political opinions, religious or philosophical beliefs, trade union membership or concerning the health or sex life of the individual.[60]

Overall there is a clear trend in relation to data collection and data sharing among civilian and intelligence organisations. As with the new practices of control at airports themselves, questions need to be raised as to the 'cosmopolitan nature' of the risk categories used in contemporary aviation security. Invariably, private sector actors are deeply involved in initiatives such as the Registered Traveller (RT) programme, which facilitates speedier clearance of a passenger who is deemed to pose lower risks. 'RT is a public–private partnership, like any other, it faces the natural tension between private sector companies expecting returns from its investment of capital, with a governmental agency like the TSA tasked with ensuring aviation security.'[61] One of the challenges of using data profiling is the incomplete picture security services have. The Richard Reid 'shoe-bomber' incident and the British born individuals in the July 2005 London bombings confounded expectations about the typical profile of a would-be terrorist. Furthermore, although precise profiling techniques remain secret, terrorists may actively seek to recruit outside their 'typical' peer group in order to outwit profile-based security traps.[62] Consequently, there has also been substantial investment in new technologies designed not only to detect concealed weapons or explosives but also to detect suspicious behavioural patterns or physiological signs that an individual is a potential security risk. Although the technology remains in the testing stage it does provide an interesting example of risk-based technologies.[63] If it proves possible to use subconscious non-verbal cues to detect risky individuals then the dataveillance regime will be able to escape suspicions of racial profiling or bias, a topic we return to in the evaluation part of this chapter.

Reforming aviation security: a case of 'institutionalised cosmopolitanism'?

The events of 9/11 stimulated new attempts of states like the US and existing international institutions like the EU to adapt to the new challenges of aviation security, while also exposing the inadequacies of others like the ICAO to respond. At the same time, non-state global industry groups like the IATA alliance of airlines sought to refocus its efforts towards this problem, in partnership with an array of relevant actors. In what follows we offer a multilevel analysis of responses to 9/11 from states (US), regional (EU) to global (ICAO, IATA). Indeed, the new risk-based technologies and approaches developed in the US or the EU mentioned above would prove more useful if they were integrated into a globally coordinated governance structure. The US *National Strategy for Aviation Security* has after all declared its intention to create what it calls a 'risk-based, cross-discipline, and global approach to aviation security'.[64] Hence, in thinking about aviation security, there does appear to be a case to echo Beck's calls for 'institutionalised cosmopolitanism' and a 'cosmopolitan opening' of the governance system:

> because of the complexity and global nature of the Aviation Transportation System, responsibility for preventing, responding to, and, if necessary, recovering from attacks in the Air Domain extends across all levels of government and across private and public sectors ... it is only through such an integrated approach among all aviation partners, governmental and non-governmental, public, and private, that the United States can improve the security of the Air Domain.[65]

The increasing participation of private non-state actors in global aviation security issues, as we have seen with the FATF and PSI, is justified in terms of greatest stake and ownership, 'substantial segments of the Nation's aviation transportation infrastructure are owned and operated by private sector entities'.[66] The goal then is summed up as follows, to 'create a web from government-to-government and government-to-private sector companies'.[67] This is particularly crucial with the idea of 'layered security', which informs aviation security. The premise being that 'layered systems cannot be breached by the defeat of a single security feature ... interleaved layers can confound the would-be terrorist'.[68] This involves the coordination of and involvement of several actors, particular the private sector. Coordination remains a difficult problem for various reasons such as lack of funding or the sheer complexity of actors involved.

Aviation security has historically been approached quite differently by the United States and Europe. The question now is whether the shock of risks to global aviation exposed by 9/11 is sufficient to bring about reform and innovative change in response. After all, attempts to standardise or radically reform global aviation security were placed on the long finger prior to 9/11 largely due largely to a lack of what one might term a 'cosmopolitan' consensus:

> The establishment of a more powerful global aviation security regime would require a degree of consensus among the member states of ICAO.... In our new world disorder, governments, regulatory agencies and the aviation industry are more likely to muddle through, responding to each crisis as it comes.[69]

Hainmuller and Lemnitzer further noted: 'Despite the generally high interest of citizens in safe air travel, a systematic cross-national comparison reveals that the performance of airport security regimes on both sides of the Atlantic is diverging widely, with Europe at the top.'[70] With regards to America, Frederickson and LaPorte observe:

> The organization and management of commercial air travel in the United States is a complex, fragmented array of horizontal, vertical and lateral

linkages between multiple jurisdictions at all levels of government; a wide range of types of corporations and unions; and a wide range of types of contractors – a system rather than a hierarchy or an organizations.[71]

In the EU by comparison, generally with a few exceptions, aviation security was firmly controlled at the national level by a single overarching authority.[72]

The events of 9/11 highlighted the impetus to generate new global, even 'cosmopolitan' consensus in terms of approaches to aviation security: the international character of Al Qaeda and the global nature of its aims meant that any adequate response would have to be equally global in its reach. Entry and exit points of the global aviation system link national boundaries, oftentimes quite distant states are rendered effectively contiguous by air transport links. Yet the dynamics of change took the US and the EU in quite different directions, albeit they talk the same language of risk. America created a new federal agency the Transportation Security Administration (TSA) to assume almost all of the security tasks that had hitherto been spread across a number of different actors.[73] The TSA employs risk-based analysis towards aviation security, which, when coupled with public–private risk-based initiatives on sharing passenger information discussed earlier, and intelligence with international partners, can be seen as evidence of a shift towards a risk management approach. Within Europe the direction of change is more clearly geared towards the establishing of best-practice standards and coordination. Regulation 2320/2002 established the world's first supranational airport security regime giving the Commission power to demand compliance with established best practices and authority to inspect airports.[74] Here we have an established international institution like the EU working to confront the new demands of aviation security risks. The EU influence stretches to include most if not all of the members of the European Civil Aviation Conference (ECAC), which states on its website that:

> this work [development of the aviation security audit programme] has been carried out in close co-ordination with the European Union, which in 2002 for the first time issued regulations in the security area. This co-operation effectively ensures a single 42-State European aviation security policy.[75]

The ECAC is arguably another example of institutionalised cosmopolitanism. The ECAC has sought to coordinate and facilitate cooperation among governments in the aviation sector. It also has maintained close links with the global trade body IATA. In relation to security, the ECAC is involved in both standard-setting and auditing to ensure best practice among member states, including the production and updating of a standard 'Aviation Security Handbook'.[76] The organisation works closely with the EU on security issues with implications for broader aspects of the world's aviation security regime. 'ECAC and the EU have reached a modus operandi for close co-operation with the aim of ensuring a single comprehensive aviation security policy for the Wider Europe.'[77] Since 2002, the ECAC has been working closely with the US in order to 'consolidate the quality of their mutual aviation security relationship'.[78] But more importantly in the context of the current discussion, the ECAC actively seeks links and 'cosmopolitan' outreach to develop new security standards beyond its member states and even the 'wider Europe'. It has established memoranda of understanding (MoUs) with the African Civil Aviation Commission, the Latin American Civil Aviation Commission, the Arab Civil Aviation Commission and most recently with the West African Economic and Monetary Union. The purpose of these MoUs is revealing in the context of what Beck might term 'institutionalised cosmopolitanism', as the ECAC website notes:

> the general objectives of these co-operations are to:
>
> - Facilitate the mutual understanding of regional aviation security requirements.
> - Share best practices on implementing security measures.
> - Strengthen the knowledge and skills of security experts in each region.
> - Harmonise security measures between ECAC and these regions.[79]

These MoUs allow for the extension of security standards and best practice beyond the ECAC's own remit and to encourage the adoption of such standards by non-member states, clearly reminiscent of the FATF's FSRB initiatives targeted at regional organisations. One question that could be raised here is the extent to which the cooperating states view the ECAC standards as reflecting their own security concern or whether this was a case of a limited vision of security being adopted by external states in return for lesser restrictions on access to European airspace.

The European Aviation Security Association (EASA) is another example of private sector actors taking initiatives and interlinking with the 'cosmopolitan' opening of the global aviation security regime to non-state actors. It comprises the seven largest companies in the provision of civil aviation security in Europe including Brinks Security Services, Group 4, ICTS, Kotter Aviation Security, Prosegur Compania de Securidad, Securitas Transport Aviation Security and Trigion Beveiliging.[80] Acutely aware of their front-line position in aviation security, in 2007 EASA announced two initiatives to improve European aviation security standards. First the creation of an industry quality charter that all members will be required to sign and second is the goal of establishing a binding European standard of quality that would cover all private actors in the aviation security sector.[81]

At the broader global level though, and typical of global governance issues, much of the problem 'arises from the absence of any international authority that can enforce regulations and mandates'.[82] The ICAO has tried to adapt its pre-existing Annex 17 of rules on security to develop international best practices but these were the lowest common denominator and many governments were unwilling or unable to do so. After 9/11, in 2002, it launched the Aviation Security Plan of Action to audit and harmonise security practices and identify deficiencies. The plan however was to be funded by voluntary contributions, of which little was forthcoming. The ICAO, which traditionally used to be primarily a standard-setting organisation, does recognise the need to adapt after 9/11. Besides simply setting benchmarks, it is now reorienting itself towards capacity-building as well. Programmes now include a comprehensive security audit unveiled in November 2002. Where substantial deficiencies are uncovered, the ICAO now also provides technical assistance to states to help bolster their capacity to comply with international standards. However, scholars such as Wallis question whether the ICAO as a 'political' state-centric UN agency is best suited to the task of responding to the global aviation challenge that transcends state boundaries. For instance it has had problems securing compliance with its best practices and many state parties to it simply do not share the same perception of aviation security risks. Furthermore, attempts to institute an evaluation regime of states' airport security are often bedevilled by self-interested fear of foreign inspections having an ulterior motive; 'wheels turn slowly within the UN agency'.[83] Global aviation risk has not built bridges, amongst states at least.

In comparison with the 'political' nature of ICAO impairing responses to new global challenges, we have private global organisations composed of international airlines in the IATA. It rationalises its existence as, 'when governments don't communicate, IATA's role is to broker effective solutions'.[84] It can be seen at one level as a global lobby group that fights for the interests of airlines across the globe. Since its inception, it has developed a whole range of commercial standards that helped grow the industry. These include standards on issues such as invoicing, reservations and fuel data, and scheduling. Ironically, the IATA possesses a more formalised and physical presence than our other cases, the FATF or PSI. It has 84 offices in 73 countries covering 115 nations; and has annual general meetings to formalise the industry position on policy issues; and corporate governance structures.

After 9/11, the IATA has added standard security measures to its previously separate safety audit systems. In 2007 it set about establishing the Global Air Cargo Security Industry Task Force with a view to:

> positively influencing developments in cargo security regulation, harmonization of global standards, promoting and developing the principle and practice of air cargo supply chain security and improving communication of relevant issues amongst and between members. Key principles will include 'many voices, one message' and 'developing talk into action'.[85]

The group that emerged from these meetings is the Air Cargo Security Industry Forum (ACSIF), membership of which is not open to individual airlines but rather what are termed 'stakeholders'. These include the Association of European Airlines, Universal Postal Union, International Road Transport Union, EASA and a broad range of other participants spread across a number of aviation sectors and locations.[86] It is another example of the 'cosmopolitan' opening up of 'institutionalised cosmopolitanism' due to recognition of the interlinked nature of the risk. The forum seeks to use its members' influence to help to standardise cargo security globally, in particular to ensure that security standards are based on 'threat and risk assessment'. As the ACSIF notes: 'Regulated security standards are becoming more complex and rigorous. Regulatory developments sometimes appear politically motivated and too often do not improve security proportionate to the burden they create.'[87] Like FATF evaluation activities, IATA also conducts surveys of airport security when nominated by airlines to do so or at the request of national airport authorities. What sets IATA inspection activities apart from say the difficulties experienced by the ICAO in the past, is that the self-interested commercial motives of airlines to protect their passengers and crew at any airport in the world was understood, as Wallis suggests, as 'having no hidden political motivation'. IATA inspections have been touted by the Council of Europe as the 'only objective survey program available to the industry and governments'.[88] Where the ICAO had mooted similar programmes in the past, 'the political nature of the UN agency made implementation difficult to achieve ... [and] still have to contend with difficulties of national sovereignty'.[89] Not only does IATA set global standards, IATA's Partnership for Safety (PfS) programme is a capacity-building initiative. It helps airlines especially in developing countries prepare for an IATA Operational Safety Audit (IOSA) through seminars on industry best practices and gap analysis. Also, its Security Management System (SEMS) pro-gramme is designed to 'help air carriers achieve "best practice" standards which would be in compliance with requirements of all States where the air carrier operates'. SEMS can also 'help air carriers meet IOSA Security Standards and Recommended Practices'.[90] The US too has recognised a need to build capacities of other actors who might pose vulnerabilities in the interlinked global air trans-port system. It 'will continue to work closely with other governments and interna-tional and regional organizations to enhance the aviation security capabilities of other key nations by offering aviation and airport security assistance, training, and consultation'.[91]

'Risk-cosmopolitanism': global standard-setting and capacity-building

We now turn to discuss in more detail the standard-setting aspects of the global aviation security regime and how the impact of 9/11 might help to generate a new risk-cosmopolitanism centred on a consensus over the need collectively to manage shared aviation security risks. However, a major problem is that 'the airlines and other private sector firms have not been interested, historically, in investing in security measures' for fear of raising costs and driving passen-gers away.[92] The logic of 'collective action' is also at play: 'no single airline had an incentive to enhance its security by making costly investments because effective security requires an integrated approach and the lower standards of its competitors would continue to endanger it'.[93] Perhaps a new sense of 'risk-cosmopolitanism' might generate greater consensus and cooperation.

What is interesting, as Wessel and Wouters observe, is that civil aviation rules and regulations, amongst other issues, now originate also from multilevel international cooperation.[94] Indeed, one of the key aspects of reform in the aviation security sector has to create and disseminate international standards. At the nation state level, the White House has declared that global standards-setting is crucial because protecting global air travel is about 'collective security' and therefore all 'nations of the world have a shared interest in maintaining and strengthening global aviation security by adopting comprehensive and cohesive policies, programs, and procedures'.[95] To that end, in 2007, TSA created its Office of Global Strategies because:

> we are faced with the challenge of aviation security as a complex and global issue, where each State has its own laws, capabilities, technology, competing interests and threats. The goal of our Global Strategies Office is to develop and harmonize these diverse methods.[96]

As we have seen in previous chapters, standards-setting and best practices are key aspects of a 'risk-cosmopolitanism' bringing nations and actors together on a new framework to manage global risk, and this seems to be the suggestion by the White House as well. However some caveats have to be made in relation to the claim to 'global' relevance, as most of the standardised aspects of dataveillance adopted are focused in Western countries, although not entirely so. In relation to international standard-setting there are then two dynamics of relevance here, one is the establishment of international standards of security practices at airports and passenger/baggage/cargo screening; the other is the adoption of standard approaches to data acquisition, retention, profiling and sharing.

At the global level, 'formal' global aviation standards, as defined and adopted by ICAO members, are contained in Annex 17 to the Chicago convention. Indeed, much of the world's aviation security guidelines are based on this Annex. After 9/11, in January 2006, ICAO approved new global standards for the 100 per cent screening of hold luggage. Work on aviation security standards has continued in ICAO's Aviation Security Panel. These rules however have not been adopted by all governments. The problem with ICAO is that it is a 'political' and official UN agency. Thus 'ICAO rules – the standards – are always the minimum acceptable.'[97] Oftentimes, smaller member states might not have the money or technical capacity to implement these standards to begin with. Most damning of all for the notion of 'risk-cosmopolitanism', 'in most instances, they do not perceive a threat to their national carriers. Because of this, they often block recommendations seen as important to the developed world.'[98] Wallis suggests that recognising the inability of ICAO to ensure global implementation of its supposedly global benchmark SARPs, the private sector in the form of the airlines most affected then developed their own response. This was far from an altruistic desire, but rather recognition that global coordination was the best way to manage their collective risks in aviation security.

The global industry group IATA thus seeks to set global standards in the aviation industry, albeit from a sectoral rather than a governmental perspective. Director General and CEO Giovanni Bisignani stresses that 'IATA is not a government.'[99] At the same time, there is a working relationship between 'national' governmental agencies such as the American TSA, which has its Office of Global Strategies working closely with IATA. The IATA Security Group is composed of ten IATA Member Airline Heads of Security, meeting twice a year to address aviation security issues and propose solutions. IATA's main objective is to ensure that international security requirements are mutually accepted between states: 'global harmonisation' is one of the key security issues being addressed. The CEO of IATA argues that 'the world's economy depends on efficient international transportation made possible by global standards – largely coordinated by IATA. Poorly coordinated security procedures put the system at risk.'[100] After 9/11, IATA proposed a globally coordinated list of prohibited items for use throughout the world by air carriers. Member airlines were receiving customer complaints about items confiscated at screening checkpoints at stopovers that had been permitted on the originating leg of their flight. A recent controversy over security issues further illustrates the need for global standards. As Georgina Graham, Director of Security and Facilitation at IATA, explains, harmonisation

> is about making the journey from check in to boarding the same wherever you travel, allowing airlines and governments to focus on reducing the risk by adopting a proactive, systems approach ... if we take the example of liquids and gels in hand luggage, at the moment it is very difficult for passengers to know what they are allowed, as there are different rules in different countries. You could leave one country and be complying with that country's requirement and land in another and be breaking their rules.[101]

The situation eventually become more uniform and as the CEO of IATA put it:

> global standards are critical for security. The common approach to liquids and gels is a step in the right direction towards harmonization. The next step is for governments to harmonize a risk-based approach to security.... We need a constant level of vigilance that is constantly adjusted to deal with specific threats or events. To achieve this, we must develop a common risk-assessment methodology.[102]

Indeed, IATA has consistently promoted 'a risk-based approach to security among governments, developing a common risk-assessment methodology'.[103] Its CEO claims that one of three core challenges for industry and governments is 'to harmonise risk-based security measures globally'.[104] Here the global trade body is in other words, endorsing the use of risk as a possible global platform to bring all actors together to negotiate on and manage shared aviation security risks. Risk-based security means a channelling of resources towards identifying and managing the high risks, not the low ones. It is simply about risk management, not universal security protection.

As such the IATA's attempt to harmonise global security standards is an important example of private activity in the global governance of aviation security risk. Under IATA agreements each airline is expected to have a SEMS in place that meets industry standards and best practices as set out by the Association and is subject to audit under the IOSA since March 2007.[105] Highlighting again the overlapping multilevel global nature of aviation security standard-setting, SEMS is based on ICAO Annex 17 security standards and the IOSA Security Standards. As a result, the difficulties ICAO faced with implementing its own Annex 17 standards due to its 'political nature', have been somewhat circumvented, as private global trade associations like the IATA now incorporate those very same standards into its own global benchmark practices for its members. As part of SEMS, each airline is expected to include 'risk and threat assessment' as part of 'security operations'. An efficient SEMS must include general procedures and methods for 'risk management' and 'threat assessment', as well as more particular 'passenger risk assessment'.[106] This is where the dataveillance techniques and governance by risk that we discussed earlier also come into play.

To build global 'cosmopolitan' consensus on security issues further, IATA is part of the Global Aviation Security Action Group (GASAG) composed of worldwide aviation industry organisations, including Airbus and the Association of Asia Pacific Airlines, working together to 'coordinate the aviation industry's inputs to achieve an effective worldwide security system'.[107] The GASAG lists three of its guiding principles as the following, all of which are highly pertinent to our present discussion:

1　concept of layered security
2　risk management
3　harmonisation of security measures.

For instance, GASAG supports the development of ground security measures 'to be applied using a globally agreed Risk Management Matrix', and that 'carefully defined individual passenger assessments, based on internationally accepted standards as an element of risk analysis' should define individual passenger risk assessments.[108]

Beck might applaud the 'risk-cosmopolitanism' underpinning attempts at establishing global risk-based standards to bring together various actors worldwide. From within the private aviation sector, the IATA and GASAG have become effectively responsible for a section of global risk governance. Indeed, it recommends that the IATA 'SEMS template should serve as a guide of what should be achieved after full implementation of SEMS'.[109] IATA is now promoting its template as a baseline for global standards-setting: 'adoption of "best practice" standards must be the goal'.[110] That the private sector, albeit with some prodding from governments, is engaged in this kind of standard-setting operation is indicative of the global nature of the aviation security risk and the 'risk-cosmopolitan' nature, at least in part, of the response. The combination of the multilevel overlapping global governance attempts of the ECAC, ICAO and IATA, go some way in closing off the potential weaknesses in a global aviation security regime by setting best practice standards and engaging in the cooperative adoption of these standards by both governments and the private sector.

Standards-setting can also have impact on the local individual level as well in terms of daily routine activities. As with the FATF and PSI, there are 'everyday' dimensions of aviation security as well. Salter writes, 'the public imaginary has become fixated on the inconveniences of travel and not the increased securitization of everyday life'.[111] Training staff in order better to implement internationally agreed specifications is 'a truly vital part of air transportation's fight against terrorism, yet too many governments, air administrators and airline managements fail to ensure their staff are adequately prepared for the role'.[112] As such, an 'effective national aviation security strategy must be supported by a private sector that internalizes a strong security culture, embedding best practices and government requirements into day-to-day operations'.[113] Indeed, the global industry association IATA realises this important point, 'security awareness training sessions should be attended by all employees, periodically, in order to promote a security culture' and to 'manage security as an integral part of its overall business, making security one of the company's core values by developing a security culture'.[114] However, as Wallis points out, the danger of having such routinised security provisions is 'boredom' as 'acts of unlawful interference are not everyday occurrences' and the 'likelihood that a screener will actually be in a position to prevent a tragedy is extremely remote'.[115]

Evaluating aviation security and global risk management

As in the previous chapter serious questions need to be addressed as to the precise nature of risk and global governance being engaged by the emergent multilevel global aviation security architecture. Two aspects need to be assessed here. On the one hand we need to evaluate how the risk-based approach is being implemented in the aviation security sector. We also need to address the criticisms of the new aviation security regime as a reflection of a biased, politicised and even racialised view of riskiness. As with the FATF and PSI the question needs to be addressed as to how risks are constructed. In this case the question is, what does the construction of risky individuals tell us about the nature of power relations lying behind the present aviation security regime? Are we dealing with a version of Beck's 'risk-cosmopolitanism' or simply impositions of what is portrayed as the appropriate global solution by powerful developed states? For instance, the 'Europeans found that a tiered structure of baggage screening provided maximum security against the baggage bomb ... but this is not possible in many parts of the developing world'.[116]

As mentioned previously, a risk management approach seeks to mitigate risks in three ways: reshape the environment where the risk exists by adding layers of difficulty and altering terrorist intentions. The overall aim is to reduce the likelihood of the risk being realised. The events of 9/11 indeed sharpened the awareness of cross-boundary aviation security risks as well as a need to generate a new 'cosmopolitan' consensus on how to manage that risk through what Beck might term new forms of 'institutionalised cosmopolitanism'. Subsequently, the aviation security regime in both the US and Europe and those touted by global bodies like ICAO and IATA have transformed along the lines of a risk-based governance approach as a global basis for regulation. In the US, as outlined above, responsibility for security has been placed in the form of the TSA, which actively promotes a risk-based analysis to identify the greatest level of risk and works with partners overseas to implement risk-based standards. In the EU there has been a focus on capacity-building, standard-setting and 'cosmopolitan' out-reach attempts at the EU level and beyond via the ECAC and the various MoUs with other regional aviation organisations. The IATA also recommends that gov-ernments should harmonise their risk-based approaches to security, and has been involved in the standardisation of many procedures adopted by airports and air-lines. The net effect of this is where once there was a patchy and inconsistent set of security standards globally, the post-9/11 reforms based around a concern with risk, have in some ways shifted that environment through attempts at stand-ardising the approach both of states and private actors. What is more, this has been achieved while allowing passenger numbers to recover to pre-9/11 levels.[117] Whether these reforms are actually *effective* in terms of reducing the risk of attack is something we'll return to below, but certainly that the environment in which an attack might take place has been reshaped is relatively uncontentious. However much more does need to be done in terms of greater global coopera-tion and implementation of uniform risk-based standards. As the IATA's CEO put it bluntly, 'security is an uncoordinated mess. Governments are not cooperat-ing; and nobody is taking leadership. They must focus on risk management, har-monise global standards, use technology and intelligence effectively and take responsibility for the bill'.[118] Signor Bisignani further argued that after 9/11, 'governments strengthened security but missed the boat on harmonisation'.[119]

Moving on to the addition of layers of difficulty to inhibit risk emerging. As we have already seen, risk management entails identifying vulnerabilities and reducing them. One way of doing so is to employ 'scalable, layered secu-rity to minimize single points of vulnerability'.[120] Adding layers of difficulty and security is a crucial component of aviation security governance. Particularly interesting are ideas about injecting 'randomness' and 'uncertainty' and 'unpre-dictability' to airport security where the goal is to 'increase complexity for terrorists ... unpredictable change can effectively disrupt those [terrorist] efforts and provide an additional layer of security'.[121] This might mean changing inspec-tion routines daily or hourly and interrupting terrorist attempts at exploiting vulnerabilities. As a means of risk management, this also alters the calculations and intentions of would-be terrorists or the capabilities they intended to deploy. Through multilevel cooperation with partners in private industry to governments and global trade bodies like IATA, layered security can include security meas-ures at all levels starting from when a flight booking is made in the first place anywhere in the world, to watch lists and PNR international agreements, to screening of passengers and restrictions on their luggage before they board the plane as well as when they are in the airport lounges. Even when they have boarded, there are still measures being adopted such as reinforced cockpit doors. TSA estimates suggest up to 20 layers of security subject a passenger to checks before they board aircraft. A layered approach is often seen as the best way to raise the hurdles for terrorists to succeed. As TSA boss Kip Hawley notes, 'We've added layers ... additional layers that have been added since 2005'.[122] Aviation security observers see the 'evolution of a layered security system'.[123] The layered system recognises that no single security measure is impenetrable. Instead, the goal is simply to generate a greater number of opportunities to foil and confound would-be terrorists and hence reduce their chances of success. If one layer was breached, others would remain as back up to create more hurdles to cross. In a globalised world, these layers should extend globally as well.

The main changes here focused on the control both of 'risky' people and objects that had access to aircraft and areas of the airport complexes. In the US, improvements in baggage screening was tackled in two ways: federalising the screeners, moving those responsible from undertrained understaffed menial jobs to better paid public jobs[124] and, second, improving the standard of screening technology including the new explosive detecting equipment.[125] Further restrictions were placed on risky items that could be taken on board, for example between February 2002 and March 2003:

> federal screeners have intercepted more than 4.8 million dangerous items, including 1101 firearms, nearly 1.4 million knives, 39,842 box cutters, 125,273 incendiary or flammable objects, and 15,566 clubs. This is an impressive figure, but it has to be kept in mind that most of these items were by and large permissible prior to September 11.[126]

On both sides of the Atlantic though, further restrictions were introduced on an ad hoc basis. For example, when Richard Reid attempted to bring down American Airlines Flight 63 with a bomb concealed in his shoe in December 2001,[127] new risk-based measures were introduced requiring the removal of shoes at airports in the EU and US. Likewise, and one of the more far reaching changes, after UK authorities foiled a plot to blow up ten American bound flights using liquid explosives smuggled on board in separate components, reminiscent of a similar plan known as Bojinka to blow up 12 American jets in the Pacific, liquids, gels and pastes were restricted to not more than 100 ml. Some exceptions were made for baby food and verifiable medical needs.[128] Similar restrictions were placed on the amount of hand luggage allowed although these restrictions have varied more widely. The restrictions on liquids have been questioned though, both in terms of their effectiveness and relevance. In September the European Parliament voted strongly in favour of scrapping the restrictions unless evidence of its effectiveness could be provided.[129] Serious questions have been raised about the likelihood of a successful liquid explosive attack, with some suggesting that the restrictions were a 'placebo' for a nervous public rather than an effective security measure.[130] In Europe, these restrictions were driven at the EU level; however they are best perceived as reactions to exogenous shocks rather than concerted governance efforts. Even so, the constant ongoing redefinition and construction of who or what poses aviation risks does implicate a familiar nexus of private and public actors.

This nexus of private and public actors is also evident in the new global governance measures introduced to restrict access to certain high-risk individuals to the aviation system. One of the problems that needed to be addressed was how to identify potentially threatening individuals. At a House subcommittee meeting in February 2002, a group of private sector experts were called in to advise on how to restrict the activities of terrorists through the application of risk profiling techniques. The experts argued that 'our enemies are hiding in open and available information'[131] and that technologies used in the private sector should be applied to border and visa regimes in order to reduce the risks of terrorists gaining access to either the United States or the aviation system itself. There is clearly a private side to the global governance dimension as Amoore puts it:

> Accenture's [the private consultancy that heads up the *Smart Border Alliance* responsible for developing the US-Visit programme] self-styled 'virtual border', the promise 'is designed to operate far beyond US boundaries', enabling the DHS [Department of Homeland Security] to 'assess the security risks of all US-bound travellers and prevent potential threats from reaching US borders'.[132]

Thus a further significant layer of difficulty has been added to terrorists hopeful of launching attacks against US aviation targets. Arguably though this approach only shifts the risk of attacks to other targets, rather than reducing the likelihood of the risk occurring. Furthermore, there is clear recognition that the fluid nature of aviation security risks is constantly in flux:

> Our fundamental challenge is to protect passengers, freight, and our transportation network in a constantly changing, unpredictable threat environment. We know that terrorists will seek to exploit weaknesses in our transportation system and its security measures. We also know that terrorists will adapt to the security measures we put into place.[133]

This is a reason why organisations like the IATA and ICAO work with industry and airline partners to keep up to date with evolving challenges. The question here is really, 'if we keep putting up barriers and they go around them, how do we get ahead of them?'[134] Whether such layered systems really do alter intentions is open to question. Indeed, Hoffman argues that to overcome the setback of losing their territorial base in Afghanistan, Al Qaeda chose to demonstrate its resolve by continuing to target Western targets such as in the plan to bomb simultaneously ten transatlantic aircraft:

Just as disturbing is the fact that these attacks were not directed against the softer, more accessible targets like subway and commuter trains, hotels and tourist destinations that the conventional wisdom held a de-graded al Qaeda only capable of: but against arguably the most internationally-hardened target set since 9/11 – commercial aviation. This alarming development calls into question some of our most fundamental assumptions about al Qaeda's capabilities and intentions, given that the movement seems undeterred from the same grand homicidal ambitions it demonstrated on 9/11.[135]

It seems that Al Qaeda's intentions had not been altered by the new layers of security introduced to manage the risk.

The differential effects of the initiatives outlined above suggest that any assessment of the effectiveness of current aviation security risk management in terms of the reduction of the likelihood of the risk occurring is going to be difficult. There have been public and notable successes such as the disruption of the plot to blow up transatlantic airliners using liquid explosives. However, sceptics such as security consultant Bruce Schneir derided such measures as 'security theater' because they are 'designed to make us feel safer but not actually safer'.[136] There have also been a number of smaller-scale incidents such as the attempted attack at Glasgow airport in 2007 and most recently when two men of Somali origin were arrested on a flight about to take off from Cologne-Bonn airport. The men were alleged to have been planning some form of attack and had left suicide notes in their apartments.[137] Although in those cases it is less clear whether domestic law enforcement or aspects of the new aviation regime or even chance and good old-fashioned intelligence were more important in preventing the risk of attack being realised. However, the current aviation security regime is relatively more robust and coherent than the one that pertained prior to 9/11: that there have been no major terrorist incidents on Western airlines since 9/11 suggests that these changes might have been at least somewhat effective if not sufficient to reduce risks.

However the focus and implementation of dataveillance techniques as a tool of governance by risk does raise some significant questions about the constructed nature of the aviation security risk and the differentiated implications of applying particular measures of riskiness in sorting airline passengers by biographical and behavioural indices. Indeed, O'Malley argues that there are significant legal and ethical implications of this 'shift from a bureaucratic rule-based system of airport security to one based on risk'.[138] Anecdotally, there has been evidence of racial profiling and concerns for domestic civil liberties in relation to passenger profiling and the risk-based approaches to aviation security. For example, the American Civil Liberties Union (ACLU) is pursuing a civil rights lawsuit on behalf of Raed Jarrar who was refused permission to board his flight ostensibly because he was wearing a t-shirt with text in both Arabic and English stating 'We will not be silent'. Ultimately a compromise was reached to allow Mr Jarrar to board the flight if he wore another t-shirt. The ACLU claimed the case is indicative of a pattern in the application of security standards in US airports and that Mr Jarrar was targeted because of his ethnicity, rather than any security risk real or perceived. The ACLU claims to have received similar complaints in relation to discrimination by the TSA or airline carriers against individuals of Arab descent every month.[139] Another high-profile incident involved the well-known musician Cat Stevens, who had converted to Islam and changed his name to Yusuf Islam. He was allowed on board a flight from London to Washington but the flight was diverted to Maine where Mr Islam was questioned and ultimately deported on 'national security' grounds. Apparently concerns over his contributions to Islamic charities viewed as fronts for terrorist financing were the main reason.[140] The two examples above raise questions as to the effectiveness of the security net created by passenger risk profiling. There is little evidence to support the idea that either of the two cases mentioned contributed to reducing the risk of terrorist attacks, if anything high-profile missteps such as the above are counter-productive. One of the strongest claims of the 'war on terror' was that it was not targeted against Muslims in general but specific wrongdoers. The perception that aviation security is racially partial can only serve to undermine its potential to become a 'cosmopolitan' regime premised on managing shared global risks.

A second concern in relation to the dataveillance regime is the source of the data. Law enforcement and other intelligence databases provide terror-watch lists against which passenger manifests are checked. The problem being that these lists can suffer from being out of date or based on incomplete or inaccurate information. In one case a family was unable to get boarding passes because as it turned out their son, James Robinson, then aged five was on the terror watch list.[141] Nobel laureate, Nelson Mandela, was only removed from the list in July of this year.[142] The above examples do demonstrate serious flaws in the aviation security system but are also ones that are rectifiable. A more fundamental challenge to the 'cosmopolitan' nature of the regime is the sources from which information is taken to populate these watch lists. As Reveron has noted:

> assimilating all of these nations into the coalition against terrorism is not without challenges. Some relationships do not measure up to American moral standards, and U.S. intelligence agencies risk becoming associated with the misdeeds of foreign intelligence services and alienating America's allies.[143]

Reveron is referring to the use of intelligence from agencies in Saudi Arabia, Pakistan and elsewhere, but from a more global perspective concerns can similarly be raised about the US' own intelligence-gathering practices in Guantanamo and elsewhere. The challenge of creating acceptable standards in intelligence gathering and judgements is yet to be addressed fully by the world's intelligence communities. There is however some evidence of an opening up of the system in intelligence practice marked by increased cooperation, standardisation and the growth of private intelligence companies using 'open source intelligence' (Osint) to provide analysis to state and non-state actors alike.[144] However, whether the involvement of a broader range of actors in intelligence analysis will construct a more 'cosmopolitan' set of risks to be managed remains to be seen.

A further aspect of the differential and exclusionary nature of the risk-based dataveillance approach to aviation security is the impact it has on immigration policy and by extension on different national, ethnic and particularly socio-economic groups. When Roger Clarke coined the term one of his key concerns was the issue of implications of the use of computer technology for privacy and how to balance legitimate policy concerns against state abuse of private information.[145] However, there is some evidence of concern that the use of passenger data is being expanded beyond security issues to broader issues of migration and border control. This apparatus of exclusion has broader social implications. As Louise Amoore notes: 'The war on terror not only separates "our war" from "their terror", but also "our globalization" of legitimate and civilised business and leisure travel from "their globalization" of trafficking and illegal migration.' As such the management of individuals through airports and other border crossings is an exclusionary practice that helps to reinscribe the distinctions between 'us' and 'them' at the heart of the violent world views driving the terrorism it is designed to combat. Therefore it is difficult to argue for the cosmopolitan nature of this approach at face value, as with the PSI and the FATF, we again find ourselves looking at the pursuit of specific and interested policy ends using risk-based analytical tools and methods that are far from 'cosmopolitan' in nature.

Subjective and greatly different risk perceptions about the utility of PNR agreements and Advanced Passenger Information System (APIS) passenger data are also creating problems for global standardisation. Designed to manage terrorism risk for the US, requiring passenger data has led the data to be used for other risks as well. China for instance wanted more detailed information such as seat allocation in order to keep tabs on passenger movement during the SARS crisis. In general then:

> a single global standard will be difficult to achieve as long as the perceived need for APIS is so varied: in the US and Europe it is viewed more as a crime and security tool, but in the southern hemisphere it is generally perceived as a facilitation tool, helping to streamline the passenger travel experience.[146]

Conclusion

As with the previous two cases then, we find ourselves confronted with a global terrorist risk to aviation security that demands a global response in order to manage it effectively. As we have argued above, certain elements of the reform of the multilevel aviation security regime after 9/11 do reflect the potential for a 'institutionalised cosmopolitan' response to this challenge. While pre-existing UN agencies like the ICAO have had difficulty responding flexibly, others such as the EU and especially private trade bodies like the IATA found themselves in a position to do so. This was mainly due to the perception that ICAO was 'political' and limited by 'national sovereignty', while IATA was private, and 'commercial' with fewer political agendas to grind in promoting particular programmes. Like the cases before then, the response has taken the form of global standards-setting and capacity-building. New forums and norms are being developed to manage new risks that at the same time are attempting a 'cosmopolitan' opening up of global governance in the field of aviation security to include more non-state actors. Although the new risk-based dataveillance initiatives mentioned and the harmonisation of airport security within the EU and creation of the TSA in the US are state based and typical of the formal institutions to which the FATF and PSI differ so much, a number of elements of aviation security governance merit further attention. The involvement of private actors in the form of the IATA, GASAG, private intelligence analysts and indeed the role of the private sector in not just designing technologies but shaping the response to aviation security reform as in the case of Accenture. The cooperative efforts of the ECAC and other regional bodies, and the attempt to implement evidence-based risk models as tools of counter-terrorism, all point towards a coordinated response to the risk of aviation terrorism. Whether it is the TSA, ICAO or the IATA, it appears that the benefits of a risk-based approach to aviation security are being proposed as a way to generate global consensus on the appropriate ways to manage the shared risks involved. Beck's understanding of 'risk-cosmopolitanism' does seem to explain at least some of the rationale behind this enforced integration of people and actors around the world. However, these security standards are not being uniformly implemented in the developing world due either to lack of will or capability. Again, this highlights the disparities in wealth and power between those who set the standards and others who have to implement them. Hence there is a real need for more capacity-building programmes to help airports and airlines in the developing world to fulfil their international standards.

As with the FATF and PSI, we have again had to highlight caveats about the subjective constructed nature of the risk in question and the differential manner in which both the risk itself and the response to it were to a large degree shaped by power considerations. Developing countries especially did not think their national aviation systems were at the same level of risk as those from Western states. On the other hand, perceptions of the risk and creating a need for global action were mostly being driven by politicians and private actors mainly in the West who had the most at stake. After all their aviation systems were the most globalised and integrated, and paradoxically also the most at risk. Nor did developing countries feel aviation security risks trumped their other more pressing issues such as economic growth and climate challenges. Furthermore, the dataveillance approach to identifying risky individuals raises serious questions in relation to civil liberties and indeed the 'politicised' nature of the construction of terrorist risk. The intersection between migration management and aviation security cannot but help suggest that the current attempt to manage population flows goes beyond immediate aviation security concerns. In one sense it can be seen almost as the opposite of a truly 'inclusive' cosmopolitan approach to global risk, and instead as an attempt to insulate and exclude one section of the globe from the anger, resentment and discontent of the remaining segments. Rather than reducing the risk of terrorism such an approach is likely to stoke the resentments that fuelled anti-Western terrorism to begin with. This is not to say that the current risk-based security regime is either unnecessary or even nefarious, but rather that it needs to be carefully calibrated to ensure that in attempting to provide safe transportation systems for the West it does so in a manner that doesn't appear racist, discriminatory or unfair. As President Bush reminded citizens in his address to the nation in 2001:

> I also want to speak tonight directly to Muslims throughout the world. We respect your faith. It's practiced freely by many millions of Americans, and by millions more in countries that America counts as friends. Its teachings are good and peaceful, and those who commit evil in the name of Allah blaspheme the name of Allah. The terrorists are traitors to their own faith, trying, in effect, to hijack Islam itself. The enemy of America is not our many Muslim friends; it is not our many Arab friends. Our enemy is a radical network of terrorists, and every government that supports them.[147]

6 Whither the other war on terror?

If we're an arrogant nation, they'll resent us. If we're a humble nation, but strong, they'll welcome us.

One way for us to end up being viewed as the Ugly American is for us to go around the world saying, 'We do it this way, so should you.'

George W. Bush, 2000[1]

Introduction

We began writing and researching this book, perturbed by the widespread critiques of the unilateral militarist manner in which the Bush administration has waged its war on terror since 9/11. Perhaps, another side to the story needs to be told. Indeed, somewhat ironically, when he was first running for the presidency of the United States in 2000, George W. Bush initially raised a glimmer of hope for a multilateral approach, talking of humility and being humble to win the respect of others. After all, he did seem to have a real grasp and self-conscious desire to avoid the 'Ugly American' syndrome. How completely contrary things have turned out, and of course this abiding perception of American unilateralism did not begin with the 9/11 attacks. Early in the Bush administration, the Kyoto Protocol on global warming was rejected, to howls of dismay and criticism from Europe particularly from then French Foreign Minister Lionel Jospin who suggested, 'this is not an isolationist administration.... This is more like a unilateralist administration.'[2]

After a brief honeymoon period immediately after 9/11 where *Le Monde* could declare 'we are all Americans now', America's standing in the world slid quickly downhill. As the US-led war on terror progressed, the excesses associated with the Bush White House were widely panned. Topping the list was the hubris, militarism and unilateralism visibly manifested in the naked display of brute military power in the 'Shock and Awe' campaigns against Iraq.[3] The prevalent image had become one of an adversarial, confrontational Ugly American with a swagger in its walk that prefers either to go its own way or the highway: the very caricature that candidate Bush sought to avoid in 2000. For the disregard of both constitutional and international law in its counter-terror policies from torture to Iraq, Bush's America has been labelled a 'Cowboy Republic'.[4]

Former vice-president turned Nobel Laureate Al Gore too criticised Bush for a 'do-it-alone, cowboy-type reaction to foreign affairs'.[5] The president's own gun-slinging rhetoric, and Wild West catchphrases like 'bring it on' and 'dead or alive' did not help.

With the benefit of hindsight, in the twilight of his presidency and concerned about historical legacies, President Bush admitted in a June 2008 interview with *The Times* that he was 'troubled about how his country had been misunderstood' as a result of his rhetoric, and that he 'in retrospect, could have used a different tone'.[6] Like the president, we were similarly perplexed and wondered if American actions in the war on terror were indeed being misconstrued, and whether we might be missing some pieces of the bigger picture. That is to say, the headline-grabbing violent outrages in the war on terror might have had rather more mundane, behind-the-scenes, 'everyday' and less-visible counterparts that were being overlooked. Was the Bush administration then, in the president's own words, misinterpreted as 'really anxious for war'?[7] Was there more to it than meets the eye? With this in mind, we set out to uncover patterns in the war on terror that might have helped to dispel this militaristic 'cowboy' image of unilateralism, dominance and undisguised power. Indeed, we were in the good company of figures like Daniel Dreudner in thinking there might be more going on in the broader scheme of US grand strategy than the highly visible unilateralism displayed so far. After all, complicated global discussions and slow-moving negotiations can hardly jostle with footage of air strikes on TV screens. This led us to consider the flip side of the coin, multilateralism and cooperation.

Of course the Bush administration has been notorious for thumbing its nose at formalised and institutionalised global governance on a grandiose scale such as the Kyoto Protocol, but we argue that a seldom-noticed aspect is its use of more informal and flexible forms of global cooperation. If terrorism today is intrinsically linked to interdependence, as we are often told, then the notion of global governance should come into play, besides military force alone. As Javier Solana observed:

> global governance is an awful term but a vital concept. We need it because of a simple reality: interdependence.... You know the list; terrorism, non-proliferation, climate change, pandemics, failing states, none can be solved by a single a government acting alone.... So the question is, how do we organize this globalized world and especially how do we tackle the dark sides of globalization.[8]

Posed in this way then, the key issue that confronted us was how less-noticed global governance arrangements might have been enacted, so as to curb more effectively global systemic risks from terrorism.

But the equation is not complete without making the link to risk and security: that other key part of the title of this book. At the same time that the Bush administration was being accused of hubristic unilateralism and war-mongering, it also appeared paradoxically to be fearful, ill at ease and insecure. Senior figures like

Donald Rumsfeld talked of 'unknown unknowns' and 'anticipatory defense'. Condoleezza Rice warned of 'mushroom clouds'. As officials talked the language of risk, academics too inevitably zeroed in on this pervasive obsession with averting risks of all sorts, mostly in a critical fashion. Officials and bureaucrats and the media, in speculating about how to cope with uncertainty after 9/11, had become what Didier Bigo called the 'managers of unease'.[9] The narrative of fear that drove official reactions to terrorism, as Frank Furedi suggests, created a sense of apprehension that both precedes and extends beyond acts of terror.[10]

In such a climate of fear and uncertainty, the negative implications of this politics of risk have most commonly been criticised. For instance a self-conscious deployment of imagination in the media and visual industries to anticipate a range of possible risk scenarios has been shown by de Goede to feed economies of both anxiety and desire.[11] Of course scholars like de Goede and Bigo are entirely justified in adopting their own peculiar understandings and interpretations of risk's significance after 9/11. That after all is the nature of the beast that is risk studies. What we are more concerned with is how a socio-political understanding of risk might help in bringing different actors together for a common risk management purpose. This aspect has been glossed over in academic commentaries. In other words, how might a new self-awareness of risk help to bring about new global governance arrangements to manage global security? Indeed, following in the footsteps of sociologist Ulrich Beck in his various analyses of the *World Risk Society* and *Cosmopolitan Vision*, we suggest that what Beck termed the positive 'integrative' aspect of global risk at least deserves more critical academic attention, particularly its relationship to global governance in the war on terror. Indeed, authors such as Aradau and Munster have examined what it meant to 'govern through risk',[12] while Renn and Walker have mooted the notion of 'global risk governance'.[13] Hence, understanding and unearthing the theoretical convergence between risk, global governance and security has been our guiding principle throughout this book. We had hoped that in the process of researching and writing, this 'other' war on terror might reveal some hitherto less-visible aspects to serve as a much-needed corrective and counter-balance to the explicit displays of undisguised power, controversy, dissension and disregard for legality that have so often plagued the war on terror. Our conclusions are however mixed and to some degree even worryingly mirrors the type of problems already encountered in the war on terror in the first place. The alternatives we have examined in the 'other' war on terror might not necessarily turn out to be more palatable. In the following, drawing on the case studies we have presented so far, we will attempt to sum up and consider the issues and problems that a theoretical perspective built on risk, global governance and security has helped us to illuminate in the 'other' war on terror.

Risk and the 'other' war on terror

In adopting a sociological interpretation of risk as understood by Ulrich Beck, we set out to examine the role that risk has played in the 'other' war on terror. In particular we disentangled Beck's 'cosmopolitan vision' for the *World Risk*

Society in which he lays out various features such as 'cosmopolitan outlook', 'risk-cosmopolitanism', 'cosmopolitan realism', 'institutionalised cosmopolitanism'. One claim is that a 'reflexive' self-awareness of shared global risk can build new bridges, bring about enforced integration and new global frameworks to negotiate and manage risk, leading to a political reconfiguration of the global system. While Beck is clearly cognisant of the very 'political' nature and vast potential for disagreement and debate on how best to manage global risks, he is at the same time hopeful that a 'global cosmopolis' would eventually emerge that is open and inclusive of all actors working together on a principle of equality, not hierarchy. Our findings suggest that several key shortcomings continue to dog this hope, and these are laid out below.

Subjective perceptions of risk differ

It is striking how many of the problems related to the issue of risk that have plagued the war on terror find many parallels in the 'other' war on terror as well. For instance, differences in risk perception creating divisions even among erstwhile NATO allies, the fundamentally subjective and socially constructive nature of risk, the negative implications for democratic accountability, civil liberties and human rights: these are all problems that we have encountered both in unilateral military campaigns *and* non-military multilateral cooperative efforts to combat terrorism. For EU foreign policy chief, Javier Solana, 'Iraq was the toughest moment for me because it showed the limits of multilateralism.'[14] Solana observed that fundamentally 'there are different perceptions of risk on both sides', between America and 'old' Europe.[15] This in turn created massive problems for coordinated action on the risk that was acknowledged to exist but was perceived differently as to its severity, urgency and, most crucially, management options. Clearly, risk in the military war on terror was divisive and often such divisions on risk perception showed up very visibly, most notably in the case of Donald Rumsfeld's distinction between 'Old' and 'New' Europe.

These problems are by no means confined to the war on Iraq. Solana's frustrations with the limits of multilateralism continue to bubble over in more cooperative forms of non-military global governance. Rather than shared global risk serving as a 'cosmopolitan' tool of 'enforced integration' to smooth over differences in Beck's formulation, the socially and culturally constructed nature of risk does continue to shape differing perceptions to a large degree. It has created dissension and difference rather than a new 'cosmopolitan' consensus for global governance. Not only was this apparent in the case of Iraq, this can be seen in the less-visible issue of the global campaign against terrorist financing. Shared global risk in this case, exposure to terrorist financing in the global financial system, had to be socially constructed by interested states as a global governance problem in the first place. This was then perceived to pose different levels of risk to different countries, depending on whether they were in the developing or developed world. The Third World simply had different priorities, such as HIV/AIDs or development, rather than concerns over terrorist financing. Somalia's economy for example was brought to a standstill as a side effect of ATF efforts when a 'Hawala' system, al-Barakaat, was shut down. Somalia had no formal banking system to speak of and the closure of al-Barakaat cut off vital remittances from Somalis abroad, who were largely responsible for keeping the economy afloat.[16]

Similarly in the case of the PSI, the American assumption was that 'proliferation was a universal threat and proactive, collective action must be taken to ensure that deadly weapons do not fall into the possession of terrorists or rogue states'.[17] Here again, we have a shared global risk of proliferation that supposedly should generate collective responses to manage that risk. But at the same time, there is recognition that 'in fact, no two countries share identical risks from nuclear smuggling or nuclear terrorism ... risk assessments and our programs [must] account for country and region-specific factors'.[18] Risk can be shared but is not experienced or perceived uniformly. Beck of course does not deny that the 'national' or 'local' still remains and his understanding of 'cosmopolitan' is simply a world view or horizon beyond the nation state. But when it boils down to the detail of practical policy making on what are 'cosmopolitan' issues, 'national' considerations remain very much in contention perhaps to a greater degree than Beck might have considered desirable. As a result there is far from universal support for the PSI, particularly from key holdout countries like China, India and South Korea. It is also hard to assess the degree to which shared WMD proliferation risk has brought actors together in the PSI because the nature of 'membership' is downplayed in favour of 'activities', which can vary quite considerably among participants.

In the case of aviation security and restrictions on liquids in hand luggage, these were justified by the UK Department of Transport as 'we are also right to require these restrictions internationally as, potentially, we are all at risk'.[19] But there are different rules in place at different airports around the world, creating confusion. Hence we have the private sector global trade body IATA calling for harmonisation of risk-based standards. Bottles of 'saline solution' are allowed on board in the US, where you are allowed to travel with as much as you wish. But at a British airport, liquids in volumes greater than 100 ml are seized and disposed of. As a result of different perceptions of the threat, both sides of the Atlantic take divergent approaches. These different perceptions of the risk in turn influence different attitudes to aviation security in the UK, the EU and the US. Travellers in different parts of the world will experience different security standards as states assess the same risk differently depending on their previous historical or contextual experiences with terrorism or based on their political cultures. More broadly speaking, this has impeded global attempts to generate a new consensus on global aviation security standards at the ICAO. Differences in risk perceptions mean that developing states do not feel their national carriers face the same exposure to risk.

Privacy, human rights, exclusion and inclusion: risk and the degrading of democratic accountability

If the high-profile detention of terrorist suspects at Guantanamo Bay or Abu Ghraib, as Admiral Mike Mullen claims, was an attempt to mitigate global risks, but that generated a massive outcry over human rights concerns, and its lower-profile counterparts too were not immune from similar criticism. Practices such as profiling airline passenger data and scrutinising financial transactions too raised questions about civil liberties and privacy, although these are admittedly different types of human rights issues at stake. While most of the world rightly recoils at the brutal interrogation methods used in Gitmo, more subtle and less visible techniques employed in global risk governance too are cause for concern. Whether it is airline security or terrorist financing or WMD proliferation, risk-profiling techniques select suspicious or unusual patterns and often the effects strongly correlate with certain ethnic/religious backgrounds. As a result Muslims and migrant communities in particular face extra hurdles to their legitimate activities, raising the danger of excluding otherwise perfectly innocent minority communities.

Whether it is participation in the PSI, or in FATF standards and airline security screening, there are concerns about exclusion rather than 'cosmopolitan' inclusion. One particular downside of the FATF standards is that they tend to marginalise further those sectors of society that are already on the fringes through risk profiling. Developing countries have raised issues about the 'exclusive club' model in which FATF standards were formulated by wealthy developed states and which as a result might lack legitimacy. Uniform international standards too should not reflect a one-size-fits-all approach. India too has voiced concerns about the 'two-tiered structure' of the PSI that seems, in the Indian view, to differentiate between the core group and other members. In other words, it was concerned about the legitimacy of the exclusive 'club' model of rule making. In response, the US argued, 'the core group was never conceived as an exclusive club. Its objective was to lay out the basic terms of the initiative and open up the membership to others.'[20] Initially a group of core members helped establish the PSI and facilitate its expansion. But amid concerns over a lack of transparency, the core group disbanded and is now replaced by an Operational Experts Group.

As for aviation security, the American Civil Liberties Union has denounced the practising of 'identity-based security' and filed a class-action lawsuit against the Federal Government's 'no-fly' list arguing that many innocent passengers are unfairly excluded. The Automated Targeting System also assigns passengers that cross US borders with a risk assessment rating that infringes privacy. Indeed, O'Malley argues that there are significant legal and ethical implications of this 'shift from a bureaucratic rule-based system of airport security to one based on risk'.[21] Airline security systems premised on a risk-based approach will pick up abnormal patterns of behaviour that might not necessarily pose risks and exclude people based on a suspicion. US Airways for instance were accused of racial profiling for removing a group of Muslim imams who, their supporters maintain, were only guilty of 'flying while Muslim' and that 'there was some peculiar behaviour'.[22]

The increasing emphasis on governing by risk is raising eyebrows about democratic accountability as well as the delegation of responsibility to mid-ranking bureaucrats or airline and banking employees now tasked with taking decisions simply based on risk profiles: whether you board a plane or you are allowed to open a bank account or whether a particular cargo manifest is classified a WMD proliferation 'red flag'. 'The process through which FATF standards has been promulgated, applied and implemented raises issues of political legitimacy and accountability. After all, the standards are essentially determined by wealthy OECD countries.'[23]

Risk and the implications for legality

If the war on Iraq created a storm of protests over its illegal nature, similar questions are being asked of the PSI's legality in relation to whether it contravenes the United Nations Conference on the Law of the Sea. (UNCLOS) Problematically, 'currently international law does not explicitly permit the use of interdiction as a tool of counter-proliferation'.[24] Under UNCLOS, intercepts are legal by a coastal state in its territorial waters but not on the high seas (except in the case of slavery or pirate ships). Although the PSI's Statement of Principles is an attempt to establish international authority for multilateral cooperative intercepts, it is more focused on action. Yet PSI supporters see it as 'a first step in the implementation of United Nations Security Council Resolution 1540, the first ever resolution on non-proliferation issues, adopted on 28 April 2004'.[25] For new flexible initiatives like the PSI seeking to combat global proliferation risks, as Beck observes, a great deal more global negotiations do need to be conducted to clarify its emerging international legal position.

In terms of terrorist financing risks, financial data mining and spying on SWIFT transactions have also raised legal questions and conflicting legal jurdisdictions over the transnational nature of financial flows. The NCCT 'blacklisting' initiative too has no binding legal obligation or sanction under international law. With aviation security risk, legal controversies too have been thrown up with the EU–US Passenger Name Records (PNRs) agreement, initially rejected by the European Court of Justice as illegal because European data protection law prevents data being sent to another country (the US in this case) that doesn't have equivalent protections. PNRs contain personal data that might be sensitive such as medical conditions and religion. Here again, attempts to profile and manage risk have generated legal controversies, for legal systems have to be adapted to the new demands of managing global risk. Yet, the EU is no laggard in its surveillance activities, as de Goede has pointed out. It is planning its own PNR system for travellers entering Europe not just for counter-terrorism but for immigration and law enforcement as well.

Risk and global governance

Beyond the 'formal' attempts at institutional reform to tackle new global challenges, most notably the painfully long-running discussions on expanding the UN Security Council, or including ever more participants to the G8 Summits, our view of global governance encompasses a whole gamut of governance activities that are less formal and less institutionalised. That is where we suggest global governance is actively being reshaped by a new awareness of shared global risk. As Forman and Segaar rightly observe:

> while much has been made of an alleged 'crisis in multilateralism' in the wake of the Security Council's failure to mediate the 2003 Iraq crisis and the US withdrawal from and abrogation of a number of treaties ... collective action to address a range of global and transnational problems is in fact highly dynamic and adaptable.[26]

Risk-based approaches and harmonising of global standards

New forms of collective action, our case studies suggest, might be emerging in the form of harmonising global standards based on collective risk. If risk is a probabilistic scenario accompanied by a policy proposal to avert that scenario materialising, it follows that risk-based planning or risk-based approaches are now seen to form a new global basis to manage shared risks. Risk is defined as a function of threat, vulnerability and consequence. Risk-based approaches are thus designed to identify vulnerabilities and remedy them. This is why the US Transport Security Administration (TSA) employs a 'systematic and analytical risk management process, which is considered a best practice, to assess the threats and vulnerabilities of general aviation'.[27] For instance, risk-based computer-assisted prescreening of passengers is conducted before a boarding pass is issued. TSA 'continues to modify its checkpoint screening program based on a number of factors including passenger feedback, risk-based planning, and its own internal review and testing process'.[28] The US *National Strategy for Aviation Security* seeks to transplant this to the global level through what it calls a 'risk-based, cross-discipline, and global approach to aviation security'.[29] This:

> requires a common understanding of, and a coordinated effort for, action on a global scale, nations have a common interest to protect global air travel. Since all nations benefit from this collective security, the United States must encourage all nations to share the responsibility for maintaining aviation security by countering the threats in this domain.[30]

The International Civil Aviation Organisation also promotes the utility of a risk-based framework, 'it is now widely-recognized that the traditional reactive approach to improving safety is no longer appropriate nor sufficient and that there is a need to shift to a proactive and predictive, risk-based safety regime'.[31] The ICAO has its own list of Standards and Recommended Practices (SARPs) on security, much like the FATF Recommendations.[32] The private sector too is calling for similar moves in harmonisation of risk-based approaches. As the CEO of the International Air Transport Association (IATA) put it:

global standards are critical for security. The common approach to liquids and gels is a step in the right direction towards harmonization. The next step is for governments to harmonize a risk-based approach to security.... We need a constant level of vigilance that is constantly adjusted to deal with specific threats or events. To achieve this, we must develop a common risk-assessment methodology.[33]

Hence, the IATA recommends that the ICAO develop a crucially relevant global function in promoting a common risk-based approach to security among governments. Indeed, Washington seems ready to cooperate:

the United States Government will further cooperate with foreign partners to enhance and encourage adoption of international standards and best practices as well as to align regulation and enforcement measures. This will include initiatives pursued through international organizations, such as the International Civil Aviation Organization (ICAO), that include industry participation.[34]

With regards to WMD proliferation, through the PSI's engagement with private sector bodies, especially the transportation industry, the rationale is that 'they are now more likely to recognise "red flags" – for example, inadequate information about end-uses or unusually favourable payment terms – that may signal a proliferation ambition'.[35] The use of 'red flags' does seem to indicate an awareness of a risk-based approach although this is not explicitly enshrined in its Statement of Principles to the same degree as the FATF standards or IATA risk management processes for aviation security are. The PSI's 'Statement of Interdiction Principles' does however attempt at the very least to 'codify a set of internationally-agreed-upon standards for interdiction'.[36] The State Department describes it as a 'global initiative', that 'does not create formal "obligations" for participating states, but does represent a political commitment to establish "best practices" to stop proliferation-related shipments'.[37] More broadly speaking the PSI is one cog in a larger global wheel of activities designed to reduce vulnerabilities in the global transportation system. The Bush administration has recognised a need to ensure global consistency by harmonising global standards and recommended procedures with organisations such as the World Customs Organisation, the International Organisation for Standards and the International Maritime Organisation:

standards are the only meaningful way that the government will be able to ensure that a certain level of security across the supply chain can be expected and achieved. Accurate data, secure cargo, and secure transit goals are all areas where internationally accepted standards would substantially improve the system.[38]

One of its key goals is to arrive at a global 'standardized risk management approach' to securing cargo that uses information to stratify the cargo into levels of risk so that resources can be directed towards the high-risk cargo.[39]

Perhaps the best template for success in harmonisation of global risk-based standards should be the FATF's 40+9 Recommendations, which set the global 'gold standard' for counter-terrorist financing. 'The risk-based approach is either incorporated into the Recommendations in specific and limited ways, or it is inherently part of or linked to those Recommendations.'[40] As we have pointed out earlier, the FATF's mandate is dedicated to global standards-setting, of which the development and issuance of risk-based approach guidance notes in collaboration with various sectors is uppermost. The motivation behind such guidance was to facilitate the development of a common global understanding of the risk-based approach and its implementation.

Does power matter more than 'cosmopolitan' solidarity?

Previously we have observed that risk-based frameworks and best practices are being touted as a new global platform for bringing nations and actors together in standard-setting. However, in truth power continues to shape the process and implementation of standard-setting and they manifest in different forms. Brute military force might be the most obvious explicit form of coercion in the war on Iraq, but the 'other' war on terror has no lack of coercive mechanisms as well. It might be less explicit, becoming more subtle, discursively mediated and implicit, for instance in compelling developing countries to accept FATF risk-based standards. Nonetheless, it was a 'deliberate and calculated use of power by the FATF to impose policies that elicited instrumental compliance by states'.[41] Power differentials, coercion and narrow self-interests still remain a key factor in determining why some actors, particularly those in the developing world, comply with these standards, rather than any notion of 'cosmopolitan' solidarity.

Likewise, the PSI is still viewed with suspicion, particularly through the lens of power and concerns about US leadership. Although the White House claims the PSI Statement of Principles constitutes a broad political consensus against proliferation, China in particular has kept it at arms-length distance, concerned both about the legality and America's perceived hegemonic position in the PSI. Compared to the FATF's global success with explicit UN Security Council endorsement in the form of Resolution 1517, the PSI Principles have been 'supported' by 90 countries, publicly revealed according to the US State Department's count. It is noteworthy that many of these 'supporters' have not declared publicly their statement of support. It is unclear what 'support' for the PSI means and how robust it is.[42] This 'reluctance to publicly endorse the PSI principles in itself indicates less than stalwart support in general, let alone in time of specific need'.[43] In September 2004, the Malaysian Prime Minister, Abdullah Badawi, declared there was a need for multilateral negotiations for 'universal, comprehensive and non-discriminatory agreements and arrangements'.[44] Here further expansion of the PSI seems to be stymied by its perception as a disguised vehicle for American dominance that targeted only specific states such as North Korea, rather than striving for universal and uniform application of its norms.

With aviation security, the requirement for biometric fingerprinting in the attempt to classify and code risks in the general population is being seen in many quarters as intertwined with and constitutive of new manifestations of state power.[45] Rather than a statistically neutral approach, it is highly political. The invocation of the language of risk belies the underlying power relationships underpinning the emerging norms to manage aviation risk. Indeed, many of the new risk-based initiatives in global aviation security are driven by states in the developed world that have the capacity to implement new security measures. The developing world simply lacks the capacity or will to do so. It is striking that the rich developed countries of the EU and the US often develop new risk-based mechanisms such as expensive biometric passports that other countries in turn then have to subscribe to in order to gain access to their aviation infrastructure. Indeed, many of these initiatives seem designed to keep people out, rather than be inclusive in the 'cosmopolitan' sense of the word. New aviation security standards are also sometimes beyond the reach of less well-off countries. This in turn necessitates capacity-building efforts that, in a rather 'teaching' tone, often sound patronising.

Institutionalised cosmopolitanism

The need to reorient and reinvigorate global governance for tackling twenty-first century risks is summed up in the following passage:

> established intergovernmental organizations are challenged to meet new demands and requirements while accommodating new mandates and members as well as non-state actors with global reach. A proliferating and fluctuating set of intergovernmental and multi-stakeholder arrangements with more assertive and diverse actors best describes the international operating environment for collective decision-making and action across a range of global issues.[46]

The cases we have examined support the claim that a more inclusive form of global governance is emerging to tackle global risks, among which a public–private partnership seems foremost on the agenda. This appears to reaffirm the arguments put forth by Biersteker and Hall about the importance of private actors in global governance as a source of knowledge, expertise and capacity. While Methuen and Taylor have assessed the role of private security actors in Africa,[47] and indeed the upsurge in private military contractor armies in Iraq and Afghanistan have garnered most visible attention, we suggest that the private sector is involved in other global governance issues as well, particularly as international arrangements nowadays inevitably seek to have them on board. First off, the FATF was a pre-existing international arrangement that quickly became re-equipped for the war on terror. 'The FATF has become adaptive, facilitating trans-national effectiveness in the fight to counterterrorist financing and compliance through globally recognized standards, peer review evaluations, and sanctions.'[48] In the process, it actively sought collaboration on global standards-setting with relevant actors including global business consortiums in the form of the International Banking Federation. The events of 9/11 'highlighted existing and new elements of shared vulnerability; ways in which the state might seek more help from business to tackle threats; ways in which business might need more help from the state'.[49] The crisis served also to 'refocused attention much more specifically on the role of business as a partner for government. One of the first initiatives ... was to block private-sector financial transfers to known terrorists and to freeze their assets.'[50] Such approaches that opened up the system of global governance were mirrored elsewhere as well. As the White House observed, 'aviation security is best achieved by integrating public and private aviation security global activities into a coordinated effort to detect, deter, prevent, and defeat threats to the Air Domain, reduce vulnerabilities'.[51] It goes on to conclude that 'aviation security is best achieved by combining public and private aviation security activities on a global scale into a comprehensive and integrated effort that addresses all aviation threats'.[52] While the government provides guidance, enforces regulatory requirements and standards, the 'bulk of the responsibility for assessing and enhancing security falls on airport operators'.[53] After 9/11, like the FATF, organisations concerned with aviation security such as ICAO and IATA have evolved and taken on new tasks of auditing implementation of its international Standards and Recommended Practices (SARPs) in aviation security.

The PSI, even more so than the FATF, could be seen as a poster boy of 'institutionalised cosmopolitanism'. It was created by a 'cosmopolitan realist' state in America that realised that global cooperation was essential if the global risk of WMD proliferation to terrorists was to be curbed. Recognising that pre-existing multilateral approaches in the form of the Non-Proliferation Treaty were outmoded and international legal frameworks like UNCLOS were 'not fit for purpose', it developed a new more flexible international forum and mechanism to do so. Using the PSI as an example, US National Security Advisor Stephen Hadley argued that 'the President believes that new international partnerships and arrangements among willing nations offer the possibility of quick and measurable results'.[54] The PSI has been cultivating partnerships with relevant non-state actors, particularly the private sector. The reasoning behind what Beck might term this 'cosmopolitan' opening up is straightforward: 'the private sector – especially the carriers of cargo – know the supply chain ... [they can] play a role in how PSI interceptions are accomplished, whether that's an oceangoing maritime carrier, or an international air cargo or express carrier'.[55] Thus, 'the private sector has been engaged in the PSI through annual meetings on particular subjects on which industry representatives contribute knowledge and expertise on relevant technical issues related to interdiction'.[56]

Informal global governance

If institutionalised cosmopolitanism discussed above meant the embracing of new multilevel partnerships against global risks, one of the most intriguing outcomes is the relatively 'informal' nature of the PSI and FATF.[57] Instead of operating through formal treaty legislation or binding international law, they function according to 'Statements of Principles' or 'Standards and Recommendations'. Back in 1991, the Organisation for Economic Cooperation and Development recommended that FATF 'should remain as flexible and informal as it is now'.[58] The wisdom of that approach was seen after 9/11 as the FATF, nominally an ad hoc 'Task Force' and not a formal international institution, was re-adapted to the new challenges of counter-terrorist financing because it was seen to have a relatively informal flexible structure. The PSI too is a 'flexible, more dynamic, ad-hoc alliance ... intended to mitigate the threats that traditional non-proliferation policies have failed to adequately address'.[59] That the PSI is different from 'traditional' multilateral institutions is summed up by the *Wall Street Journal*, 'do not mistake PSI for a multilateral institution in the conventional sense. There's no headquarters, no secretary-general, no talkfests – and, perhaps most important of all, no French or Russian veto.'[60] Instead, participants simply agree to share information and to act when needed. The much-used slogan of the PSI is that 'it is an activity, not an organisation'.[61] It goes even further than the FATF in that it prefers 'supporters' or 'partners' rather than 'members' in the formal sense. These 'supporters' are encouraged, but not legally obliged, to commit to a Statement of Principles.[62] The *SIPRI Yearbook 2007* helpfully points out, 'there is neither a public list of PSI partners nor a membership procedure'.[63] But the State Department did eventually move to list PSI 'partners' publicly on its website as of 22 May 2008.[64] In terms of aviation security, the harmonisation of hand luggage restrictions were quickly put in place in airports worldwide on liquids and gels after an aborted terrorist plot involving liquid explosives in August 2006. The ability to be flexible and respond to new challenges is crucial. TSA Administrator Kip Hawley places 'a high premium on being nimble, agile and flexible' in developing a model to handle the risks faced by the aviation industry. TSA wants a model that will 'work well against known risks but also build in a margin that allows you to be flexible'.[65]

A benefit of the relative flexibility of these arrangements is they can be tweaked to meet new challenges and achieve synergies with other initiatives. For instance, the PSI overlaps to a significant degree with the CSI, while the FATF is looking at whether the 40+9 Recommendations can be reinforced to counter vulnerabilities associated with WMD proliferation financing mechanisms. Whether it is the PSI or the FATF, the increasing use of these 'ad hoc informal arrangements raises the spectre of an increased tendency to rely on non-institutional mechanisms to deal with these major threats to international peace and security'.[66] There is a serious trade-off to consider here. In swapping the formality and rigidity of the UN system for flexibility and informality, the legitimacy and universality that comes with being under the truly global UN umbrella is lost. Furthermore, 'although these features may enhance its flexibility, as well as the speed of decision-making and resultant action, they also constrain its capacity'.[67] The informal nature of support also means that 'given the flexibility of cooperation, many if not most of these 80 so-called supporters would not be obligated to interdict vessels or aircraft at the behest of the United States and might well decline doing so'.[68] With its informal nature, the FATF too lacked legal enforcement mechanisms formally to ensure compliance and had to resort to 'blacklisting' processes to coerce recalcitrant states into submission.

Risk management goes global?

Previously, we have summarised our conclusions on the relationship between risk both as a motivating factor and suggested policy solutions for global governance frameworks in the 'other' war on terror. What remains for us to address is the final piece in the puzzle: once the various risk-based global standards and benchmarks have been harmonised and adopted, how can they function to reduce global security risks? To recap, according to the US General Accounting Office, 'a risk management approach includes assessments of threats to security, vulnerabilities to those threats, and the criticality, or relative importance, of addressing the identified vulnerabilities'.[69] We shall now assess how this approach manifested in our case studies.

Globalisation and the vulnerability of global infrastructure

We begin by identifying and assessing vulnerabilities. Both the global financial infrastructure and transportation network was deemed to be vulnerable as a result of globalisation and the massive flows of people or funds across borders. With terrorist financing, as Richard Clarke observed, 'the terrorists moved their money through old-fashioned smuggling but also by bank transfers through the unsuspecting (and often unregulated) holes in the global financial system'.[70] It is these 'holes' or gaps in global infrastructure that pose risks. Hence the FATF Recommendations has been designed to identify and plug weak points in the global financial system to reduce susceptibility to terrorist financing. The global aviation network is deemed to be another soft under-belly of globalisation. Airports form the backbone of the global air travel infrastructure and indeed, 'few sites are more symbolic of both the opportunities and vulnerabilities of contemporary globalization than the international airport'.[71] The US *National Strategy for Aviation Security* observes:

> Globalization, technological advances, the proliferation of WMD, and the emergence of terrorism as a global phenomenon have enabled threats to the Air Domain to extend in reach, accelerate in speed, and increase in potential. Aviation is a global enterprise with a distributed infrastructure and multiple access points.[72]

As airports become securitised in their attempts to identify separate safe from potentially risky passengers, risk-based procedures are designed to reduce vulnerabilities identified in the system such as security procedures of some air carriers and airports.

Similar concerns with the vulnerabilities of global infrastructure exist for the PSI. Tangredi observes that globalisation has affected all aspects of human civilisation, creating an increase in non-state and transnational threats to the United States, increased traffic and trade on the seas, new areas of military intervention, a restructuring of alliances and the proliferation of information, technology and weapons.[73] The same global infrastructure has also enabled the proliferation of dangerous capabilities, such as advanced technical knowledge and weapons of mass destruction.[74] As Harbaugh points out, 'While the maritime transport system has been a critical component of the global economy, it is wrought with security vulnerabilities, permitting terrorists to smuggle drugs, people, contraband, and arms, critical to financing their operations.'[75] The PSI seeks to build partner capacity and cooperation to reduce these vulnerabilities, by coordinating intercept procedures and operations. These come in the form of exercises and actual interdictions. Likewise, the IATA and FATF work to help those who cannot implement ICAO SARPs or FATF Recommendations.

Layered security and increasing difficulties

Having identified vulnerabilities, one way of remedying these vulnerabilities is increasing layers of difficulty in order to reduce the likelihood of terrorists achieving their goals. This was a common feature of all three global governance cases we examined, although they did so in different ways. The combined effect amounts to a reshaping of terrorists' operating environment (wherever that may be: in airports, financial infrastructure or on the high seas) to make their tasks harder.

The PSI's goal is, as John Bolton remarks, to 'lengthen the time that proliferators need to acquire new weapons capabilities, increase their cost, and demonstrate our resolve to combat proliferation'.[76] Bolton further suggests the ultimate intention is to 'create a web of counter-proliferation partnerships through which proliferators will have difficulty carrying out their trade'.[77] Bush declared the purpose was 'taking cooperative action to stop the proliferation trade and to deny terrorists, rogue states, and their supplier networks access to weapons of mass destruction (WMD), their delivery systems, and related materials'.[78] Overall, 'the initiative is designed to make it more costly and risky for proliferators to acquire the weapons or materials they seek'.[79] As Australia's Foreign Minister pointed out, the aim was to 'make the trafficking of the world's most dangerous weapons as near to impossible as we can'.[80] National Security Advisor Stephen Hadley argues that:

> a robust, layered defense against such weapons and the means to deliver them can discourage the effort to acquire such weapons by denying our enemies the ability to achieve the benefits they seek in these weapons in the first place.[81]

As a risk management tool targeted at altering the capabilities and intentions of terrorists, the PSI affects the strategic calculations of terrorists and rogue states to discourage them from acquiring or using weapons of terror. Senior Bush administration officials contended that 'the PSI's greatest success lies in the way it has helped shape the international environment to enable interdiction of WMD and related materials'.[82]

In evaluating the PSI, it is important to note that it is not a stand-alone initiative. Together with other counter-proliferation mechanisms like the NPT, CSI and multilateral export control regimes such as the Nuclear Suppliers Group, it forms a 'layered defence system'.[83] The White House claims that the PSI has 'made significant strides in shaping a new environment to combat trafficking to and from states and non-state actors of proliferation concern of weapons of mass destruction, their delivery systems, and related materials'.[84]

Aviation security too is predicated on adding layers of security to make it more difficult for terrorists to succeed. TSA estimates suggest up to 20 layers of security subject a passenger to checks before they board aircraft. A layered approach is often seen as the best way to raise the hurdles for terrorists to succeed. As TSA boss Kip Hawley notes, 'We've added layers … additional layers that have been added since 2005.'[85] Aviation security observers see the 'evolution of a layered security system'.[86]

The layered system, one that recognised that no single security measure was flawless or impenetrable, was designed to provide a greater number of opportunities to foil and confound would-be terrorists. If one layer was breached, then others would remain to provide back up. These layers can start piling up even before a passenger arrives in another country's airspace. A global coordinated layered approach can help ensure the security of commercial aviation, involving multiple diverse and coordinated measures. These measures include enhancing passenger and checked baggage screening, matching with watch lists, observing behaviours through surveillance, offering security training for flight and cabin crews to handle potential threats onboard aircraft, expanding the Federal Air Marshal Service.

The aim of layered security is to minimise any individual single points of vulnerability that might be exploited. There is also an international dimension to this as extra layers are added in travel originating overseas with the PNR agreement. The US *National Strategy for Aviation Security* points out, 'aviation security is best achieved by integrating public and private aviation security global activities into a coordinated effort … involving appropriate Federal, State, local, and tribal governments and the private sector to provide active layered aviation security'.[87] The benefit of layered security is explained in these terms:

> Each one of these layers alone is capable of stopping a terrorist attack. In combination their security value is multiplied, creating a much stronger, formidable system. A terrorist who has to overcome multiple security layers in order to carry out an attack is more likely to be pre-empted, deterred, or to fail during the attempt.[88]

The FATF too attempts to increase the obstacles by adding various layers of checks and scrutiny from risk-based approaches checking customers opening bank accounts to data mining of financial transactions. Overall, it is claimed that the campaign against terrorist financing has:

> made it harder and costlier for al-Qaida and other terrorist groups to move money around the world and have built more stringent barriers in the international financial system to prevent its abuse … better practices across the international financial system have raised higher institutional hurdles for terrorists to circumvent.[89]

What is clear is the emphasis on raising the bar to successful terrorist financing and as a result hopefully reducing the risk in the process. Disruption is a key word both in the FATF and PSI activities to reduce risk. However, one sceptic of this approach, which essentially seeks to inconvenience terrorists, is security expert Bruce Schneir. He wrote regarding Gordon Brown's security measures around airports and sports stadiums, 'UK Spends Billions To Force Terrorists To Drive A Little Further'.[90]

'Everyday' war on terror

The idea of inconveniencing terrorists to reduce risks has some parallels in a recent development in contemporary crime control that 'de-dramatizes crime and presents it as a routine activity, carried out by ordinary individuals exposed to everyday criminogenic situations'.[91] By presenting crime as a 'routine' activity that happens if criminals find the chance to do so, then the assumption is that crime can be avoided if these opportunities are expunged from daily activities. In the war on terror too, the 'threat of terrorism has entered our everyday life and now shapes where we may go, how we travel and what we may do'.[92] One risk management implication, as our case studies suggest, is that counter-terrorism efforts now aim at reducing the opportunities of unwanted outcomes by altering our daily pattern of activities. It is the 'everyday' mundane nature of the 'other' war on terror that is highlighted when global governance and risk come together, for global standards to regulate risk are becoming embedded in the routines of modern life. Each time we go to the bank or pass through airport security restrictions on liquids, we are participating in the 'other' war on terror on an ordinary routinised basis. For instance the FATF's flexibility means it recently became concerned with the financing of WMD proliferation. It recommends that 'know your customer' (KYC) and 'customer due diligence' (CDD) and identifying suspicious activity can help reduce the risk of WMD proliferation financing.[93] One of its prescriptions is compiling a 'red flag' checklist that identifies potential risks of proliferation financing to be implemented on a daily basis. As for aviation security, since most of the aviation infrastructure is in private hands, 'effective national aviation security strategy must be supported by a private sector that internalizes a strong security culture, embedding best practices and government requirements into day-to-day operations'.[94] In other words, the risk-based approach must now become fully incorporated into operational structures and standard procedures to be employed globally at airports worldwide.

Recognising that private owners and operators of maritime transport infrastructure are the first line of defence against WMD proliferation, the US *National Strategy for Maritime Security* too highlights a need to 'embed security into commercial practices to reduce vulnerabilities … a close partnership between government and the private sector is essential to ensuring critical infrastructure and key resource vulnerabilities are identified and corrected quickly'.[95] As the Homeland Security Department puts it, 'the more we can integrate security into common business practices and modern information systems, the better we will be able to sustain increased levels of security'.[96] Here, the PSI's outreach activities play a part through the development of best practices and building the capacity of partners and shipping officials such that looking at cargo manifests or port activities for suspicious patterns becomes part and parcel of their standard operating procedures at shipping companies or freight forwarders.

Boomerang effects and evolution of risk

What our case studies of global governance finally reinforce is the constant evolution of risk. The need to keep up is as much a common feature of aviation security as it is in terrorist financing and WMD proliferation. The *National Strategy for Aviation Security* warns that 'threats to the Air Domain are numerous, complex, and adaptive. The terrorist threat is changing in form and intensity as terrorists' intentions and capabilities change and countermeasures are instituted.'[97] From straightforward hijackings to shoe bombs to liquid explosives, the risk constantly evolves. Likewise, terrorist funding methods have now moved into the informal remittance sector, charities and even morphed into organised criminal activities. With WMD proliferation too, it is important to note that the risk continually evolves and changes. 'The WMD proliferation landscape is dynamic … our responses must similarly evolve.'[98] The genesis of the PSI itself reflects attempts to respond to changing circumstances where traditional nonproliferation mechanisms such as NPT were no longer sufficient on their own, and had to be adapted to new threats. The built-in flexibility of the FATF and PSI as an informal arrangement allows them to be quickly adapted in response to the evolution of risks. One such recent demand includes the need to reorient the PSI towards considering air interdictions, port inspections. The PSI is being billed as just such a multilateral platform suited for cooperation on such efforts. Both the FATF and PSI are also now turning their attentions to the intersection between WMD proliferation and terrorist financing.

A happy ending?

In drawing the final curtains on this book, we have now come full circle in showing how several key but so far divergent strands of academic and policy debates on the war on terror can in fact be interwoven to reach a more complete understanding of the endeavour. To begin with, the Bush White House's penchant for unilateralism and militarism has fuelled musings among intellectuals in the Beltway such as Strobe Talbott about multilateral cooperative alternatives in a greatly expanded reconfigured form of global governance that does *not* centre on the formalised UN system alone. At the same time, there is a growing call for recognising that perhaps, *just perhaps*, the Bush administration's less obvious policies in reshaping global institutions might have been overshadowed by raging controversies over Iraq and other high-profile military excesses. Indeed, discussion of 'quiet' fronts in the war on terror has been drowned out by continuing problems in Iraq and Afghanistan. The last, and by no means least, development underlines the bourgeoning proliferation of risk-related ideas such as Beck's 'risk-cosmopolitanism', Renn's 'global risk governance' and Amoore and de Goede's 'governing by risk', which have sprouted like veritable mushrooms after the rain. Somewhat against the grain of academic works that have rightly criticised the negative implications for human rights and civil liberties, we wondered whether risk could perhaps fulfil more positive integrative functions in bringing about new forms of global cooperation in the war on terror that might possibly have been overlooked. Here, sociologist Ulrich Beck's theories about 'cosmopolitan vision' and 'risk-cosmopolitanism' in the *World Risk Society* underpinned our analyses.

Building upon these three observations on the state of the art in current thinking about the war on terror, our basic overarching premise then is that the 'Long War' embodies several elements – the FATF, PSI and avation security – that are *relatively* more cooperative, less visible and lower-profile but no less important than their 'violent' dramatic counterparts seen so far in Iraq and Afghanistan, Guantanamo and Abu Ghraib. As Rumsfeld put it, 'some steps will be visible, as in a traditional conflict, and in other cases they will be not visible'.[99] Paying particular attention to the intersection between theories of risk, global governance and security, we then proposed how this theoretical perspective can help shed light on the rationale, implementation and implications of these less-noticed initiatives under the rubric of what we term the 'other' war on terror.

A new concern with shared global risk does seem to have injected momentum and creativity into new flexible cooperative efforts at risk management. To reiterate, risk can be seen as a probabilistic undesirable scenario followed by a policy proposal to avert that unwanted outcome. The function of risk here is thus twofold: as a probabilistic scenario to be averted it is serving as a motivating force, but at the same time it also provides the suggested policy solution to prevent that scenario materialising. Hence, new 'informal' forms of global governance such as the PSI and FATF and the IATA have arisen not just in response to awareness of shared global risks but a risk-based regulatory framework also supplies the basic global scaffolding for negotiations to harmonise global standards ranging from FATF to IATA recommended best practices. Our understanding of global governance expanded beyond the relatively rigid formalised institutionalised UN or state-centric system. Multilevel overlapping arrangements are being established with the recognition that the cross-boundary elusive nature of global risk brings with it a whole new ball game, as states alone are not up to the task. Reminiscent of Beck's 'institutionalised cosmopolitanism', the negotiation and implementation of these global risk-based standards has brought more actors into the fold, ranging from global businesses to regional bodies, NGOs, the private sector right down to individuals. These actors are seen as having agency in shaping the global risk environment in their own ways. As a technique of risk management, these standards not only helped to identify vulnerabilities and remedy them but also in the process introduced multiple layers of difficulty to make it harder for terrorists to succeed. Indeed, 'layered security' and 'shaping the environment' are now favoured terms of the Bush administration. Adoption of these new risk-based approaches was becoming routinised as part of day-to-day activities. As a result, the 'other' war on terror was now in danger of becoming mundane and everyday.

The less visible nature of these risk-based global governance approaches however cannot conceal the continuing gulf in subjective risk perceptions as well as power differentials that significantly dilute any emergent sense of 'risk-cosmopolitanism'. Indeed, the very undesirable downsides of the war on terror that first soured many people's opinions of the entire enterprise unfortunately also continue to stalk the 'other' war on terror. Coercion, power, exclusion, discrimination, infringement of human rights and civil liberties, and questions of murky legality are just some of the long list of concerns that bedevil global risk governance. The controversial involvement of the private sector in the 'hot' wars on Iraq, Abu Ghraib and Afghanistan have their less visible counterparts in airline security and financial data-mining companies who profit from a new politics of fear in what Hughes has termed the 'War on Terror, Inc'. 'The war on terror was a strange new hybrid: the British and US governments seized new powers and then quickly delegated them to private companies, giving rise to the new security industries.'[100] Any hint of a 'cosmopolitan outlook' can also quickly evaporate under the power of subjective risk perceptions and national interests. A case in point would be Ireland's unilateral 'national' response to the global credit crisis of October 2008 in guaranteeing its national bank deposits. Widely denounced as a 'beggar thy neighbour' policy, this should not have happened in Beck's supposedly 'cosmopolitan' Europe. Even worse, Germany then followed suit. Although there has been some shift back towards the global via coordinated interest rate cuts and agreements between Eurozone members and Britain, it is clear that what should have been a definitive and ideal test case of globally shared economic risks bringing about enforced integration initially led to dissensus, rather than consensus. The 'cosmopolitan' nature of a response is, therefore, not a foregone conclusion. Let us of course not forget that besides transnational terrorism, global economic contagion risk forms the other crucial pillar of Beck's *World Risk Society*. Finally, what Beck's notion of 'cosmopolitan realism' fails to make clear is the precise relationship and continuing tension between continuing selfish interests of 'cosmopolitan realist' states and at the same time the recognition that these very states have crucial roles to play in managing global risks in the first place. The coercion of weaker states into acceptance of new risk-based 'cosmopolitan' norms is also a function of power relationships.

In thinking through the longer-term implications of the less visible 'other' war on terror, it is perhaps useful to take a leaf out of the books of other similar 'rhetorical' wars on crime and drugs of which the world has longer experience. Former Democratic presidential candidate John Kerry was once famously ridiculed for suggesting that terrorism should be reduced to a 'nuisance':

> We have to get back to the place we were, where terrorists are not the focus of our lives, but they're a nuisance.... As a former law-enforcement person, I know we're never going to end prostitution. We're never going to end illegal gambling. But we're going to reduce it, organized crime, to a level where it isn't on the rise. It isn't threatening people's lives every day, and fundamentally, it's something that you continue to fight, but it's not threatening the fabric of your life.[101]

While Kerry was widely criticised and slated for his suggestion, it took America's top military office to give more credibility to this line of thinking. The former US Joint Chiefs of Staff General Peter Pace too made a similar comparison between terrorism and crime. Both ills can never be completely eradicated but can be controlled and managed:

> all major cities have crime, but the police forces keep the crime rate below the level at which the normal population can live and work and prosper ... and that is really, I believe, the end state for the war on terrorism.[102]

Pace felt that global cooperation can help achieve this end game. A close reading of these two statements combined hints very strongly at global governance and risk management, not elimination. It is a case of constant ongoing adaptation and responding to the evolution of risk and 'boomerang effects', recognising that there is no such thing as decisive victory. Of course the negotiation and implementation of these norms contain within themselves undesirable downsides such as power, coercion, exclusion and infringement of civil liberties. Indeed, the cost–benefit analysis might not work out in some instances as the compliance costs simply outweigh any perceived gains. This is an issue that requires careful consideration to avoid any defections. Yet the relatively 'informal' means of global governance we have discussed can potentially bring about the harmonisation of global risk-based standards to 'routinise' the war on terror in areas as diverse as aviation security to terrorist financing such that it becomes part of everyday life at all levels of human and political activity. Once it is no longer seen as an extraordinarily dramatic security measure but a rather mundane cooperative risk management exercise, at the end of the day, this is perhaps what the 'other' war on terror can realistically hope to achieve. As Donald Rumsfeld once said:

> there's not going to be a D-Day as such, and I'm sure there will not be a signing ceremony on the Missouri as such. This is not something that

begins with a significant event or ends with a significant event. It is something that will involve a sustained effort over a good period of time ... making a series of incremental steps that create an environment that's inhospitable to people who are determined to kill other people through terrorist acts.[103]

Notes

1 The other war on terror

1 This is an idea also floated by Louise Amoore and Marieke de Goede, 'Transactions after 9/11: the banal face of the preemptive strike', *Transactions of the Institute of British Geographers*, Vol. 33 No. 2, January 2008, p. 182.
2 Bruce Hoffman, 'Remember Al Qaeda? They're baaack!' *LA Times*, 20 February 2007. Online, available at: www.latimes.com/news/opinion/la-oe-hoffman20feb20,0,2283472. story (accessed 17 October 2008).
3 Annual Threat Assessment of the Intelligence Community for the Senate Armed Services Committee 27 February 2008, p. 4. Online, available at: www.dni.gov/ testimonies/20080227_testimony.pdf (accessed 14 August 2008).
4 Remarks by Ted Gistaro, National Intelligence Officer for Transnational Threats, the Washington Institute for Near East Policy, Washington, DC, 12 August 2008. Online, available at: www.odni.gov/speeches/20080812_speech.pdf (accessed 14 August 2008).
5 See 'A not very private feud over terrorism', *New York Times*, 8 June 2008; and Marc Sageman and Bruce Hoffman, 'Does Osama still call the shots?' *Foreign Affairs*, Vol. 87 No. 4, July/August 2008, pp. 163–166.
6 Amoore and de Goede, 'Transactions after 9/11: the banal face of the preemptive strike', pp. 173–174.
7 Daniel W. Drezner, 'The new new world order', *Foreign Affairs*, March/April 2007, pp. 34–46.
8 Joseph Nye, 'Global governance', *Washington Post*, 27 January 2008, p. BW04.
9 Hearing of the House Armed Services Committee, 10 September 2008. Online, available at: www.jcs.mil/j_directors/10SEP08_CJCS_HASC_testimony.pdf (accessed 12 September 2008).
10 For a sample selection, see William Vlcek 'Money, terror and protecting the West', *The Round Table: The Commonwealth Journal of International Affairs*, Vol. 97 No. 395, April 2008, pp. 305–311; Ibrahim Warde, *The Price of Fear: Al-Qaeda and the Truth Behind the Financial War on Terror*, London: I.B. Tauris, 2007; Thomas J. Biersteker and Sue E. Eckert (eds), *Countering the Financing of Terrorism*, London and New York, Routledge, 2007.
11 Louise Amoore and Marieke de Goede, 'Governance, risk and dataveillance in the war on terror', *Crime, Law and Social Change*, Vol. 43 No. 2–3, 2005, pp. 149–173; Claudia Aradau and Rens van Munster, 'Governing terrorism through risk: taking precautions, (un)knowing the future', *European Journal of International Relations*, Vol. 13 No. 1, 2007, pp. 89–115; Gabe Mythen and Sandra Walklate, 'Terrorism, risk and international security: the perils of asking "what if?"' *Security Dialogue*, Vol. 39 No. 2–3, 2008, pp. 221–242; Amoore and de Goede, 'Transactions after 9/11: the banal face of the preemptive strike', pp. 173–185; Jon Coaffee, *Terrorism, Risk and the City: The Making of a Contemporary Urban Landscape*, Aldershot, Ashgate, 2003.

12 Daniel Byman, *The Five Front War: The Better Way to Fight Global Jihad*, New Jersey: Wiley, 2007.

13 David Cortwright and George Lopez (eds), *Uniting Against Terror: Cooperative Non-military Responses to the Global Terrorist Threat*, Cambridge, MA:MIT Press, 2007.

14 Drezner, 'The new new world order'.

15 Drezner, 'The new new world order'.

16 George W. Bush, 'President freezes terrorist assets', remarks by the president, Secretary of Treasury O'Neill and Secretary of State Powell on Executive Order on Terrorist Financing (EO 13224), The Rose Garden, 20 September 2001. Online, available at: www.whitehouse.gov/news/releases/2001/09/20010924–4.html (accessed 20 October 2006).

17 The White House, *National Strategy for Combating Terrorism*, 'Overview of America's national strategy for combating terrorism', July 2006. Online, available at: www.whitehouse.gov/nsc/nsct/2006/sectionI.html (accessed 13 September 2008).

18 The White House, *National Strategy for Combating Terrorism*, Washington, DC, 2003, p. 1

19 *National Strategy for Combating Terrorism*, 2003, pp. 20–21.

20 See for instance Giles Andreani, 'The war on terror: good cause, wrong concept', *Survival*, Vol. 46 No. 4, December 2004, pp. 31–50; Michael Howard, 'What's in a name? How to fight terrorism', *Foreign Affairs*, Vol. 81 No. 1, January/February 2002, pp. 8–13; Yee-Kuang Heng, 'Unravelling the war on terrorism: a risk management exercise in "war" clothing?' *Security Dialogue*, Vol. 33 No. 2, June 2002, pp. 227–242.

21 Cited in Eric Schmitt and Thom Shanker, 'Washington recasts terror war as "struggle"', *New York Times*, 27 July 2005.

22 An example would be Mel Gurtov, *Superpower on Crusade: The Bush Doctrine in US Foreign Policy*, London: Lynne Rienner, 2006.

23 US Department of Defense, *Quadrennial Defence Review*, February 2006, p. 22.

24 Jonathan Stevenson, 'Demilitarising the "war on terror"', *Survival*, Vol. 48 No. 2, Summer 2006, p. 37.

25 Stevenson,'Demilitarising the "war on terror"', p. 48.

26 'Morrocco's gentle war on terror', *TIME*, 6 August 2008. Online, available at: www.time.com/time/magazine/article/0,9171,1829931,00.html?xid=rss-topstories (accessed 12 September 2008). The 'Quiet war on terror' was also explored in a five-part series broadcast by NPR in November 2005.

27 Remarks at George Washington University, 16 March 2005. Online, available at: www.dhs.gov/xnews/speeches/speech_0245.shtm (accessed 12 September 2008).

28 John Hobson and Leonard Seabrooke (eds), *Everyday Politics of the World Economy*, Cambridge: Cambridge University Press, 2007.

29 Marieke de Goede, 'The politics of preemption in the war on terror', *European Journal of International Relations*, Vol. 14 No. 1, 2008, p. 162.

30 *New Scientist*, 17 September 2005, Issue 2517.

31 John Adams, 'The world's biggest ideas: risk', *New Scientist*, 17 September 2005, Issue 2517, p. 187.

32 HM Government, *Countering International Terrorism: The United Kingdom's Strategy*, July 2006, p. 1.

33 HM Government Cabinet Office, *National Risk Register*, 2008, p. 3.

34 HM Government Cabinet Office, *The National Security Strategy of the United Kingdom: Security in an Interdependent World*, Cm7291, March 2008.

35 Ulrich Beck, 'The world risk society revisited: the terrorist threat?' LSE Public Lecture, London, 14 February 2002; 'Terror and solidarity' in Mark Leonard (ed.), *Re-ordering the World*, London: Foreign Policy Centre, 2002.

36 See for instance Louise Amoore and Marieke de Goede (eds), *Risk and the War on Terror*, London: Routledge, 2008; Aradau and van Munster, 'Governing terrorism

through risk: taking precautions, (un)knowing the future', pp. 89–115; Amoore and de Goede, 'Governance, risk, and dataveillance in the war on terror'; David Lyon, *Surveillance as Social Sorting*, London: Routledge, 2003; Keith Spence, 'World risk society and war against terror', *Political Studies*, Vol. 53 No. 2, 2005, pp. 284–302; Colin McInnes, *Health, Security and the Risk Society*, London: Nuffield Trust, 2005.

37 These include Christopher Coker, *War in an Age of Risk*, New Jersey: Polity Press, 2009; Yee-Kuang Heng, *War as Risk Management: Strategy and Conflict in an Age of Globalised Risks*, London: Routledge, 2006; Mikkel Rasmussen, *The Risk Society at War*, Cambridge: Cambridge University Press, 2006; Christopher Coker, *Globalisation and Insecurity in the Twenty-first Century: NATO and the Management of Risk*, Adelphi Paper 345, Oxford: Oxford University Press, 2002.
38 Amoore and de Goede, 'Transactions after 9/11: the banal face of the preemptive strike', p. 176.
39 Ortwin Renn and Kathering D. Walker (eds), *Global Risk Governance*, Amsterdam: Springer, 2008.
40 Michael Power, *The Risk Management of Everything*, London: Demos, 2004, p. 10.
41 The White House, National *Strategy for Combating Terrorism*, 'Overview of America's National strategy for combating terrorism', 2006.
42 HM Government, *Countering International Terrorism: The United Kingdom's Strategy*, p. 2.
43 The White House, *National Strategy for Combating Terrorism*, 2006. Online, available at: www.whitehouse.gov/nsc/nsct/2006/sectionV.html#prevent (accessed 10 September 2008).
44 The White House, *National Strategy for Combating Terrorism*, 'Overview of America's National strategy for combating terrorism', 2006.
45 Christopher Banks, 'Protecting (or destroying) freedom through law: the USA Patriot Act's constitutional implications' in David Cohen and John Wells (eds), *American National Security and Civil Liberties in an Era of Terrorism*, London: Palgrave, 2004, pp. 30–31.
46 The above times and figures are taken from the *9/11 Commission Report: Final Report of the National Commission on Terrorist attacks upon the United States*, National Commission on Terrorist Attacks Upon the United States, New York: Norton, 2004.
47 See James Der Derian, 'In terrorem: war, terror, judgement' in Ken Booth and Tim Dunne (eds), *Worlds in Collision*, Basingstoke: Macmillan, 2002, pp. 101–117, for a discussion of the term '9/11' as a signifier for these events.
48 Bob Woodward, *Bush At War*, London: Pocket Books, 2003, p. 16.
49 Woodward, *Bush at War*, p. 30.
50 Woodward, *Bush at War*, p. 30.
51 George W. Bush, 'President freezes terrorist assets', 20 September 2001.
52 See John B. Taylor, *Global Financial Warriors: The Untold Story of International Finance in the Post-9/11 World*, New York: W.W. Norton, 2007.
53 *The United Nations Global Counter-terrorism Strategy*, 2006 Online, available at: www.un.org/terrorism/strategy-highlights.shtml (accessed 10 September 2008).
54 The White House, *National Strategy for Combating Terrorism*, 'Institutionalizing our strategy for long-term success', July 2006. Online, available at: www.whitehouse. gov/nsc/nsct/2006/sectionVI.html (accessed 15 September 2008).
55 Cited in Anne L. Clunan, 'The fight against terrorist financing', *Political Science Quarterly*, Vol. 121 No. 4, December 2006, pp. 569–596.
56 On terrorist financing, see Clunan, 'The fight against terrorist financing'; Bruce Zagaris, 'The merging of the anti-money laundering and counter-terrorism financial enforcement regimes after September 11, 2001', *Berkeley Journal of International Law*, Vol. 22 No. 1, 2004, pp. 123–158; Ilias Bantekas 'The international law of terrorist financing', *American Journal of International Law*, Vol. 97 No. 2, 2003, pp. 315–332. On the PSI, see Michael Byers, 'Policing the high seas: the Proliferation

Security Initiative', *American Journal of International Law*, Vol. 98 No. 3, 2004, pp. 526–545; James Cotton, 'The Proliferation Security Initiative and North Korea: legality and limitations of a coalition strategy', *Security Dialogue*, Vol. 36 No. 2, 2005, pp. 193–211.

57 Martin Navias, 'Finance warfare and international terrorism', *Political Quarterly*, Vol. 73 No. 1, August 2002, p. 76.

58 Although some scholars have examined the specific details and flaws of how these UN instruments function, they do not access it from the point of view of a multilevel overlappping counter-terrorist framework we attempt here. See for instance Eric Rosand, 'The Security Council's efforts to monitor the implementation of Al Qaeda/ Taliban sanctions', *American Journal of International Law*, Vol. 98 No. 4, October 2004, pp. 745–763.

59 *The United Nations Global Counter-terrorism Strategy*, Section II.5, 2006. Online, available at: www.un.org/terrorism/strategy-counter-terrorism.shtml (accessed 10 September 2008).

60 The White House, *National Strategy to Combat Weapons of Mass Destruction*, December 2002, p. 6.

61 The White House, *National Strategy to Combat Weapons of Mass Destruction*, December 2002, p. 4.

62 Byers, 'Policing the high seas: the Proliferation Security Initiative', p. 526.

63 Remarks by National Security Advisor Stephen J. Hadley at the Proliferation Security Initiative Fifth Anniversary Senior Level Meeting, Washington, DC, 28 May 2008. Online, available at: www.whitehouse.gov/news/releases/2008/05/20080528–3.html (accessed 24 June 2008).

64 Brad Knickerboxer, 'Silent surge in contractor armies', *Christian Science Monitor*, 18 July 2007.

65 David A. Baldwin, 'The concept of security', *Review of International Studies*, Vol. 23, 1997, p. 5.

66 Emma Rothschild, 'What is security?' *Daedalus*, Vol. 124 No. 3, 1995, p. 55.

67 It should be noted here that a concern with the security of individuals was always the concern of politics at the domestic level, what is new here is that the boundary between inside/outside are being blurred if not outrightly obliterated.

68 Rothschild, 'What is security?', p. 55

69 As discussed in Elke Krahman, 'Conceptualizing security governance', *Cooperation and Conflict*, Vol. 38 No. 1, 2003, pp. 7–9. Much of the following discussion follows Krahmann's argument with some minor additions.

70 John Mearsheimer, 'Back to the future: instability in Europe after the Cold War', *International Security*, Vol. 15 No. 2, 1990, p. 56.

71 That is with the exception of those who argue that the current dispensation represents a unipolar moment likely to be shortlived but at present providing stability, see Charles A. Kupchan, 'After Pax Americana: benign power, regional integration, and the sources of a stable multipolarity', *International Security*, Vol. 23 No. 2, Autumn 1998, pp. 40–79 and Christopher Layne, 'The unipolar illusion: why new great powers will rise', *International Security*, Vol. 17 No. 4, Spring 1993, for examples. Although the idea of unipolarity has received broad attention, it has also received much criticism, particularly for confusing the image of US power with the reality of its limitations.

72 Krahman, 'Conceptualising security governance', p. 8.

73 Thomas Ehrlich, *Human Natures*, Washington, DC: Island Press, 2000.

74 Krahmann, 'Conceptualising security governance', pp. 8–9.

75 Hedley Bull, 'Society and anarchy in international relations' in James Der Derian (ed.), *International Theory: Critical Investigations*, Basingstoke: Macmillan, 1995, p. 75.

76 Jan Aart Scholte, 'Global capitalism and the state', *International Affairs*, Vol. 73 No. 3, 1997, p. 427.

77 Ulrich Beck, *Power in the Global Age*, Cambridge, Polity Press, 2005, pp. 3–4.
78 Chris Dodd, 'Opening statement: turmoil in US credit markets', *Hearing of the Senate Banking Committee*, 23 September 2008. Online, available at: http://dodd.senate.gov/index.php?q=node/4572 (accessed 23 September 2008).
79 Ulrich Beck, *World Risk Society*, Cambridge: Polity Press, 1999, p. 14.
80 Beck, *Power in the Global Age*, p. 257.
81 Aradau and Van Munster, 'Governing terrorism through risk: taking precautions, (un)knowing the future', pp. 89–115.
82 Rasmussen, *The Risk Society at War*; Heng, *War as Risk Management*; Coker, *Globalisation and Insecurity in the Twenty-First Century*.
83 Darryl S.L. Jarvis and Martin Griffiths, 'Risk and international relations: a new research agenda', *Global Society*, Vol. 21 No. 1, 2007, pp. 1–4.
84 See for example A.W. Rhodes, *Understanding Governance*, Buckingham: Open University Press, 1996.
85 See David Senghaas, 'Global governance: how could it be conceived?' *Security Dialogue*, Vol. 24 No. 3, 1993, pp. 247–256.
86 See for example Caroline Thomas, *Global Governance, Development and Human Security*, London: Pluto, 2000; Enrst-Otto Czempiel and James N. Rosenau, *Governance without Government: Order and Change in World Politics*, Cambridge: Cambridge University Press, 1992.
87 Thomas, *Global Governance, Development and Human Security*.
88 Timothy M. Shaw, Sandra J. MacLean and David R. Black, 'Introduction: a decade of human security: what prospects for global governance and new multilateralisms?' in Sandra J. Maclean, David R. Black and Timothy Shaw (eds), *A Decade of Human Security: Global Governance and New Multilateralisms*, Aldershot, Ashgate, 2006.
89 James Rosenau, 'Towards an ontology of globlal governance', in Martin Hewson and Tim Sinclair (eds), *Approaches to Global Governance Theory*, Albany, NY: State University of New York Press, 1999, p. 288.
90 The White House, *National Strategy for Combating Terrorism*, Washington, DC, 2003, p. 12.
91 Phil Williams, 'Strategy for a new world: combating trans-national organised crime and terrorism', in John Baylis and Steve Smith (eds), *Strategy in the Contemporary World*, Oxford: Oxford University Press, 2nd edn, 2007, p. 203.
92 Remarks at George Washington University, 16 March 2005. Online, available at: www.dhs.gov/xnews/speeches/speech_0245.shtm (accessed 12 September 2008).

2 Risk, global governance and security

1 Dirk Messner and Franz Nuscheler, 'Basic outlines of German development policy' in Saori Katada, Hanns Maull and Takashi Inoguchi, *Global Governance: Germany and Japan in the International System*, Aldershot: Ashgate, 2004, p. 173.
2 Ulrich Beck, *Cosmopolitan Vision*, Cambridge: Polity Press, 2006.
3 We thank an anonymous reviewer for reminding us to clarify this point.
4 Richard Ericson, 'Ten uncertainties of risk-management approaches to security', *Canadian Journal of Criminology and Criminal Justice*, Vol. 48 No. 3, June 2006, p. 346.
5 Quoted in the *Sun* (UK), 14 November 2007.
6 UK Ministry of Defence, 'Public discussion on the new chapter for the Strategic Defence Review', London, February 2002. Online, available at: www.mod.uk/issues/sdr/new_chapter/glance.htm (accessed 1 April 2003).
7 Paul R. Pillar, *Terrorism and US Foreign Policy*, Washington, DC: The Brookings Institute, 2003, p. 141.
8 Mikkel Rasmussen, *The Risk Society at War*, Cambridge: Cambridge University Press, 2006, p. 2.

9 US Joint Inquiry, *Report of the Joint Inquiry into the Terrorist Attacks of September 11, 2001*, House Permanent Select Committee on Intelligence and the Senate Select Committee on Intelligence, 2003, p. 14.

10 Yee-Kuang Heng, *War as Risk Management: Strategy and Conflict in an Age of Globalised Risks*, London: Routledge, 2006, p. 73.

11 Michael Power, *The Risk Management of Everything*, London: Demos, 2004, p. 14.

12 P. Bracken, I. Bremmer and D. Gordon (eds), *Managing Strategic Surprise: Lessons from Risk Management and Risk Assessment*, Cambridge: Cambridge University Press, 2008.

13 Vikash Yadav, *Risk in International Finance*, London: Routledge, 2008.

14 Gabe Mythen and Sandra Walklate (eds), *Beyond the Risk Society*, Maidenhead: Open University Press, 2006.

15 Claudia Aradau, Luis Lobo-Guerrero and Rens Van Munster (eds), 'Security, technologies of risk, and the political', Special issue, *Security Dialogue*, Vol. 39 No. 2–3, 2008, pp. 147–154.

16 Gabe Mythen and Sandra Walklate, 'Terrorism, risk and international security: the perils of asking "what if?"' *Security Dialogue*, Vol. 39 No. 2–3, 2008, pp. 221–242.

17 Stefan Elbe, 'Risking lives: AIDS, security and three concepts of risk', *Security Dialogue*, Vol. 39 No. 2–3, 2008, pp. 177–198.

18 Claudia Aradau and Rens Van Munster, 'Governing terrorism through risk: taking precautions, (un)knowing the future', *European Journal of International Relations*, Vol. 13 No. 1, 2007, pp. 89–115.

19 Louise Amoore and Marieke de Goede (eds), *Risk and the War on Terror*, London: Routledge, 2008.

20 Marieke de Goede, 'Beyond risk: premediation and the post-9/11 security imagination', *Security Dialogue*, Vol. 39 No. 2–3, 2008, pp. 161–185.

21 See L. Lobo-Guerero, 'Biopolitics of specialist risk: kidnap and ransom insurance', *Security Dialogue*, Vol. 38 No. 3, September 2007, pp. 315–334.

22 Michael Dillon, 'Underwriting security', *Security Dialogue*, Vol. 39 No. 2–3, 2008, pp. 309–332.

23 Darryl Jarvis and Martin Griffiths, 'Risk and international relations: a new research agenda', *Global Society*, Vol. 21 No. 1, 2007, pp. 1–4.

24 Raoul Bianchi, 'Tourism and the globalisation of fear: analysing the politics of risk and (in)security in global travel', *Tourism and Hospitality Research*, Vol. 7 No. 1, 2007, pp. 64–74.

25 Christopher Coker, *War in an Age of Risk*, Cambridge: Polity Press, 2009; Heng, *War as Risk Management*; Rasmussen, *The Risk Society at War*; Christopher Coker, *Globalisation and Insecurity in the Twenty-first Century: NATO and the Management of Risk*, Adelphi Paper 345, Oxford: Oxford University Press, 2002.

26 Jen-Peter Voß, Dirk Bauknecht and Rene Kemp (eds), *Reflexive Governance for Sustainable Development*, Camberley: Edward Elgar, 2006.

27 Gabe Mythen and Sandra Walklate, 'Criminology and terrorism: which thesis? Risk society or governmentality?' *British Journal of Criminology*, Vol. 46 No. 3, 2006, pp. 379–398.

28 Gearoid O'Tuathail, 'Understanding critical geopolitics: geopolitics and the risk society', *Journal of Strategic Studies*, Vol. 22 No. 2/3, 1999, pp. 107–124.

29 Kristine Toohey, 'Terrorism, sport, and public policy in the risk society', *Sport in Society*, Vol. 11 No. 4, July 2008, pp. 429–442.

30 For instance Gabe Mythen, *Ulrich Beck: A Critical Introduction to the Risk Society*, Cambridge: Polity, 2004.

31 Power, *The Risk Management of Everything*, p. 38.

32 Ulrich Beck, *World at Risk*, Cambridge: Polity: 2008.

33 Ulrich Beck, *Cosmopolitan Vision*, Cambridge: Polity, 2006, p. 132.

34 Anthony Giddens, *Modernity and Self-identity*, Cambridge: Polity, 1998, p. 147.

35 Ulrich Beck, *World Risk Society*, Cambridge; Polity, 1999, p. 14.
36 Ulrich Beck, *What is Globalisation?* Cambridge: Polity, 2000, p. 133.
37 Ulrich Beck, 'Living in a world risk society', public lecture at the London School of Economics, 15 February 2006, available in *Economy and Society*, Vol. 35 No. 3, August 2006.
38 Yee-Kuang Heng is grateful to Professor Edgar Grande for pointing this out in a private discussion, March 2008. Beck's earlier works include *Risk Society*, Cambridge: Polity, 1992; *Ecological Politics in an Age of Risk*, Cambridge: Polity, 1995; *World Risk Society*. The recent trilogy of books on cosmopolitan realism include Ulrich Beck, *Power in the Global Age*, Cambridge: Polity, 2005; *Cosmopolitan Europe*, Cambridge: Polity, 2006; Ulrich Beck and Edgar Grande, *Cosmopolitan Europe*, Cambridge: Polity, 2008.
39 Ulrich Beck, 'The Cosmopolitan State: towards a realistic utopia', 2001. Online, available at: www.eurozine.com/articles/2001-12-05-beck-en.html (accessed 14 November 2007).
40 Ulrich Beck, 'In the new, anxious world, leaders must learn to think beyond borders', *Guardian*, 13 July 2007. Online, available at: www.guardian.co.uk/commentisfree/story/0,,2125317,00.html (accessed 12 November 2007).
41 Beck, *Cosmopolitan Vision*, pp. 2, 19.
42 Beck, *Cosmopolitan Vision*, p. 147.
43 Beck, *Cosmopolitan Vision*, p. 40.
44 Beck, 'In the new anxious world, leaders must learn to think beyond borders'.
45 Daniel Archibugi and Matthias Koenig-Archibugi, *Debating Cosmopolitics*, London: Verso, 2003, p. 264.
46 Beck, *Cosmopolitan Vision*, p. 2.
47 Beck, *Cosmopolitan Vision*, p. 7.
48 Ulrich Beck, 'The world risk society revisited: the terrorist threat?' LSE Public Lecture, London, 14 February 2002.
49 Beck, *Cosmopolitan Vision*, 2006, p. 19
50 Bruno Latour, 'Whose cosmos, which cosmopolitics?', *Common Knowledge*, Vol. 10 No. 3, 2004, p. 454
51 Beck, *Cosmopolitan Vision*, p. 14.
52 Beck, *Cosmopolitan Vision*, p. 3.
53 Beck, *Cosmopolitan Vision*, p. 21.
54 Ulrich Beck, 'A new cosmopolitanism is in the air', 20 November 2007. Online, available at: www.signandsight.com/features/1603.html (accessed 12 January 2008).
55 Beck, *Cosmopolitan Vision*, p. 18.
56 William Vlcek, 'Surveillance to combat terrorist financing in Europe: whose liberty, whose security?' *European Security*, Vol. 16 No. 1, March 2007, pp. 112–113.
57 Rainer Hulsse, 'Creating demand for global governance: the making of a global money-laundering problem', *Global Society*, Vol. 21 No. 2, April 2007, pp. 155–178.
58 Archibugi and Koenig-Archibugi, *Debating Cosmopolitics*, p. 264.
59 See for instance Vlcek, 'Surveillance to combat terrorist financing in Europe: whose liberty, whose security?' pp. 99–119; Mona Atia, 'In whose interest? Financial surveillance and the circuits of exception in the war on terror', *Environment and Planning D*, Vol. 25 No. 3, 2007, pp. 447–475.
60 Beck, *Cosmopolitan Vision*, p. 72.
61 Beck, 'Living in a world risk society'.
62 Beck, *Cosmopolitan Vision*, p. 35.
63 Beck, *Cosmopolitan Vision*, pp. 5–6.
64 Beck, *Cosmopolitan Vision*, p. 35.
65 Beck, *Cosmopolitan Vision*, p. 36.
66 Beck, *Cosmopolitan Vision*, p. 21.

67 Jason Sharman, 'Power and discourse in policy diffusion: anti-money laundering in developing states', *International Studies Quarterly*, Vol. 52 No. 3, September 2008, pp. 635–656.
68 Beck, *Cosmopolitan Vision*, p. 73.
69 Beck, *Cosmopolitan Vision*, pp. 17–18.
70 Speaking to Jon Snow, *Channel 4 News*, 7p.m., 15 September 2008.
71 Beck, *Cosmopolitan Vision*, p. 36.
72 Ulrich Beck, *The Reinvention of Politics: Rethinking Modernity in the Global Social Order*, Cambridge: Polity, 1997.
73 Beck, *Cosmopolitan Vision*, pp. 22–23.
74 Archibugi and Koenig-Archibugi, *Debating Cosmopolitics*, p. 265.
75 Beck, 'Living in a world risk society'.
76 Beck, 'Living in a world risk society'.
77 Beck and Grande, *Cosmopolitan Europe*, p. 21.
78 Jonathan Clarke and Geoffrey Edwards, *Global Governance in the 21st Century*, London: Palgrave, 2004, p. 7.
79 Remarks to the meeting of the General Assembly on the UN Global Counter-terrorism strategy, 4 September 2008. Online, available at: www.un.org/apps/news/infocus/sgspeeches/statments_full.asp?statID=309 (accessed 22 December 2008).
80 Peter Romaniuk, *Global Counterterrorism: How Multi-lateral Cooperation Works*, London: Routledge, forthcoming 2009.
81 Giuseppe Nesi (ed.), *International Cooperation in Counter-terrorism: The United Nations and Regional Organizations in the Fight Against Terrorism*, Aldershot: Ashgate, 2006.
82 Wyn Rees, *Transatlantic Security Cooperation: Counter Terrorism in the Twenty-First Century*, London: Routledge, 2006.
83 David Held and Anthony McGrew, 'Introduction' in David Held and Anthony McGrew (eds), *Governing Globalization: Power, Authority and Global Governance*, Cambridge: Polity Press, 2002, p. 5.
84 HM Government, *Countering International Terrorism: The United Kingdom's Strategy*, July 2006, p. 3.
85 The White House, *National Strategy for Combating Terrorism*, 'Institutionalizing our strategy for long-term success', July 2006. Online, available at: www.whitehouse.gov/nsc/nsct/2006/sectionVI.html (accessed 15 September 2008).
86 See Louise Amoore and Marieke de Goede, 'Governing by risk in the war on terror', in Amoore and de Goede (eds), *Risk and the War on Terror*; Aradau and Van Munster, 'Governing terrorism through risk: taking precautions, (un)knowing the future', pp. 89–115.
87 Clarke and Edwards, *Global Governance in the 21st Century*.
88 Larry Finkelstein, 'What is global governance?' *Global Governance*, Vol. 1 No. 3, 1995, p. 368.
89 Martin Hewson and Timothy Sinclair, 'Introduction', *Approaches to Global Governance Theory*, Albany, NY: State University of New York, 1999.
90 Ramesh Thakur and Thomas G. Weiss, *The UN and Global Governance: An Unfinished Journey*, Bloomington, IN: Indiana University Press, forthcoming.
91 Rorden Wilkinson, 'Introduction: issues and concepts in global governance' in Rorden Wilkinson (ed.) *The Global Governance Reader*, London: Routledge, 2005, pp. 4–7.
92 Clarke and Edwards, *Global Governance in the 21st Century*.
93 Hewson and Sinclair, 'Preface', *Approaches to Global Governance Theory*.
94 Wilkinson, 'Introduction', *The Global Governance Reader*, pp. 2–3.
95 Margaret Karns and Karen Mingst, *International Organisations: The Politics and Processes of Global Governance*, London: Lynne Rienner, 2004, p. 1.
96 James Rosenau, 'Towards an ontology of global governance', in Hewson and Sinclair, *Approaches to Global Governance Theory*.

97 Karns and Mingst, *International Organisations: The Politics and Processes of Global Governance*, p. 4.

98 Robert Latham, 'Politics in floating world: toward a critique of global governance' in Hewson and Sinclair, *Approaches to Global Governance Theory*, pp. 27, 32.

99 John Grin, 'Reflexive modernisation as a governance issue, or designing and re-shaping structuration', in Jan-Peter Voss, Dierk Bauknecht and René Kemp (eds), *Reflexive Governance for Sustainable Development*, Camberley: Edward Elgar Publishing, 2006, pp. 57–58.

100 Hewson and Sinclair, 'Preface', *Approaches to Global Governance Theory*, p. ix.

101 Rosenau, 'Towards and ontology of flobal governance', p. 293.

102 See for instance Karns and Mingst, *International Organisations: The Politics and Processes of Global Governance*. Also Paul Diehl, *The Politics of Global Governance: International Organisations in an Interdependent World*, London: Lynne Rienner, 2005.

103 Rosenau, 'Towards an ontology of global governance', p. 288.

104 Clarke and Edwards, 'Introduction', *Global Governance in the 21st Century*.

105 Peter Haass (ed.), *International Environmental Governance*, Aldershot: Ashgate, 2008, Parts III, VI, VII.

106 *Our Global Neighbourhood*, Commission on Global Governance, Oxford University Press, 1995, Chapter 1.

107 Latham, 'Politics in a floating world', p. 42.

108 Karns and Mingst, *International Organisations: The Politics and Processes of Global Governance*, p. 3.

109 Latham, 'Politics in a floating world', p. 43.

110 Latham, 'Politics in a floating world', p. 30.

111 E. Krahmann, 'Conceptualising security governance', *Cooperation and Conflict*, Vol. 38 No. 1, 2003, pp. 5–26.

112 Emile Kirchner and James Sperling, *EU Security Governance*, Manchester: Manchester University Press, 2008.

113 Emile Kirchner and James Sperling, *Global Security Governance*, London: Routledge, 2007.

114 Ortwin Renn and Katherine Walker (eds), *Global Risk Governance*, Amsterdam: Springer, 2008.

115 Ortwin Renn, *Risk Governance: Coping with Uncertainty in a Complex World*, London: Earthscan, 2008, p. 9.

116 Renn and Walker, *Global Risk Governance*.

117 Louise Amoore and Mariek de Goede, 'Governance, risk, and dataveillance in the war on terror', *Crime, Law and Social Change*, Vol. 43 No. 2–3, 2005, p. 150.

118 Karns and Mingst, *International Organisations: The Politics and Processes of Global Governance*, p. 14.

119 Rodney Hall and Thomas Biersteker, 'Private authority as global governance' in Rodney Hall and Thomas Biersteker (eds), *Private Authority and Global Governance*, Cambridge: Cambridge University Press, 2002, Chapter 10, p. 203.

120 Hall and Biersteker, *Private Authority and Global Governance*, p. 209.

121 Hall and Biersteker, *Private Authority and Global Governance*, p. 4.

122 Ronnie Lipschultz cited in Hall and Biersteker, *Private Authority and Global Governance*, Chapter 10, p. 204.

123 Hall and Biersteker, *Private Authority and Global Governance*, p. 214.

124 'White House ruins terrorist intel', *CBS News*, 9 October 2007. Online, available at: www.cbsnews.com/stories/2007/10/09/terror/main3346411.shtml (accessed 29 November 2007).

125 We are indebted to an anonymous reviewer for reminding us to clarify this issue.

126 Robert Paton, 'Risk management's role in countering global terrorism', *Rough Notes*, October 2003.

127 Power, *The Risk Management of Everything*, p. 9.
128 Frank Furedi, *The Culture of Fear*, London: Cassell, 1997, p. 29.
129 Henry Willis, 'Challenges of applying risk management to terrorism security policy', *Testimony to the House Homeland Security Committee*, 24 June 2008, p. 4. Online, available at: www.rand.org/pubs/testimonies/2008/RAND_CT310.pdf (accessed 1 September 2008).
130 Beck, 'Living in the world risk society'.
131 Ericson, 'Ten uncertainties of risk-management approaches to security', p. 346.
132 Louise Amoore, 'Biometric borders: governing mobilities in the war on terror', *Political Geography*, Vol. 25 No. 3, 2006, p. 336.
133 Remarks at George Washington University, 16 March 2005. Online, available at: www.dhs.gov/xnews/speeches/speech_0245.shtm (accessed 12 September 2008).
134 The White House, *National Strategy for Homeland Security*, 2007. Online, available at: www.whitehouse.gov/infocus/homeland/nshs/2007/sectionVIII.html (accessed 5 August 2008).
135 Power, *The Risk Management of Everything*, p. 12.
136 Amoore and de Goede, 'Governance, risk, and dataveillance in the war on terror', p. 149.
137 Amoore and de Goede, 'Governance, risk, and dataveillance in the war on terror', p. 150.
138 Amoore and de Goede, 'Governance, risk, and dataveillance in the war on terror', p. 151.
139 David Lyon, 'Introduction' in David Lyon (ed.), *Surveillance as Social Sorting: Privacy, Risk and Digital Discrimination*, London: Routledge, 2003, p. 8.
140 Nick Pidgeon, Christopher Hood, David Jones, Brian Turner and Robert Gibson, *Risk: Analysis, Perception and Management*, London: Report of a Royal Society Study Group, 1992, p. 53; Michael Crouhy, Dan Galai and Robert Mark, *Risk Management*, New York: McGraw-Hill, 2001, p. 109.
141 David Lyon, *Surveillance Society: Monitoring Everyday Life*, Buckingham: Open University Press, 2001, pp. 2, 47–49; also Christopher Dandeker, 'Preface', *Surveillance, Power and Modernity*, Cambridge: Polity Press, 1990, p. vii.
142 Kevin Hagerty and Richard Ericson (eds), *The New Politics of Surveillance and Visibility*, Toronto: University of Toronto Press, 2006.
143 Michael Levi and D.S.Wall, 'Technologies, security, and privacy in the post-9/11 European information society', *Journal of Law and Society*, Vol. 31 No. 2, 2004 pp. 194–220.
144 Amoore and de Goede, 'Governance, risk, and dataveillance in the war on terror', p. 174.
145 Hagerty and Ericson, *The New Politics of Surveillance and Visibility*.
146 Louise Amoore, 'Biometric borders: governing mobilities in the war on terror', pp. 336–351.
147 See Lyon, *Surveillance Society*, pp. 89, 104; Lyon, 'Chapter 1' in Lyon, *Surveillance as Social Sorting*, pp. 24, 39.
148 Sam Nunn, 'Preventing the next terrorist attack: the theory and practice of homeland security information systems', *Journal of Homeland Security and Emergency management*, Vol. 2 No. 3, 2005, p. 4.
149 Department of Homeland Security. Online, available at: www.dhs.gov/xprevprot/programs/gc_1166037389664.shtm (accessed 1 July 2008).
150 The White House, *National Strategy for Homeland Security*, 2007. Online, available at: www.whitehouse.gov/infocus/homeland/nshs/2007/sectionVI.html (accessed 4 August 2008).
151 Quoted in 'Guantanamo mission mitigates global risk, Mullen says', *American Forces Press Service*, 14 January 2008. Online, available at: www.defenselink.mil/news/newsarticle.aspx?id=48649 (accessed 15 January 2008).

152 Eric Williamson and David Winget, 'Risk management and design of critical bridges for terrorist attacks', *Journal of Bridge Engineering*, Vol. 10 No. 1, January/February 2005, pp. 96–106.

153 Jon Coaffee, *Terrorism, Risk and the City: The Making of a Contemporary Urban Landscape*, Aldershot: Ashgate, 2003.

154 Gordon Hughes, *Understanding Crime Prevention: Social Control, Risk and Late Modernity*, Buckingham: Open University Press, 1998, pp. 60–63.

155 Remarks by Mr Ted Gistaro, National Intelligence Officer for Transnational Threats at the Washington Institute for Near East Policy, Washington, DC, 12 August 2008. Online, available at: www.odni.gov/speeches/20080812_speech.pdf (accessed 14 August 2008).

156 The White House, *National Strategy for Combating Terrorism*, 'Strategic vision for the war on terror', July 2006. Online, available at: www.whitehouse.gov/nsc/nsct/2006/sectionIV.html (accessed 10 September 2008).

157 The White House, *National Strategy to Combat Weapons of Mass Destruction*, December 2002, p. 2.

158 The White House, *National Strategy to Combat Weapons of Mass Destruction*, December 2002, p. 4.

159 Thomas Lehrman, Acting Director, Office of Weapons of Mass Destruction, Terrorism Remarks at the Fourth Annual Toxic Industrial Chemicals/Toxic Industrial Materials Symposium, Richmond, VA, 12 July 2006. Online, available at: www.state.gov/t/isn/rls/rm/69690.htm (accessed 11 August 2008).

160 Ericson, 'Ten uncertainties of risk-management approaches to security', p. 352.

161 Ericson, 'Ten uncertainties of risk-management approaches to security', p. 345.

162 Thomas Lehrman, Remarks at the Fourth Annual Toxic Industrial Chemicals/Toxic Industrial Materials Symposium, Richmond, VA, 12 July 2006.

163 Ericson, 'Ten uncertainties of risk-management approaches to security', p. 346.

3 The Financial Action Task Force

1 William Vlcek, 'Surveillance to combat terrorist financing in Europe: whose liberty, whose security?' *European Security*, Vol. 16 No. 1, March 2007, p. 100. On 28 September 2001, the United Nations Security Council unanimously adopted Resolution (UNSCR) 1373, requiring all member states to '[f]reeze without delay funds and other financial assets or economic resources of persons who commit, or attempt to commit, terrorist acts'.

2 9/11 Public Discourse Project, Final Report on 9/11 Commission Recommendations, 12 December 2005. Online, available at: www.9–11pdp.org/press/2005–12–05_summary.pdf (accessed 10 January 2008).

3 George W. Bush, 'President freezes terrorist assets', remarks by the president, Secretary of Treasury O'Neill and Secretary of State Powell on Executive Order on Terrorist Financing (EO 13224), The Rose Garden, 20 September 2001. Online, available at: www.whitehouse.gov/news/releases/2001/09/20010924–4.html (accessed 20 October 2006).

4 This was revealed in Bob Woodward's *Bush at War*, New York: Simon & Schuster, 2002.

5 'President holds prime-time news conference', 11 October 2001. Online, available at: www.whitehouse.gov/news/releases/2001/10/20011011–7.html (accessed 10 January 2008).

6 John Taylor, *Global Financial Warriors: The Untold Story of International Finance in the Post-9/11 World*, New York: W.W. Norton, 2007.

7 US Treasury, 'Counter terrorist financing rewards program' Online, available at: www.rewardsforjustice.net/index.cfm?page=Treasury&language=english (accessed 15 September 2008).

8 John Snow, 'Financial intelligence', *Washington Post*, 14 April 2006.
9 Juan Carlos Zarate, 'Bankrupting terrorists', *E-Journal USA The Global War on Terrorist Finance*, September 2004.
10 A statement made by Treasury Under Secretary for Enforcement Jimmy Gurule, in 'Treasury's Gurule on strategy to fight money laundering', *US Department of State: International Information Programs*, 22 October 2001.
11 Martin Navias, 'Finance warfare and international terrorism', *Political Quarterly*, Vol. 73 No. 1, August 2002, p. 77.
12 See Taylor, *Global FinancialWarriors*, 2007.
13 Wolfsberg Statement on suppression of the financing of terrorism, 11 January 2002. Online, available at: www.wolfsberg-principles.com/pdf/ws_on_terrorism.pdf (accessed 10 January 2008).
14 FATF, *Annual Report 2001/02*, p. 6.
15 Taylor, *Global Financial Warriors*, 2007, p. 28.
16 Council on Foreign Relations, *The War on Terrorism: The Financial Front*, Transcript, 10 January 2007. Online, available at: www.cfr.org/publication/12432/war_on_terrorism.html (accessed 4 April 2008).
17 Louise Amoore and Marieke de Goede, 'Governance, risk, and dataveillance in the war on terror', *Crime, Law and Social Change*, Vol. 43, No. 2–3, 2005 p. 178.
18 FATF, *Money Laundering and Terrorist Financing Risk Assessment Strategies*, 18 June 2008, p. 2. Online, available at: www.fatf-gafi.org/dataoecd/46/24/40978997.pdf (accessed 5 July 2008).
19 FATF, *Annual Report 2007–08*, 30 June 2008, p. 20.
20 Michael Levi, 'Lessons for countering terrorist financing from the war on serious and organised crime', in Thomas Biersteker and Sue E. Eckert (eds), *Countering the Financing of Terrorism*, London: Routledge, 2007 p. 277.
21 FATF, *Money Laundering and Terrorist Financing Vulnerabilities of Commercial Websites and Internet Payment Systems*, 18 June 2008, p. 4. Online, available at: www.fatf-gafi.org/dataoecd/57/21/40997818.pdf (accessed 22 December 2008).
22 British Bankers' Association. Online, available at: www.bba.org.uk/bba/jsp/polopoly. jsp?d=143&a=11848 (accessed 19 September 2008).
23 FATF, *RBA Guidance for Accountants*, 17 June 2008, p. 5. Online, available at: www.fatf-gafi.org/dataoecd/19/44/41092947.pdf (accessed 23 July 2008).
24 Jimmy Gurule, 'The global effort to stop terrorist financing', *American Internationalism*, August 2003. Online, available at: http://usinfo.state.gov/journals/itps/0803/ijpe/pj81gurule.htm (accessed 5 August 2008).
25 Vlcek, 'Surveillance to combat terrorist financing in Europe', p. 100.
26 'Remarks on protecting the homeland: meeting challenges and looking forward', George Washington University, 14 December 2006. Online, available at: www.dhs. gov/xnews/speeches/sp_1166137816540.shtm (accessed 2 July 2008).
27 FATF, *Annual Report 2007–08*, p. 1.
28 Current membership: Argentina; Australia; Austria; Belgium; Brazil; Canada; Denmark; European Commission; Finland; France; Germany; Greece; Gulf Co-operation Council (Bahrain; Kuwait; Oman; Qatar; Saudi Arabia; United Arab Emirates); Ireland; Italy; Japan; Luxembourg; Mexico; Kingdom of the Netherlands; New Zealand; Norway; Portugal; Russian Federation; Singapore; South Africa; Spain; Sweden; Switzerland; Turkey; United Kingdom; United States.
29 FATF, *Annual Report 2001–02*, June 2002, p. 1.
30 For instance see Martin Levi, 'Lessons for countering terrorist financing from the war on serious and organised crime'.
31 Bruce Zagaris, 'The merging of the anti-money laundering and counter-terrorism financial enforcement regimes after September 11, 2001', *Berkeley Journal of International Law*, Vol. 22 No. 1, 2004, p. 141.

32 The White House, *National Strategy for Combating Terrorism*, 'Institutionalizing our strategy for long-term success', July 2006. Online, available at: www.whitehouse.gov/ nsc/nsct/2006/sectionVI.html (accessed 15 September 2008).

33 Peter Shields, 'When the "information revolution" and the US security state collide', *New Media and Society*, Vol. 7 No. 4, 2005, pp. 483–512.

34 Navias, 'Finance warfare', p. 77.

35 Anne Clunan, 'The fight against terrorist financing', *Political Science Quarterly*, Vol. 121 No. 4, 2006, p. 595.

36 Clunan, 'The fight against terrorist financing', p. 581.

37 Biersteker and Eckert, *Countering the Financing of Terrorism*, p. 293.

38 Biersteker and Eckert, *Countering the Financing of Terrorism*, p. 253

39 *The United Nations Global Counter-terrorism Strategy*, Section II.10, 2006. Online, available at: www.un.org/terrorism/strategy-counter-terrorism.shtml (accessed 10 September 2008).

40 FATF, *Annual Report 1991/92*, Annex, p. 31.

41 FATF, *Annual Report 1997/98*, p. 34.

42 Vlcek, 'Surveillance to combat terrorist financing in Europe', p. 100.

43 *Speech Before the Anti-Money Laundering Compliance Conference*, Securities Industry Association, New York, 4 March 2004. Online, available at: www.fincen. gov/foxsia030404.pdf (accessed 22 December 2008).

44 Michael Power, *The Risk Management of Everything*, London: Demos, 2004, p. 21.

45 FATF, *The 40 Recommendations*, 2003. Online, available at: www.fatf-gafi.org/ dataoecd/7/40/34849567.pdf (accessed 12 January 2008).

46 FATF, *Guidance on the Risk-based Approach to Combating Money Laundering and Terrorist Financing*, 2007, p. 5. Online, available at: www.fatf-gafi.org/ dataoecd/43/46/38960576.pdf (accessed 10 January 2008).

47 FATF, *RBA Guidance for Accountants*, 17 June 2008, p. 5. Online, available at: www.fatf-gafi.org/dataoecd/19/44/41092947.pdf (accessed 23 July 2008).

48 FATF, *The 40 Recommendations*, 'Introduction'.

49 Zagaris, 'The merging of the anti-money laundering and counter-terrorism regimes', p. 156.

50 The Egmont Group is an organisation focused on assisting and encouraging the exchange of financial intelligence involving Financial Intelligence Units from over 100 countries worldwide.

51 FATF, *Money Laundering and Terrorist Financing Typologies*, 2004–05, p. 92.

52 Jason Sharman, 'Power and discourse in policy diffusion: anti-money laundering in developing states', *International Studies Quarterly*, Vol. 52 No. 3, 2008 p. 641.

53 FATF, *Annual Report*, 2005–06, p. 4.

54 FATF, *Annual Report*, 2005–06, p. 5.

55 Mark Pieth, 'Financing of terrorism: follow the money', *European Journal of Law Reform*, Vol. 4 No. 2, 2002, pp. 365–376.

56 FATF, *Annual Report 2007–08*, p. 21, 30 June 2008.

57 FATF, *Annual Report 2007–08*, 'Foreword', 30 June 2008. Online, available at: www.fatf-gafi.org/dataoecd/58/0/41141361.pdf (accessed 4 July 2008).

58 FATF, *Guidance on the Risk-based Approach*, p. 1.

59 FATF, *Guidance on the Risk-based Approach*, p. 10.

60 Mark Pieth and Gemma Aiolfi, 'The private sector becomes active: the Wolfsberg Process', *Journal of Financial Crime*, Vol. 10 No. 4, 2003, pp. 359–365.

61 'Global banks: global standards', *Wolfsberg AML Principles*. Online, available at: www.wolfsberg-principles.com/ (accessed 10 January 2008).

62 Pieth and Aiolfi 'The private sector'.

63 British Bankers' Association. Online, available at: www.bba.org.uk/bba/jsp/polopoly. jsp?d=143&a=11848 (accessed 19 September 2008).

64 See for instance FATF, *RBA Guidance for Accountants*.

65 Amoore and de Goede, 'Governance, risk, and dataveillance in the war on terror', p. 177.
66 Amoore and de Goede, 'Governance, risk, and dataveillance in the war on terror', pp. 178–180.
67 FATF, *Guidance on the Risk-based*, p. 28.
68 New Zealand Society of Risk Management, 'Process of risk management'. Online, available at: www.risksociety.org.nz/what_is_risk_management/index.php?page=process_risk_management (accessed 10 January 2008).
69 Remarks at George Washington University, 16 March 2005. Online, available at: www.dhs.gov/xnews/speeches/speech_0245.shtm (accessed 12 September 2008).
70 John Hobson and Leonard Seabrooke (eds), *Everyday Politics of the World Economy*, Cambridge: Cambridge University Press, 2007.
71 Sharman, 'Power and discourse in policy diffusion: anti-money laundering in developing states', p. 653.
72 William Vlcek, 'Surveillance to combat terrorist financing in Europe', p. 100.
73 Rainer Hulsse, 'Creating demand for global governance: the making of a global money-laundering problem', *Global Society*, Vol. 21 No. 2, April 2007, p. 155.
74 Hulsse, 'Creating demand for global governance'.
75 Sharman, 'Power and discourse in policy diffusion', p. 641.
76 Power, *The Risk Management of Everything*, p. 29.
77 Ibrahim Warde, *The Price of Fear: The Truth Behind the Financial War on Terror*, London: University of California Press, 2007.
78 Hulsse, 'Creating demand for global governance', p. 155.
79 Hulsse, 'Creating demand for global governance', pp. 155–178.
80 Hulsse, 'Creating demand for global governance', p. 156.
81 John Braithwaite and Peter Drahos, *Global Business Regulation*, Cambridge: Cambridge University Press, 2000, p. 553.
82 Hulsse, 'Creating demand for global governance', p. 168.
83 Hulsse, 'Creating demand for global governance', p. 175.
84 Hulsse, 'Creating demand for global governance', p. 169.
85 Hulsse, 'Creating demand for global governance', pp. 167–168.
86 Hulsse, 'Creating demand for global governance', p. 169.
87 Hulsse, 'Creating demand for global governance', p. 171.
88 Hulsse, 'Creating demand for global governance', p. 173.
89 Hulsse, 'Creating demand for global governance', p. 177.
90 Stephen Gill, 'American transparency capitalism and human security: a contradiction in terms?' *Global Change, Peace and Security*, Vol. 15 No. 1, February 2003, pp. 9–25.
91 Henry Willis, 'Challenges of applying risk management to terrorism security policy', *Testimony to the House Homeland Security Committee*, 24 June 2008, p. 5. Online, available at: www.rand.org/pubs/testimonies/2008/RAND_CT310.pdf (accessed 1 August 2008).
92 Hulsse, 'Creating demand for global governance', p. 170.
93 Taylor, *Global Financial Warriors*, pp. 12, 18. We are grateful to William Vlcek for pointing this out to us.
94 Sharman, 'Power and discourse in policy diffusion', p. 652.
95 Marieke de Goede, 'The politics of preemption and the war on terror in Europe', *European Journal of International Relations*, Vol. 14 No. 1, 2008, pp. 161–185.
96 Sharman, 'Power and discourse in policy diffusion', p. 652.
97 Sharman, 'Power and discourse in policy diffusion', pp. 635–656.
98 FATF, *Annual Review of NCCT 2005–06*, 2006, p. 2.
99 FATF, *Annual Review 2006*, pp. 2–3.
100 Jackie Johnson, 'Repairing legitimacy after blacklisting by the Financial Action Task Force', *Journal of Money Laundering Control*, Vol. 7 No. 1, 2003, pp. 38–49.

101 Sharman, 'Power and discourse in policy diffusion', p. 647.
102 Sharman, 'Power and discourse in policy diffusion', p. 650.
103 Sharman, 'Power and discourse in policy diffusion', p. 651.
104 Hulsse, 'Creating demand for global governance', p. 174.
105 Hulsse, 'Creating demand for global governance', p. 164.
106 Sharman, 'Power and discourse in policy diffusion', p. 636.
107 Bretton Woods official quoted in Sharman, 'Power and discourse in policy diffusion', p. 646.
108 Sharman, 'Power and discourse in policy diffusion', p. 644.
109 Sharman, 'Power and discourse in policy diffusion', p. 643.
110 Sharman, 'Power and discourse in policy diffusion', p. 644.
111 Quoted in Sharman, 'Power and discourse in policy diffusion', p. 651.
112 Sharman, 'Power and discourse in policy diffusion', p. 645.
113 Sharman, 'Power and discourse in policy diffusion', p. 646.
114 William Vlcek, 'Money, terror and protecting the west', *Round Table*, Vol. 97 No. 395, April 2008, p. 305.
115 Vlcek, 'Money, terror and protecting the west', p. 310.
116 Vlcek, 'Money, terror and protecting the west', p. 311.
117 Eleni Tsingou, 'Targeting money laundering: global approach or diffusion of authority', in Elke Krahmann (ed.), *New Threats and New Actors in International Security*, Basingstoke: Palgrave, 2005, pp. 101–102.
118 De Goede, 'The politics of preemption', p. 175.
119 De Goede, 'The politics of preemption', p. 176.
120 Judith Butler, *Precarious Life: The Powers of Mourning and Violence*, London: Verso, 2004 p. 6, cited in de Goede, 'The politics of preemption', p. 176.
121 Mona Atia, 'In whose interest? Financial surveillance and the circuits of exception in the war on terror', *Environment and Planning D: Society and Space*, Vol. 25 No. 3, 2007, pp. 447–475.
122 Richard Ericson, *Crime in an Insecure World*, Cambridge: Polity, 2007, pp. 31, 35.
123 Amoore and de Goede, 'Governance, risk, and dataveillance in the war on terror', p. 183.
124 R.T. Naylor, *Satanic Purses: Money, Myth and Misinformation in the War on Terror*, Toronto: McGill-Queen's University Press, 2006.
125 See Richard V. Ericson, 'Ten uncertainties of risk-management approaches to security', *Canadian Journal of Criminology and Criminal Justice*, Vol. 48 No. 3, June 2006, p. 353. Also Michael Ignatieff, *The Lesser Evil: Political Ethics in an Age of Terror*, Princeton, NJ: Princeton University Press, 2004.
126 Vlcek, 'Surveillance to combat terrorist financing in Europe', p. 110.
127 Vlcek, 'Surveillance to combat terrorist financing in Europe', p. 109.
128 Vlcek, 'Surveillance to combat terrorist financing in Europe', p. 100.
129 FATF, *Guidance on the Risk-based Approach*, p. 2.
130 Robert Castel, 'From dangerousness to risk', in Graham Burchill, Colin Gordon and Peter Miller (eds), *The Foucault Effect: Studies in Governmentality*, London: Harvester Wheatsheaf, 1991, p. 288.
131 Levi, 'Lessons for countering terrorist financing', p. 269.
132 FATF, *Annual Report 2007–08*, 'Foreword', p. ii, 30 June 2008.
133 Levi, 'Lessons for countering terrorist financing from the war on serious and organised crime'.
134 The White House, *9/11 Five Years Later: Successes and Challenges – Foreword*, Washington, DC, 2006. Online, available at: www.whitehouse.gov/nsc/waronterror/2006/sectionI.html (accessed 10 January 2008).
135 William J. Fox, *Statement Before the United States House of Representatives*, Committee on Financial Services, 16 June, 2004. Online, available at: www.fincen.gov/hfscommitteestatement061604.pdf (accessed 5 July 2008).

136 Levi, 'Lessons for countering terrorist financing', p. 271 (italics added).
137 9/11 Commission, *Monograph on Terrorist Financing*, 2004, p. 16 (italics added). Online, available at: http://govinfo.library.unt.edu/911/staff_statements/index.htm (accessed 10 January 2008).
138 FATF, *Guidance on the Risk-based Approach*, p. 10.
139 FATF, *Guidance on the Risk-based Approach*, p. 3 (italics added).
140 Douglas Farah, 'Al Qaeda and the gemstone trade', in Biersteker and Eckert, *Countering the Financing of Terrorism*, p. 202 (italics added).
141 Text of letter dated 9 July 2005. Online, available at: www.globalsecurity.org/security/library/report/2005/zawahiri-zarqawi-letter_9jul2005.htm (accessed 10 January 2008).
142 'Looking in the wrong places – financing terrorism', *Economist*, 22 October 2005, pp. 81–83.
143 Peter Reuter and Edwin Truman, *Chasing Dirty Money: The Fight Against Money-laundering*, Washington, DC: Institute for International Economics, 2004, p. 7.
144 Sharman, 'Power and discourse in policy diffusion', p. 642.
145 Biersteker and Eckert, 'Conclusion' in Biersteker and Eckert, *Countering the Financing of Terrorism*, p. 292.
146 Levi 'Lessons for countering terrorist financing', p. 267.
147 Vlcek, 'Surveillance to combat terrorist financing in Europe', p. 114.
148 Biersteker and Eckert, 'Conclusion' in Biersteker and Eckert, *Countering the Financing of Terrorism*, p. 292.
149 FATF, *RBA Guidance for Accountants'*, 17 June 2008, p. 6.
150 Paul Williams, 'Terrorist financing and organised crime: nexus, appropriation or transformation' in Biersteker and Eckerts, *Countering Financing of Terrorism*.
151 Vlcek, 'Surveillance to combat terrorist financing in Europe', pp. 110–111.
152 Ericson, 'Ten uncertainties of risk-management', p. 345.
153 Vlcek, 'Surveillance to combat terrorist financing in Europe', p. 112.
154 Levi, 'Lessons for countering terrorist financing', pp. 267–268.
155 Levi, 'Lessons for countering terrorist financing', p. 272.
156 Clunan, 'The fight against terrorist financing', p. 596.
157 James Fallows, 'Declaring victory', *Atlantic Monthly*, September 2006. Online, available at: www.theatlantic.com/doc/200609/fallows_victory/2 (accessed 12 November 2007).
158 Fallows, 'Declaring victory'.
159 Fallows, 'Declaring victory'.
160 Richard Clarke cited in Fallows, 'Declaring victory'.
161 Taylor, *Global Financial Warriors*, p. 8.
162 'Basel Committee issues consultative document on consolidated KYC risk management', 20 August 2003. Online, available at: www.bis.org/press/p030820.htm (accessed 11 January 2008).
163 Interview with Jeremy Paxman on *BBC Newsnight*, 21 September 2001. Online, available at: http://news.bbc.co.uk/2/hi/events/newsnight/1563074.stm (accessed 11 January 2008).
164 Levi, 'Lessons for countering terrorist financing', pp. 275–276.
165 Levi, 'Lessons for countering terrorist financing', p. 278.
166 Vlcek, 'Surveillance to combat terrorist financing in Europe', p. 107.
167 Wolfsberg Group, 'Wolfsberg statement – guidance on a risk based approach for managing money laundering risks', March 2006, p. 1.
168 Sharman, 'Power and discourse in policy diffusion', p. 640.
169 Levi, 'Lessons for countering terrorist financing', p. 269.
170 Quoted in 'Brown steps up fight against money laundering', *Guardian*, 15 October 2001. Online, available at: www.guardian.co.uk/world/2001/oct/15/september11.usa1 (accessed 9 January 2002).

171 See for instance Amitav Acharya and Arabinda Acharya, 'The myth of the second front: localising the "war on terror" in Southeast Asia', *Washington Quarterly*, Vol. 30 No. 4, Autumn 2007.

172 The White House, *National Strategy for Combating Terrorism*, 'Institutionalizing our strategy for long-term success', July 2006. Online, available at: www.whitehouse.gov/nsc/nsct/2006/sectionVI.html (15 September 2008).

173 Levi, 'Lessons for countering terrorist financing', pp. 267–268. Also see Michael Kenny, *From Pablo to Osama: Trafficking and Terrorist Networks, Government Bureaucracies, and Competitive Adaptation*, University Park, PA: Penn State University Press, 2007.

174 Vlcek, 'Surveillance to combat terrorist financing in Europe', p. 113.

4 The Proliferation Security Initiative

1 See for example Robert J. Bunker Weapons of mass disruption and terrorism', *Terrorism and Political Violence*, Vol 17 No. 3, 2005.

2 Sharon Squassoni, 'Proliferation Security Initiative (PSI)', *CRS Report for Congress*, Order RS21881, 14 September 2006, p. 1.

3 Andrew C. Winner, 'The Proliferation Security Initiative: the new face of interdiction', *Washington Quarterly*, Vol. 28 No. 2, Spring 2005, pp. 129–143.

4 John C. Rood, Acting Under Secretary of State for Arms Control and International Security Remarks at the Twenty-fifth International Workshop on Global Security Rome, Italy, 21 June 2008.

5 John C. Rood, Acting Under Secretary of State for Arms Control and International Security Remarks at the Twenty-fifth International Workshop on Global Security Rome, Italy, 21 June 2008.

6 Squassoni, 'Proliferation Security Initiative (PSI)', p. 5.

7 Testimony before the House International Relations Committee, 'The Bush administration's nonproliferation policy: successes and future challenges', 30 March 2004.

8 Jonathan Tucker, *War of Nerves: A History of Chemical Weapons from World War 1 to Al-Qaeda*, New York: Pantheon, 2006.

9 *Convention (II) with Respect to the Laws and Customs of War on Land*, The Hague, II, 29 July 1899. Online, available at: www.opcw.org/chemical-weapons-convention/related-international-agreements/chemical-warfare-and-chemical-weapons/hague-convention-of-1899/ (accessed 12 September 2008).

10 *Convention (IV) respecting the Laws and Customs of War on Land and its annex: Regulations concerning the Laws and Customs of War on Land*, The Hague, 18 October 1907. Online, available at: www.opcw.org/chemical-weapons-convention/related-international-agreements/chemical-warfare-and-chemical-weapons/hague-convention-of-1907/ (accessed 12 September 2008).

11 The Geneva Protocol, 1928. Online, available at: www.opcw.org/chemical-weapons-convention/related-international-agreements/chemical-warfare-and-chemical-weapons/the-geneva-protocol/ (accessed 12 September 2008).

12 One study notes the use of such weapons by Italy in Abyssinia in 1935, by Japan in China in 1936, Egypt in Yemen 1963–67 and 1980–88 by Iraq against Iran. See Demetrius Evison, David Hinsley and Paul Rice, 'Chemical weapons', *British Medical Journal*, Vol. 324, 2002, pp. 332–335.

13 See for discussion Malcolm Dando, 'Scientific and technological change and the future of CWC: the problem of non-lethal weapons', in the *CWC Conference Review*, No. 4, 2002, online, available at: www.unidir.ch/pdf/articles/pdf-art1824.pdf (accessed 3 September 2008), and Nick Lewer, 'Non-lethal weapons', *Medicine, Conflict and Survival*, Vol. 11 No. 2, 1995, pp. 78–90.

14 Jozef Goldbalt, *Can Nuclear Proliferation be Stopped?* Geneva: Geneva International Peace Research Institute, 2007, p. 1.

15 For an overview of the arguments involved see Lyle J. Goldstein, *Preventive Attack and Weapons of Mass Destruction: A Comparative Historical Analysis*, Stanford, CA: Stanford University Press, 2006, Chapter 2.

16 President Dwight D. Eisenhower, 'Address to the 470th plenary meeting of the United Nations General Assembly', 8 December 1953. Online, available at: www.iaea.org/ About/history_speech.html (accessed 13 September 2008).

17 David Fisher, *History of the IAEA: The First Forty Years*, Vienna: IAEA, 1997.

18 'Nuclear weapons: who has what at a glance', Factsheet, Arms Control Association. Online, available at: www.armscontrol.org/factsheets/Nuclearweaponswhohaswhat (accessed 11 September 2001).

19 John C. Rood, Acting Under Secretary of State for Arms Control and International Security Remarks at the Twenty-fifth International Workshop on Global Security Rome, Italy, 21 June 2008.

20 See Donna Miles, 'Report provides strategic vision for countering WMD', *American Forces Press Services*, 24 March 2006. Online, available at: www.defenselink.mil/ news/Mar2006/20060324_4592.html (accessed 8 April 2006).

21 Remarks at US–NATO Missions Annual Conference, Brussels, Belgium, 19 January 2002.

22 The White House, *National Strategy to Combat Weapons of Mass Destruction*, December 2002, p. 1.

23 Cited in Jack Boureston, 'Al Qaeda's WMD capabilities', *Strategic Insights*, Vol. 1 No. 7, September 2002. Online, available at: www.ccc.nps.navy.mil/si/sept02/wmd. asp (accessed 1 February 2003).

24 David Albright, Kathryn Buehler and Holly Higgins, 'Bin Laden and the bomb', *Bulletin of Atomic Scientists*, January/February 2002, pp. 23–24.

25 Quoted in 'Al-Qaida weapon access worries U.S.', *Guardian*, 18 July 2002.

26 Testimony before the Senate Committee on Intelligence, 6 February 2002.

27 See Akiva J. Lovenz, 'Al-Qaeda's maritime threat', Maritime Terrorism Research Centre, 15 April 2007. Online, available at: www.maritimeterrorism.com/wp-content/ uploads/2008/01/al-qaedas-maritime-threat.pdf (accessed 1 October 2008).

28 As quoted on Eagle Speak, 8 May 2008. Online, available at: www.eaglespeak. us/2008/05/al-qaeda-calling-for-choke-point.html (accessed 16 September 2008).

29 Peter Grier and Faye Bowers, 'How Al Qaeda might strike the US by sea', *Christian Science Monitor*, 15 May 2003. Online, available at: www.csmonitor.com/2003/0515/ p02s02-usgn.html (accessed 16 August 2008).

30 Grier and Bowers, 'How Al Qaeda might strike the US by sea'.

31 The White House, *National Security Strategy of the United States*, Section V, Washington, DC, 2006.

32 Richard Lugar, 'The Lugar doctrine', 6 December 2001. Online, available at: http://lugar.senate.gov/bio/doctrine.cfm (accessed 4 February 2002).

33 Canadian Department of Defence, 'Backgrounder: the Proliferation Security Initiative', 19 May 2006. Online, available at: www.dnd.ca/site/Newsroom/view_news_e.asp? id=1329 (accessed 9 July 2006).

34 'Proliferation Security Initiative: statement of interdiction principles', agreed at Paris, 4 September 2003. Online, available at: www.whitehouse.gov/news/releases/2003/09/ 20030904-11.html (accessed 12 August 2008).

35 For example UNSCR 814, 1993, highlighted the lack of a responsible authority within the territory of Somalia as one of the reasons that international forces were required to restore some semblance of the rule of law and to allow the delivery of vital humanitarian aid. Online, available at: http://daccessdds.un.org/doc/ UNDOC/GEN/N93/226/18/IMG/N9322618.pdf?OpenElement (accessed 1 August 2008).

36 Judge Van Den Wyngaert, *Case Concerning the Arrest Warrant of 11 April 2000 (Democratic Republic of Congo v Belgium), Judgement*, as quoted in Douglas

Guilfoyle, 'Maritime interdiction of weapons of mass destruction', *Journal of Conflict and Security Law*, Vol. 12 No. 1, 2007, p. 4.

37 See for discussion Larry J. Sechrest, 'Privateering and national defense: naval warfare for profit' in Hans-Hermanne Hoppe (ed.), *The Myth of National Defense: Essays on the Theory and History of Security Production*, Auburn, AL: Ludvig Von Mises Institute, 2003, pp. 239–274.

38 See for discussion I. Nelson Rose, 'Casinos on cruiseships, why not on airplanes?' *Gaming Law Review*, Vol. 10 No. 6, 2006, pp. 519–520.

39 Nelson Rose, 'Casinos on cruiseships, why not on airplanes?', p. 519.

40 See Art. 110, UN Convention on the Law of the Sea. Online, available at: www.un.org/Depts/los/convention_agreements/texts/unclos/closindx.htm (accessed 4 August 2008).

41 Guilfoyle, 'Maritime interdiction', p. 6.

42 Andreas Persbo and Ian Davis, *Sailing into Uncharted Waters? The Proliferation Security Initiative and the Law of the Sea*, British American Security Information Council, Research Report 2004.2, June 2004, p. 8.

43 James Cotton, 'The Proliferation Security Initiative and North Korea: legality and limitations of a coalition strategy', *Security Dialogue*, Vol. 36 No. 2, 2005, p. 193.

44 See for discussion Cotton, 'The Proliferation Security Initiative and North Korea', pp. 196–197.

45 Cotton, 'The Proliferation Security Initiative and North Korea', p. 198.

46 Press briefing, 11 December 2002, as quoted in Michael Byers, 'Policing the high seas: the Proliferation Security Initiative', *American Journal of International Law*, Vol. 98 No. 3, 2004, p. 526.

48 James Cotton, 'The Proliferation Security Initiative', p. 196.

49 See US Department of Defense, *1996 Annual Defense Report*, Chapter 7: 'Counter-proliferation and Treaty Activities'. Online, available at: www.dod.mil/execsec/adr96/toc.html (accessed 10 September 2008).

50 See George Perkovich, 'Bush's nuclear revolution: a regime change in nonproliferation', *Foreign Affairs*, Vol. 82, No. 2, 2003, pp. 2–8. For an alternative account of disarmament see William J. Long and Suzette R. Grillot, 'Ideas, beliefs, and nuclear policies: the cases of South Africa and Ukraine', *Non-Proliferation Review*, Spring 2000, pp. 24–40.

51 Jason D. Ellis, 'The best defense: counterproliferaton and U.S. national strategy', *Washington Quarterly*, Vol. 26 No. 2, 2003, pp. 129–130.

52 Senior US Official cited in Carla Anne Robbins, 'Why U.S. gave U.N. no role in plan to halt arms ships', *Wall Street Journal*, 21 October 2003, p. 1.

53 John C. Rood, Acting Under Secretary of State for Arms Control and International Security, Remarks at the Twenty-fifth International Workshop on Global Security Rome, Italy, 21 June 2008.

54 See Sheryl Gay Stolberg, 'Threats and responses: Washington talk; an order of fries, please, but do hold the French', *New York Times*, 12 March 2003.

55 Rumsfeld, 'Department of Defense newsbriefing', 25 September 2001.

56 Andrew C. Winner, 'The Proliferation Security Initiative: the new face of interdiction', *Washington Quarterly*, Vol. 28 No. 2, Spring 2005, p. 130.

57 Winner, 'The Proliferation Security Initiative', p. 132.

58 Winner, 'The Proliferation Security Initiative', p. 130.

59 John Rood, Acting Under Secretary of State for Arms Control and International Security Foreign Press Center, Roundtable Briefing, Washington, DC, 27 May 2008.

60 As issued in a statement by the British government as part of its chairman's conclusions following a meeting of PSI participants in London in October 2003, as quoted in 'The Proliferation Security Initiative (PSI) at a glance', Arms Control Association. Online, available at: www.armscontrol.org/factsheets/PSI (accessed 15 August 2008).

61 Winner, 'The Proliferation Security Initiative', p. 130.
62 'Chairman's statement at the first anniversary PSI meeting', Foreign Ministry of Poland, 1 June 2004. Online, available at: www.nuclearfiles.org/menu/key-issues/nuclear-weapons/issues/proliferation/psi/2004–06–01_krakow-chairmans-statement_fco_gov_uk.pdf (accessed 10 August 2008).
63 Adam Ingram remarks on 'Preventing WMD proliferation', PSI Maritime Industry Conference, London, 25 August 2006.
64 Patricia McNerney, Principal Deputy Assistant Secretary of State for International Security and Nonproliferation, Testimony before the HFAC Subcommittee on Terrorism, Nonproliferation and Trade, 18 April 2007.
65 Press release, 'London PSI meeting advances public private partnership to combat WMD proliferation', Office of the Spokesman, US Department of State, 26 September 2006. Online, available at: www.state.gov/r/pa/prs/ps/2006/73177.htm (accessed 21 September 2008).
66 'The Proliferation Security Initiative (PSI) – maritime industry workshop', HMRC Ref: JCCC(07) 14. Online, available at: http://customs.hmrc.gov.uk/channelsPortal-WebApp/channelsPortalWebApp.portal?_nfpb=true&_pageLabel=pageLibrary_Pub licNoticesAndInfoSheets&propertyType=document&columns=1&id=HMCE_PROD1_027044 (accessed 21 September 2008).
67 John Rood, Acting Under Secretary of State for Arms Control and International Security Foreign Press Center, Roundtable Briefing, Washington, DC, 27 May 2008.
68 Elaine Ganley, 'French troops save 2 hostages from Somali pirates', *Associated Press*, 16 September 2008. Online, available at: http://ap.google.com/article/ALeqM5hMp1INkR0b8KWv0f2qtYIXFtHafQD937SJCO1 (accessed 17 September 2008).
69 Jeffrey Gettleman, 'Pirated arms freighter cornered by U.S. Navy', *New York Times*, 30 September 2008. Online, available at: www.nytimes.com/2008/09/30/world/Africa/30pirate.html?_r=1&bl=&ei=5087&en=040eb2 (accessed 1 October 2008).
70 Press Office, US Department of Homeland Security, 'Fact sheet', 1 October 2007. Online, available at: www.cbp.gov/linkhandler/cgov/trade/cargo_security/csi/csi_fact_sheet.ctt/csi_fact_sheet.doc (accessed 20 September 2008).
71 Press Office, US Department of Homeland Security 'Fact Sheet', 2007.
72 Jon D. Haveman, Ethan M. Jennings, Howard J. Shatz and Greg C. Wright, 'The Container Security Initiative and ocean container threats', *Journal of Homeland Security and Emergency Management*, Vol. 4, No. 1, 2007, p. 12.
73 Haveman *et al.*, 'The Container Security Initiative', pp. 2–3.
74 *The National Strategy for Maritime Security*, 2005. Online, available at: www.whitehouse.gov/homeland/maritime-security.html (acccesed 21 September 2008).
75 Chairman's Conclusions, PSI Meeting, London, 9–10 October 2003. Online, available at: www.fco.gov.uk/resources/en/press-release/2003/10/fco_npr_101003_strawpsiprogress (accessed 8 August 2004).
76 Cited in 'The Proliferation Security Initiative serves notice to WMD traffickers', PSI Meeting, London, 9–10 October 2003. Online, available at: www.fco.gov.uk/resources/en/press-release/2003/10/fco_npr_101003_strawpsiprogress (accessed 14 February 2005).
77 Canadian Department of Defence, 'Backgrounder: the Proliferation Security Initiative'.
78 F. Record, Acting Assistant Secretary, International Security and Nonproliferation, Statement before the House Committee on Homeland Security, Subcommittee on Prevention of Nuclear and Biological Attacks, Washington, DC, 25 May 2006. Online, available at: www.state.gov/t/isn/rls/rm/69307.htm (accessed 5 June 2006).
79 Indian Chief of Naval Staff Arun Prakash, cited in 'Proliferation Security Initiative: New Delhi discussing reservations with Washington', *Hindu*, 22 May 2005.
80 Prakash, 'Proliferation Security Initiative: New Delhi discussing reservations with Washington'.

81 James Holmes, 'Sea power with Asian characteristics: China, India and the Prolifer-ation Security Initiative', *Southeast Review of Asian Politics*, 1 January 2007.

82 Rita Grossman-Vermaas, 'Proliferation and development – exposing the link', *NATO Review*, Autumn 2007. Online, available at: www.nato.int/docu/review/2007/issue3/english/art3.html (accessed 9 November 2007).

83 These were Australia, France, Germany, Italy, Japan, the Netherlands, Poland, Portugal, Spain and the UK.

84 Erin Harbaugh, 'The Proliferation Security Initiative: counterproliferation at the crossroads', *Strategic Insights*, Vol. III No. 7, July 2004. Online, available at: www.ccc.nps.navy.mil/si/2004/jul/harbaughJul04.asp (accessed 1 September 2008).

85 'The Proliferation Security Initiative', June 2004. Online, available at: http://usinfo. state.gov/products/pubs/proliferation/ (accessed 9 November 2006).

86 Wade Boese, 'Interdiction initiative successes assessed', Arms Control Association, 2008. Online, available at: www.armscontrol.org/act/2008_07–08/interdiction (accessed 9 August 2008).

87 John Rood, Acting Under Secretary of State for Arms Control and Interna-tional Security Foreign Press Center, Roundtable Briefing, Washington, DC, 27 May 2008.

88 'PSI maritime industry workshop preventing WMD proliferation', 26 September 2006. Online, available at: www.fco.gov.uk/resources/en/pdf/pdf14/fco_fpg_intsec_prolifsecpsimari (accessed 9 January 2007).

89 Quoted in British American Security Information Council, *Proliferation Security Initiative*. Online, available at: www.basicint.org/nuclear/counterproliferation/psi.htm (accessed 8 April 2006).

90 Boese, 'Interdiction initiative successes assessed'.

91 John Rood, Acting Under Secretary of State for Arms Control and International Security Foreign Press Center, Roundtable Briefing, Washington, DC, 27 May 2008.

92 John F. Sopko, 'The changing proliferation threat', *Foreign Policy*, No. 105, Winter 1996–97, p. 4.

93 Sopko, 'The changing proliferation threat', pp. 4–5.

94 See 'Fact sheet on dirty bombs', United States Nuclear Regulatory Commission. Online, available at: www.nrc.gov/reading-rm/doc-collections/fact-sheets/dirty-bombs. html (accessed 7 September 2008).

95 See for discussion Laura Eichelberger, 'SARS and New Yorks Chinatown: the poli-tics of risk and blame during an epidemic of fear', *Social Science and Medicine*, Vol. 65 No. 6, September 2007, pp. 1284–1295.

96 *Annual Report of the Department of Defense*, Department of Defense, 1996 Chapter 7. Online, available at: www.dod.mil/execsec/adr96/chapt_7.html (accessed 15 September 2008).

97 Ido Oren and Ty Solomon, 'WMD: words of mass distraction', unpublished manuscript, presented at the ISA Annual Convention, San Francisco, March 2008, *passim*.

98 As reflected, for example, in the increasing use of UNSC sanctions against non-state actors. See Thomas G. Weiss, *Humanitarian Intervention* Polity, 2007 p. 44.

99 White House, *National Strategy to Combat Weapons of Mass Destruction* (WMD), December 2002, p. 2.

100 Statement at the PSI Meeting, Krakow, Poland, 31 May 2004.

101 Former US Senator Jim Talent, co-chair of the Commission on the Prevention of Weapons of Mass Destruction Proliferation and Terrorism (WMD), remarks at public hearing, New York, 11 September 2008. Online, available at: www.preventwmd.gov/9_11_2008/ (accessed 1 October 2008).

102 Stephen Flynn, 'The continued vulnerability of the global maritime transportation system', Written Testimony before the House of Representatives, 9 March 2006. Online, available at: www.cfr.org/publication/10074/ (accessed 28 May 2007).

103 Office of the Press Secretary, White House, 'Fact sheet: Proliferation Security Initiative: statement of interdiction principles', 4 September 2003. Online, available at: www.state.gov/t/isn/rls/fs/23764.htm (accessed 10 September 2004).
104 Mark J. Valencia, 'Is the PSI really the cornerstone of a new international norm?' *Naval War College Review*, Vol. 59 No. 4, Autumn 2006, p. 128.
105 Oren and Solomon, 'WMD: words of mass distraction', p. 33.
106 Wade Boese, 'Interview with John Bolton', Arms Control Association, 2003. Online, available at: www.armscontrol.org/aca/midmonth/2003/November/Bolton (accessed 17 September 2008).
107 John Bolton, as quoted in Andreas Persbo and Ian Davis, 'Sailing into uncharted waters? The Proliferation Security Initiative and the Law of the Sea', *BASIC Research Report*, British American Security Council, Research Report no. 2, June 2004, p. 128.
108 Prakash, 'Proliferation Security Initiative: New Delhi discussing reservations with Washington'.
109 M. Valencia, 'Bring the PSI into the UN', *Nautilus Institute Policy Online Forum*, 05–101A, 20 December 2005. Online, available at: www.nautilus.org/fora/security/05101Valencia.html (accessed 23 January 2006).
110 Arms Control Association Fact Sheet, 'The Proliferation Security Initiative at a Glance', October 2007. Online, available at: www.armscontrol.org/factsheets/PSI (accessed 15 November 2007).
111 Speech to the meeting of the PSI, Brisbane, 9 July 2003. Online, available at: www.acronym.org.uk/docs/0307/doc04.htm#02 (accessed 24 August 2004).
112 M. Richardson, The PSI and Counterproliferation in the AsiaPacific Region, Address to the NZIIA, Victoria University, New Zealand, 20 November 2007. Online, available at: www.victoria.ac.nz/nziia/assets/talks/wn/M_Richardson_20Nov2007%20Wgtn%20BrNZIIA.pdf (accessed 12 March 2008).
113 Andrew K. Semmel, 'The U.S. Perspective on UN Security Council Resolution 1540', Remarks, Asia-Pacific Nuclear Safeguards and Security Conference, Sydney, 8 November 2004. Online, available at: www.state.gov/t/np/rls/rm/38256.htm (accessed 30 January 2005).
114 Statement by the Press Secretary: Principles for the Proliferation Security Initiative, 4 September 2003. Online, available at: www.state.gov/t/isn/rls/prsrl/23809.htm (accessed 18 January 2004).
115 Statement by the president on the fifth anniversary of the Proliferation Security Initiative, 28 May 2008.
116 John Pike, as quoted in Persbo and Davis, 'Sailing into unchartered waters', p. 38.
117 Persbo and Davis, 'Sailing into unchartered waters', p. 40.
118 Persbo and Davis, 'Sailing into unchartered waters', p. 40.
119 Again the BASIC report in discussing intelligence sharing exercises notes that the results of exercises undertaken by participating states remain out of the public domain. Persbo and Davis, 'Sailing into unchartered waters', p. 39.
120 John Bolton in an interview with Wade Boese of the Arms Control Association argued that the focus of the PSI would be on rogue states and terrorists because they 'pose the most immediate threat', 2003. Online, available at: www.armscontrol.org/print/1437 (accessed 10 August 2008).
121 Secretary of State Condoleeza Rice, 'Remarks on the second anniversary of the Proliferation Security Initiative', 31 May 2005. Online, available at: www.state.gov/secretary/rm/2005/46951.htm (accessed 8 June 2008).
122 Wade Boese, 'Interdiction initiative successes assessed'.
123 Ulrich Beck, 'The terrorist threat revisited', *Theory Culture and Society*, Vol. 19 No. 4, 2002, p. 41.
124 John Rood, Acting Under Secretary of State for Arms Control and International Security Foreign Press Center, Roundtable Briefing, Washington, DC, 27 May 2008.

125 Wade Boese, 'Interdiction initiative successes assessed'. For a more jaundiced view of the PSI and its effectiveness, see Jeffrey Lewis, 'PSI: the record to date', 6 June 2005. Online, available at: www.armscontrolwonk.com/629/psi-the-record-to-date (accessed 7 July 2008).

126 Harbaugh, 'The Proliferation Security Initiative'.

127 Kong Quan, Chinese Foreign Ministry spokesperson, as quoted in Wade Boese 'The Proliferation Security Initiative: an interview with John Bolton'. Online, available at: www.armscontrol.org/print/1437 (accessed 10 August 2008).

128 Winner, 'The Proliferation Security Initiative', p. 133.

129 Kofi Annan, 'Global strategy for fighting terrorism', Madrid Summit, Spain, 10 March 2005.

5 Aviation security

1 Parts of this chapter were previously published in Kenneth McDonagh, 'Governing global security in the departure lounge', *Journal of Global Change and Governance*, Vol. 1 No. 3, 2008. Online, available at: http://andromeda.rutgers.edu/~gdga/JGCG/archive/Summer08/MCDONAGH.pdf (accessed 22 December 2008).

2 Mark Salter, 'Imagining numbers: risk, quantification and aviation security', *Security Dialogue*, Vol. 39 No. 2–3, 2008, p. 245.

3 Salter, 'Imagining numbers', p. 243.

4 Paul Seidenstat, 'Terrorism, airport security, and the private sector', *Review of Policy Research*, Vol. 21 No. 3, 2004, pp. 275–291.

5 See Seidenstat 'Terrorism, airport security, and the private sector', pp. 275–276.

6 The term dataveillance is a neologism used as a short form of 'data-surveillance'. The term was coined by Roger A. Clarke, see Roger A. Clarke, 'Information technology and dataveillance', *Communications of the ACM*, Vol. 31 No. 5, May 1988, pp.498–512.

7 The White House, *The National Strategy for Aviation Security*, Section VI, 'Conclusion', Washington, DC, 27 March 2007. Online, available at: www.whitehouse.gov/homeland/aviation-security.html#section6 (accessed 4 February 2008).

8 Salter, 'Imagining numbers', p. 243.

9 Kip Hawley, Keynote speech at 'Anticipating the unexpected – IATA AVSEC World', Geneva, Switzerland, 26 October 2005.

10 Giovanni Bisignani, Director General and CEO, IATA, 'Leading change', International Aviation Club, Washington, DC, 20 April 2004.

11 *The National Strategy for Aviation Security*, Section IV, 'Strategic actions', 27 March 2007. Online, available at: www.whitehouse.gov/homeland/aviation-security.html#section4 (accessed 4 February 2008).

12 Available at ICAO, *Annual Report of the Council*, 2007, Doc. 9898, 2007.

13 Salter, 'Imagining numbers', p. 243.

14 Joseph S. Szyliowicz, 'Aviation security: promise or reality?' *Studies in Conflict and Terrorism*, Vol. 27 No. 1, 2004, p. 58.

15 Kip Hawley, Keynote speech at 'Anticipating the unexpected'.

16 Hawley, 'Keynote speech at 'Anticipating the unexpected'.

17 *The National Strategy for Aviation Security*, Section IV, 'Strategic Actions'.

18 See for instance Rodney Wallis, *How Safe are our Skies? Assessing the Airlines' Responses to Terrorism*, Westport, CT: Greenwood Publishing, 2003, p. 65.

19 Testimony before the United States House of Representatives Committee on Oversight and Government Reform, 15 November 2007. Online, available at: www.tsa.gov/press/speeches/111507_hawley_house.shtm (accessed 6 January 2008).

20 GAO report number GAO-08–48T, 'Aviation security: vulnerabilities exposed through covert testing of TSA's passenger screening process', 15 November 2007. Online, available at: www.gao.gov/htext/d0848t.html (accessed 9 December 2007).

21 ICAO, *Annual Report of the Council*, Doc. 9898, p. 31.

22 Salter, 'Imagining numbers', p. 244.

23 Bruce Schneir, *Beyond Fear: Thinking Sensibly About Security in an Uncertain World*, New York: Copernicus Books, 2003.

24 *The 9/11 Commission Report*, Chapter 1, 22 July 2004, Washington DC. Online, available at: http://govinfo.library.unt.edu/911/report/index.htm (accessed 4 May 2007).

25 For the early response, including reference to a possible Middle Eastern connection, to the Oklahoma bombing see, for example, 'Terror in Oklahoma City: the investigation; at least 31 are dead; scores missing after car bomb attack in Oklahoma City wrecks 9 storey Federal Office building', *New York Times*, 20 April 1995.

26 Slavoj Zizek has explored the effects of the cinematic qualities of the events of 9/11 as a frame for interpreting. See Slavoj Zizek, *Welcome to the Desert of the Real*, London: Verso, 2002.

27 President G.W. Bush, 'Address to a Joint Session of Congress and the American People', 20 September 2001. Online, available at: www.whitehouse.gov/news/releases/2001/09/20010920–8.html (accessed 6 September 2008).

28 *Associated Press*, 'American among Yemen militants killed', 7 November 2002. Online, available at: www.cbsnews.com/stories/2002/11/09/attack/main528782.shtml (accessed 7 September 2008).

29 Ellen Knickmeyer and Jonathan Finer, 'Insurgent leader Al-Zarqawi killed in Iraq', *Washington Post*, 8 June 2006. Online, available at: www.washingtonpost.com/wp-dyn/content/article/2006/06/08/AR2006060800114.html (accessed 8 September 2008).

30 Oliver Kessler and Wouter Werner, 'Extrajudicial killing as risk management', *Security Dialogue*, Vol. 39 No. 2–3, 2008, pp. 289–308.

31 'US anthrax attacks'. Online, available at: www.gwu.edu/~cih/anthraxinfo/public/publicthreat_attacks.htm (accessed 20 August 2008). The alleged main suspect in the case, a US scientist that had worked for US Army Medical Research Institute for Infectious Diseases, committed suicide in 2008. See Bob Considine, 'Anthrax suspect's colleague blames FBI for suicide', MSNBC. Online, available at: www.msnbc.msn.com/id/26007186/ (accessed 20 August 2008).

32 David Heyman, *Lessons from the Anthrax Attacks: Implications for US Bioterrorism Preparedness*, Centre for Strategic and International Studies and the Defense Threat Reduction Agency, April 2002, p. VII. Online, available at: www.fas.org/irp/threat/cbw/dtra02.pdf (accessed 21 July 2008).

33 Heyman, *Lessons from the Anthrax Attacks*, p. 28.

34 Michael Elliott, 'The shoe-bombers world', *Time*, 16 February 2002. Online, available at: www.time.com/time/world/article/0,8599,203478,00.html (accessed 20 July 2008).

35 As quoted in Mike Allen, 'Bush reacts to attacks, moves to Nebraska', *Washington Post*, 11 September 2001. Online, available at: www.washingtonpost.com/wp-srv/nation/articles/bush091101.htm (accessed 6 September 2008).

36 See for discussion Richard Jackson, *Writing the War on Terrorism*, Manchester: Manchester University Press, 2006.

37 As quoted in Bruce Hoffman, 'Challenges for the US special operations command posed by the global terrorist threat: Al Qaeda on the run or on the march?' Written Testimony Submitted to the House Armed Services Subcommittee on Terrorism, Unconventional Threats and Capabilities, 14 February 2007, p. 9. Online, available at: http://armedservices.house.gov/pdfs/TUTC021407/Hoffman_Testimony021407.pdf (accessed 21 July 2007).

38 Cited in John Mueller, 'Is there still a terrorist threat: the myth of the omnipresent enemy', *Foreign Affairs*, September/October 2006.

39 Marieke de Goede, 'Beyond risk: premediation and the post-9/11 security imagination', *Security Dialogue*, Vol. 39 No. 2–3, 2008, pp. 155–176.

40 Salter, 'Imagining numbers', p. 244.
41 Zack Phillips, 'Security theatre', *Government Executive*, Vol. 39 No. 13, 1 August 2007. Online, available at: www.govexec.com/features/0807–01/0807–01s3.htm (accessed 10 January 2008).
42 Quoted in Phillips, 'Security theatre'.
43 Mueller, 'Is there still a terrorist threat: the myth of the omnipresent enemy'.
44 Randy Beardsworth, DHS Assistant Secretary for Strategic Plans, quoted in Phillips, 'Security theatre'.
45 Remarks to the Sacramento Metro Chamber of Commerce, 23 April 2007. Online, available at: www.dhs.gov/xnews/speeches/sp_1177426083887.shtm (accessed 26 May 2007).
46 Cited in *Consumer Reports Magazine*, February 2008.
47 Anna Leander, 'The power to construct international security: on the significance of private military companies', *Millennium: Journal of International Studies*, Vol. 33, 2005, pp. 813–814.
48 Salter 'Imagining numbers', p. 243.
49 Hawley, Keynote speech at 'Anticipating the nexpected'
50 'The Passenger Name Record (PNR): FAQ'. Online, available at: http://europa.eu/rapid/pressReleasesAction.do?reference=MEMO/07/294&format=HTML&aged=0&language=EN (accessed 24 January 2008).
51 Quoted in Sam Nunn, 'Preventing the next terrorist attack: the theory and practice of homeland security information systems', *Journal of Homeland Security and Emergency Management*, Vol. 2 No. 3, 2005, p. 4.
52 IATA, *Air Transportation since 11 September 2001*, Annex A, pp. 8–9.
53 Louise Amoore and Marieke De Goede 'Governance, risk and dataveillance in the war on terror', *Crime, Law and Social Change*, Vol. 43 No. 2–3, 2005, p. 150.
54 Amoore and de Goede, 'Governance, risk and dataveillance in the war on terror', p. 162.
55 Amoore and de Goede, 'Governance, risk and dataveillance in the war on terror', p. 162.
56 See 'Biometric industry to share in US$10 billion US-visit deal', *Biometric Technology Today*, Vol. 12 No. 2, 2004, pp. 1–12.
57 Louise Amoore, 'Biometric borders: governing mobilities in the war on terror', *Political Geography*, Vol. 25 No. 3, 2006, p. 345.
58 As quoted in Leander, 'The power to construct international security', p. 813.
59 Leander, 'The power to construct international security', p. 813.
60 'The Passenger Name Record (PNR): FAQ'.
61 See Charles Stone and Anne Zissu, 'Registered travellers: the financial value of registering the good guys', *Review of Policy Research*, Vol. 24 No. 5, September 2007, pp. 443–462.
62 See Atin Basuchoudhary and Laura Razzolini 'Hiding in plain sight – using signals to detect terrorists', *Public Choice*, Vol. 128, 2006, pp. 245–255.
63 See for example Allison Barrie, 'Homeland Security detects terrorist threats by reading your mind', *Fox News*, 23 September 2008. Online, available at: www.foxnews.com/story/0,2933,426485,00.html (accessed 25 September 2008).
64 The White House, *National Strategy for Aviation Security*, Section II, 'Risk methodology', March 2007. Online, available at: www.whitehouse.gov/homeland/aviation-security.html (accessed 22 December 2008).
65 The White House, *The National Strategy for Aviation Security*, Section V, 'Roles and responsibilities', 26 March 2007. Online, available at: www.whitehouse.gov/homeland/aviation-security.html#section5 (accessed 4 February 2008).
66 *The National Strategy for Aviation Security*, Section V, 'Roles and responsibilities'.
67 Kip Hawley, Keynote address at IATA Security and Facilitation Forum, Washington, DC, 18 June 2008.

68 Transportation Research Board, 'Deterrence, protection and preparation: the new transportation security imperative,' *Special Report 270*, 2002, p. 2.

69 Paul Wilkinson, 'Enhancing global aviation security?' in Paul Wilkinson and Brian Jenkins (eds), *Aviation Terrorism and Security*, London: Frank Cass, 1999 p. 165.

70 Jens Hainmuller and Jan Martin Lemitzer, 'Why do Europeans fly safer? The politics of airport security in Europe and the US', *Terrorism and Political Violence*, Vol. 15 No. 4, Winter 2003, p. 1.

71 H. George Frederickson and T.R. Laporte, 'Airport security, high reliability, and the problem of rationality', *Public Admin Review*, Vol. 62, Special Issue, 2002, p. 33.

72 Hainmuller and Lemitzer, 'Why do Europeans fly safer?' pp. 9–12.

73 Seidenstat, 'Terrorism, airport security, and the private sector', p. 284.

74 Hainmuller and Lemitzer, 'Why do Europeans fly safer?' pp. 27–28.

75 'About ECAC – five decades of shaping civil aviation in Europe 1995–2005'. Online, available at: http://ecac-ceac.org/index.php?content=historique&section=historique13 (accessed 24 January 2008).

76 See ECAC, 'Development and implementation of aviation security measures'. Online, available at: www.ecac-ceac.org/index.php?content=static&section=AVSEC%20Measures (accessed 5 October 2008).

77 ECAC, 'Development and implementation of aviation security measures'.

78 ECAC, 'Relations with third countries and other regional organisations'. Online, available at: www.ecac-ceac.org/index.php?content=static&section=SecRelations (accessed 5 September 2008).

79 ECAC, 'Relations with third countries and other regional organisations'.

80 See EASA 'Members'. Online, available at: www.easa-security.org/ (accessed 16 September 2008).

81 EASA, 'Press release', 5 November 2007. Online, available at: www.easa-security.org/Press%20release%20EASA%20on%20ACE-%20051107.pdf (accessed 16 September 2008).

82 Szyliowicz, 'Aviation security: promise or reality?' p. 49.

83 Wallis, *How Safe are our Skies?* p. 74.

84 Bisignani, 'Leading change'.

85 See IATA, 'Global air cargo security industry task force'. Online, available at: http://iata.org/whatwedo/cargo/security_taskforce.htm (accessed 16 September 2008).

86 For the full list of members see ACSIF, 'Membership at January 2008'. Online, available at: http://iata.org/NR/rdonlyres/D20C7972-AF9C-4D8B-8DA5-B5EDB0A3524F/0/ACSIF_members.pdf (accessed 16 September 2008).

87 ACSIF, online, available at: http://iata.org/workgroups/acsif.htm (accessed 16 September 2008).

88 Wallis, *How Safe are our Skies?* p. 70.

89 Wallis, *How Safe are our Skies?* p. 72.

90 IATA, 'Security management systems for air transport operations', Executive Summary, July 2007, pp. 3–4. Online, available at: http:// www.iata.org/NR/rdonlyres/5774928C-B7A8–4E32–968B-CCD2016A0E3D/58461/SEMSv32Summary.pdf (accessed 24 January 2008).

91 *The National Strategy for Aviation Security*, Section IV, 'Strategic actions'. Online, available at: www.whitehouse.gov/homeland/aviation-security.html#section4 (accessed 4 February 2008).

92 Szyliowicz, 'Aviation security: promise or reality?' p. 58.

93 Szyliowicz, 'Aviation security: promise or reality?' p. 51.

94 Ramses A. Wessel and Jan Wouters, 'The phenomenon of multilevel regulation: the global, EU and national regulatory spheres', *International Organisations Law Review*, Vol. 4 No. 2, 2008, pp. 259–291.

95 *The National Strategy for Aviation Security*, Section III, 'Strategic objectives'. Online, available at: www.whitehouse.gov/homeland/aviation-security.html#section3 (accessed 22 December 2008).

96 Kip Hawley, Keynote address at IATA Security and Facilitation Forum, Washington, DC, 18 June 2008.

97 Wallis, *How Safe are our Skies?* p. 69.

98 Wallis, *How Safe are our Skies?* p. 69.

99 Bisignani, 'Leading change'.

100 Bisignani, 'Leading change'.

101 Quoted in 'Airport security technology safe and convenient', *Public Service Review: European Union Issue 13*, 3 April 2007. Online, available at: www.publicservice.co.uk/feature_story.asp?id=7568&topic=Transport (accessed 29 July 2007).

102 IATA Director General Giovanni Bisignani, Remarks at McGill Conference – Aviation Security and Environment, 15 September 2007.

103 Giovanni Bisignani, *CEO Brief*, October 2007. Online, available at: http://iata.org/NR/rdonlyres/B71D7FEE-622C-445B-A435-A3B32D115A9E/0/ceoBrief_Oct07.pdf (accessed 4 February 2008).

104 IATA, *Industry Times*, March 2007.

105 IATA, 'Security management systems (SEMS)', pp. 1–5. Online, available at: www.iata.org/whatwedo/safety_security/security_issues/sems.htm (accessed 6 October 2008).

106 IATA, 'Security management systems for air transport operations', pp. 1–5.

107 Global Aviation Security Action Group, *Industry Positions on Security Issues*, Issue 10, 1 May 2005.

108 Global Aviation Security Action Group, *Industry Positions on Security Issues*, pp. 2–4.

109 IATA, 'Security management systems for air transport operations'.

110 IATA, 'Security management systems for air transport operations', p. 2.

111 Salter, 'Imagining numbers', p. 244.

112 Rodney Wallis, *Combating Air Terrorism*, Washington, DC: Brassey's, 1993.

113 *National Strategy for Aviation Security*, Section V, 'Roles and responsibilities', 'Private sector'.

114 IATA, 'Security management systems for air transport operations', pp. 2–3.

115 Wallis, *How Safe are our Skies?* p. 77.

116 Wallis, *How Safe are our Skies?* p. 85.

117 See, for example, Bureau of Transport Statistics, *Issue Brief No. 13*, US Department of Transportation, December 2005. Online, available at: www.bts.gov/publications/issue_briefs/number_13/pdf/entire.pdf (accessed 6 April 2008).

118 Giovanni Bisignani, Remarks on 'State of the air transport industry', 64th IATA Annual General Meeting, Istanbul, Turkey, 2 June 2008.

119 Cited in IATA, *The Air Transport Industry since 9/11*, 'Introduction', 2006.

120 *National Strategy for Aviation Security*, Section IV, 'Strategic actions'.

121 Hawley, Keynote speech at 'Anticipating the unexpected'.

122 Testimony before the United States House of Representatives Committee on Oversight and Government Reform, 15 November 2007.

123 *Business Week*, 'Airport security goes high-tech', 10 August 2006. Online, available at: www.businessweek.com/technology/content/aug2006/tc20060810_208055.htm (accessed 23 August 2006).

124 Prior to 9/11 the starting salary for a baggage screener was $6 per hour, less than could be earned in a fast food restaurant. Dirk Haubrich, 'Modern politics in an age of global terrorism: new challenges for domestic public policy', *Political Studies*, Vol. 54, 2006, p. 415.

125 Seidenstat, 'Terrorism, airport security, and the private sector', p. 288.

126 Hainmuller and Lemitzer, 'Why do Europeans fly safer?' pp. 24–25.

127 '2003: "Shoe bomber" jailed for life'. Online, available at: http://news.bbc.co.uk/onthis-day/hi/dates/stories/january/30/newsid_4081000/4081741.stm (accessed 24 January 2008).

128 See, for example, the passenger advice at Heathrow. Online, available at: www.hea-throwairport.com/portal/controller/dispatcher.jsp?ChPath=Heathrow^General^Airpo rt%20information^Security%20control&securityCountryGUID=a058b7b277c35110 VgnVCM10000036821c0a____ (accessed 24 January 2008).

129 David Charter, 'Vote to scrap flight ban on liquids', *The Times*, 6 September 2007.

130 Amitai Aviram, 'The placebo effect of law: law's role in manipulating perceptions', *George Washington Law Review*, Vol. 75 No. 1, November 2006, *passim*.

131 Amoore, 'Biometric borders', p. 337.

132 Amoore, 'Biometric borders', p. 337.

133 Kip Hawley, Keynote speech at 'Anticipating the unexpected'.

134 Kip Hawley, Keynote address at IATA Security and Facilitation Forum, Washington, DC, 18 June 2008.

135 Hoffman, 'Challenges for the US special operations command posed by the global terrorist threat: Al Qaeda on the run or on the march?', p. 15.

136 Bruce Schneir, 'Schneir on security: last week's terrorism arrests', 13 August 2006. Online, available at: www.schneier.com/blog/archives/2006/08/terrorism_secur.html (accessed 24 September 2006).

137 See 'Terror suspects held on KLM plane', *BBC News*, 26 September 2008. Online, available at: http://news.bbc.co.uk/2/hi/europe/7637226.stm (accessed 7 October 2008).

138 See Pat O'Malley, 'Risks, ethics and airport security', *Canadian Journal of Criminology and Criminal Justice*, Vol. 48 No. 3, June 2006.

139 See ACLU Press release, 'ACLU sues TSA official, Jetblue for discriminating against passenger wearing Arabic t-shirt', 9 August 2007. Online, available at: www.aclu.org/racialjustice/racialprofiling/34814prs20070809.html (accessed 10 October 2007).

140 See, 'Cat Stevens refused entry to the US', *Guardian*, 22 September 2004. Online, available at: www.guardian.co.uk/world/2004/sep/22/usa/print (accessed 9 October 2006).

141 See Drew Griffin and Kathleen Johnston, 'Airline captain, lawyer, child on terror "watch" list', *CNN*, 19 August 2008. Online, available at: www.cnn.com/2008/US/08/19/tsa.watch.list/index.html (accessed 21 August 2008).

142 'Nelson Mandela removed from terror list', *Telegraph*, 18 July 2008. Online, available at: www.telegraph.co.uk/news/worldnews/africaandindianocean/southafrica/2233256/Nelson-Mandela-removed-from-US-terror-list.html (accessed 10 August 2008).

143 Derek Reveron, 'Old allies, new friends: intelligence-sharing in the war on terror', *Orbis*, Summer 2006, p. 467.

144 See for discussion, Adam Svendsen, 'The globalization of intelligence since 9/11: frameworks and operational parameters', *Cambridge Review of International Affairs*, Vol. 21 No. 1, March 2008.

145 Clarke, 'Information technology and dataveillance', *passim*.

146 Anne Paylor, 'Wanted: a security standard', *Air Transport World*, June 2006, p. 36.

147 George W. Bush, 'Address to a joint session of Congress and the American people', 20 September 2001.

6 Whither the other war on terror?

1 Quoted in 'The second Bush–Gore presidential debate', transcript at *Commission on Presidential Debates*, 11 October 2000. Online, available at: www.debates.org/pages/trans2000b.html (accessed 4 April 2008).

2 Quoted in 'France turns heat on Bush', *BBC News*, 4 April 2001. Online, available at: http://news.bbc.co.uk/2/hi/americas/1260499.stm (accessed 8 February 2008).

3 For a typical critique, see Douglas Kellner, 'Preemptive strikes and the war on Iraq: a critique of Bush administration unilateralism and militarism', *New Political Science*, Vol. 26 No. 3, September 2004, pp. 417–440.

4 Marjorie Cohn, *Cowboy Republic: Six Ways the Bush Gang has Defied the Law*, Sausalito, CA: Polipoint Press, 2007.

5 Quoted in 'Gore blasts Bush's "cowboy" Iraq policy', *San Francisco Chronicle*, 24 September 2002.

6 Quoted in Tom Baldwin and Gerard Baker, 'President Bush regrets his legacy as man who wanted war', *The Times*, 11 June 2008.

7 As quoted in Baldwin and Baker 'President Bush regrets his legacy as man who wanted war'.

8 Javier Solana, 'Managing global insecurity', speech at Brookings Institute, Washington, DC, 21 March 2007. Online, available at: www.eu-un.europa.eu/articles/en/article_6882_en.htm (accessed 10 January 2008).

9 Didier Bigo, 'Security and immigration: toward a critique of the governmentality of unease', *Alternatives: Global, Local, Politics*, Vol. 27 No. 1, 2002.

10 Frank Furedi, *Invitation to Terror*, London: Continuum Press, 2007.

11 Marieke de Goede, 'Beyond risk: premediation and the post-9/11 security imagination', *Security Dialogue*, Vol. 39 No. 2–3, 2008, pp. 155–176.

12 Claudia Aradau and Rens Van Munster, 'Governing terrorism through risk: taking precautions, (un)knowing the future', *European Journal of International Relations*, Vol. 13 No. 1, 2007, pp. 89–115.

13 Ortwin Renn and Katherine D. Walker (eds), *Global Risk Governance*, Amsterdam: Springer, 2008.

14 Quoted in 'Solana, EU's "good cop", takes centre stage', *International Herald Tribune*, 12 August 2006.

15 Quoted in 'For old friends, Iraq bares a deep rift', *New York Times*, 14 February 2003.

16 Maryam Razavy, 'Hawala: an underground haven for terrorists or social phenomenon?' *Crime, Law and Social Change*, Vol. 44 No. 3, 2005, pp. 277–278.

17 Erin Harbaugh, 'The Proliferation Security Initiative: counter-proliferation at the cross-roads', *Strategic Insights*, Vol. 3 No. 7, July 2004. Online, available at: www.ccc.nps.navy.mil/si/2004/jul/harbaughJul04.asp (accessed 9 April 2005).

18 F. Record, Acting Assistant Secretary, International Security and Nonproliferation, Statement before the House Committee on Homeland Security, Subcommittee on Prevention of Nuclear and Biological Attacks, Washington, DC, 25 May 2006. Online, available at: www.state.gov/t/isn/rls/rm/69307.htm (accessed 5 June 2006).

19 Quoted in 'Airline urges liquids review after trial', 9 September 2008. Online, available at: http://news.bbc.co.uk/2/hi/uk_news/7606892.stm (accessed 10 September 2008).

20 US Under-Secretary of State for Non-Proliferation and International Security, Robert Joseph, quoted in British American Security Information Council, *Proliferation Security Initiative*. Online, available at: www.basicint.org/nuclear/counterproliferation/psi.htm (accessed 17 September 2008).

21 See Pat O'Malley, 'Risks, ethics and airport security', *Canadian Journal of Criminology and Criminal Justice*, Vol. 48 No. 3, June 2006.

22 'Airline checks claim of "Muslim while flying" discrimination', *CNN*, 21 November 2006. Online, available at: http://edition.cnn.com/2006/US/11/21/passengers.removed/ (accessed 5 February 2007).

23 Kern Alexander, Rahul Dhumale and John Eatwell, *Global Governance of Financial Systems: The International Regulation of Systemic Risk*, Oxford: Oxford University Press, 2006, pp. 152–154.

24 Harbaugh, 'The Proliferation Security Initiative'.

25 Proliferation Security Initiative, 'Introduction'. Online, available at: www.proliferationsecurity.info/introduction.html (accessed 23 August 2008) (website maintained and funded by the Canadian government).

26 Shepard Forman and Derk Segaar, 'New coalitions for global governance: the changing dynamics of multilateralism', *Global Governance*, Vol. 12 No. 2, April 2006, p. 206.

27 General Accounting Office, *General Aviation Security: Increased Federal Oversight Needed But Continued Partnership With Private Sector Is Critical To Long-Term Success*, GAO-05–144, Washington, DC, 10 November 2004.

28 General Accounting Office, *Aviation Security: Risk, Experience, and Customer Concerns Drive Changes to Airline Passenger Screening Procedures, but Evaluation and Documentation of Proposed Changes Could Be Improved*, GAO-07–634, Washington, DC, 16 April 2007.

29 White House, *National Strategy for Aviation Security*, Section II, 'Risk methodology', March 2007. Online, available at: www.whitehouse.gov/homeland/aviation-security. html (accessed 22 December 2008).

30 *National Strategy for Aviation Security*, Section I, 'Introduction'. Online, available at: www.whitehouse.gov/homeland/aviation-security.html#section1 (accessed 22 December 2008).

31 ICAO, *Annual Report 2007*, Doc. 9898, p. 21.

32 International Civil Aviation Organisation Day, 7 December 2007. Online, available at: www.paris.icao.int/news/20071207_ica_day.htm (accessed 9 January 2008).

33 IATA Director General Giovanni Bisignani, Remarks at McGill Conference – Aviation Security and Environment, 15 September 2007.

34 *National Strategy for Aviation Security*, Section IV, 'Strategic actions', 27 March 2007. Online, available at: www.whitehouse.gov/homeland/aviation-security. html#section4 (accessed 4 February 2008).

35 Phil Goff, *Opening Address of the Proliferation Security Initiative Operational Experts Group Meeting*, Auckland, New Zealand, 26 March 2007. Online, available at: www.beehive.govt.nz/speech/cooperating+non-proliferation (accessed 8 April 2007).

36 Harbaugh, 'The Proliferation Security Initiative'.

37 'The Proliferation Security Initiative', June 2004. Online, available at: http://usinfo. state.gov/products/pubs/proliferation/ (accessed 9 November 2006).

38 Department of Homeland Security, *Maritime Commerce Security Plan for the National Strategy for Maritime Security*, Washington, DC, October 2005, p. 8.

39 Department of Homeland Security, *Maritime Commerce Security Plan for the National Strategy for Maritime Security*, p. 8.

40 FATF, *Guidance on the Risk-based Approach to Combating Money Laundering and Terrorist Financing*, 2007, p.5. Online, available at: www.fatf-gafi.org/dataoecd/43/46/38960576.pdf (accessed 10 January 2008).

41 Jason Sharman, 'Power and discourse in policy diffusion: anti-money laundering in developing states', *International Studies Quarterly*, Vol. 52 No. 3, September 2008, p. 636.

42 Sharon Squassoni, 'Proliferation Security Initiative', Congressional Research Service, Order Code RS21881, 7 June 2005.

43 Mark J. Valencia, 'Is the PSI really the cornerstone of a new international norm?' *Naval War College Review*, Vol. 59 No. 4, Autumn 2006, p. 124.

44 Address at General Debate of the fifty-ninth session of the General Assembly of the United Nations, New York, 27 September 2004.

45 Dean Wilson, *Borders, Mobility and Technologies of Control*, Amsterdam: Springer, 2006, p. 87.

46 Forman and Segaar, 'New coalitions for global governance: the changing dynamics of multilateralism'.

47 Bernadette Methuen and Ian Taylor, 'The return of the dogs of war? The privatisation of security in Africa' in Rodney Bruce Hall and Thomas Biersteker (eds), *The Emergence of Private Authority in Global Governance*, Cambridge: Cambridge University Press, 2002, pp. 183–202.

48 Kathryn Gardner, 'Fighting terrorism the FATF way', *Global Governance*, Vol. 13 No. 3, 2007, pp. 325–345.
49 Alison J.K. Bailes, 'Business and security: public–private sector interface and inter-dependence at the turn of the 21st century', in Alison J. Bailes and Isabelle Frommelt (eds), *Business and Security: Public Private Sector Relationships In A New Security Environment*, Stockholm: SIPRI, 2004, pp. 5–6.
50 Bailes, 'Business and security', p. 7.
51 The White House, *National Strategy for Aviation Security*, March 2007. Online, available at: www.whitehouse.gov/homeland/aviation-security.html (accessed 9 May 2007).
52 *National Strategy for Aviation Security*, Section IV, 'Strategic actions'.
53 General Accounting Office, *General Aviation Security*.
54 Remarks by National Security Advisor Stephen Hadley to the United States Institute of Peace on the President's National Security Strategy, 16 March 2006. Online, available at: www.whitehouse.gov/news/releases/2006/03/20060316–8.html (accessed 27 April 2006).
55 Remarks by Commissioner Robert C. Bonner, United States Customs and Border Protection, 'Proliferation Security Initiative', Los Angeles, CA, 14 September 2005. Online, available at: www.customs.gov/xp/cgov/newsroom/commissioner/speeches_statements/archives/2005/09142005_speech.xml (accessed 2 December 2005).
56 'Non-proliferation, arms control, disarmament', *SIPRI Yearbook 2007*, Stockholm: SIPRI, 2007, p. 648.
57 Of course, the G8 is also known as an informal grouping without headquarters or permanent staff but it primarily relies on government-to-government interaction. See Sieglinde Gstöhl, 'Governance through government networks', *Review of International Organisations*, Vol. 2 No. 1, March 2007, pp. 1–37.
58 FATF, *Annual Report 1990–91*, p. 19.
59 Harbaugh, 'The Proliferation Security Initiative'.
60 'The new multilateralism', *Wall Street Journal*, 8 January 2004.
61 'Unnamed senior administration official' quoted in 'The new multilateralism'.
62 Council on Foreign Relations, 'The Proliferation Security Initiative', updated 19 October 2006. Online, available at: www.cfr.org/publication/11057/ (accessed 23 December 2006).
63 *SIPRI Yearbook 2007*, 'Non-proliferation, arms control, disarmament', p. 648.
64 PSI participants, Bureau of International Security and Non-proliferation, Washington, DC, 22 May 2008. Online, available at: www.state.gov/t/isn/c19310.htm (accessed 1 September 2008).
65 Cited in 'Security at the terminal', *National Defense*, 1 November 2005.
66 Forman and Segaar, 'New coalitions for global governance: the changing dynamics of multilateralism', p. 219.
67 Mark Valencia, 'The Proliferation Security Initiative: a glass half-full', *Arms Control Today*, June 2007. Online, available at: www.armscontrol.org/act/2007_06/Valencia (accessed 8 July 2007).
68 Valencia, 'The Proliferation Security Initiative: a glass half-full'.
69 General Accounting Office, *Homeland Security: A Risk Management Approach can Guide Preparedness Efforts*, GAO-02-208T, Washington, DC, 31 October 2001.
70 Richard Clarke, *Against All Enemies: Inside America's War on Terror*, New York: Free Press, 2004, p. 192.
71 See Mark Salter (ed.), *Politics at the Airport*, Minneapolis, MN: University of Minnesota Press, 2008.
72 *National Strategy for Aviation Security*, Section II, 'Threats to the air domain'. Online, available at: www.whitehouse.gov/homeland/aviation-security.html (accessed 22 December 2008).

73 Sam Tangredi, 'Introduction' in Sam Tangredi (ed.), *Globalisation and Maritime Power*, Washington, DC: National Defense University, 2002.
74 Harbaugh, 'The Proliferation Security Initiative'.
75 Harbaugh, 'The Proliferation Security Initiative'.
76 John Bolton, 'A response to "legitimacy" in international affairs: the American perspective in theory and operation', Remarks to the Federalist Society, Washington, DC, 13 November 2003. Online, available at: www.state.gov/t/us/rm/26143.htm (accessed 25 March 2004).
77 Testimony before the House International Relations Committee, 2004, cited in Council on Foreign Relations, 'The Proliferation Security Initiative'.
78 Statement by the president on the Fifth Anniversary of the Proliferation Security Initiative, 28 May 2008.
79 Arms Control Association Fact Sheet, 'The Proliferation Security Initiative at a glance', October 2007. Online, available at: www.armscontrol.org/factsheets/PSI (accessed 15 November 2007).
80 Speech to the meeting of the PSI, Brisbane, 9 July 2003. Online, available at: www.acronym.org.uk/docs/0307/doc04.htm#02 (accessed 24 August 2004).
81 Remarks by National Security Advisor Stephen J. Hadley at the Proliferation Security Initiative Fifth Anniversary Senior Level Meeting, Washington, DC, 28 May 2008. Online, available at: www.whitehouse.gov/news/releases/2008/05/20080528–3.html (accessed 24 June 2008).
82 Patricia McNerney, Principal Deputy Assistant Secretary, International Security and Nonproliferation, Remarks at Conference on Global Perspectives of the Proliferation Landscape: An Assessment of Tools and Policy Problems, Monterey, CA, 10 June 2008. Online, available at: www.state.gov/t/isn/rls/rm/105775.htm (accessed 19 June 2008).
83 Michael Richardson, 'The PSI and counter-proliferation in the Asia-Pacific region', address to the NZIIA, Victoria University, New Zealand, 20 November 2007. Online, available at: www.victoria.ac.nz/nziia/assets/talks/wn/M_Richardson_20Nov2007%20Wgtn%20BrNZIIA.pdf (accessed 12 March 2008).
84 Statement by the Press Secretary 'Principles for the Proliferation Security Initiative', 4 September 2003. Online, available at: www.state.gov/t/isn/rls/prsrl/23809.htm (accessed 18 January 2004).
85 Testimony before the United States House of Representatives Committee on Oversight and Government Reform, 15 November 2007.
86 *Business Week*, 'Airport security goes high-tech', 10 August 2006. Online, available at: www.businessweek.com/technology/content/aug2006/tc20060810_208055.htm (accessed 23 August 2006).
87 *National Strategy for Aviation Security*, 'Prologue', p. 2. Online, available at: www.whitehouse.gov/homeland/aviation-security.html (accessed 22 December 2008).
88 Transportation Security Administration, 'Layers of security'. Online, available at: www.tsa.gov/what_we_do/layers/index.shtm (accessed 20 March 2008).
89 Juan Carlos Zarate, 'Bankrupting terrorists', *E-Journal USA*, September 2004. Online, available at: http://usinfo.state.gov/journals/ites/0904/ijee/zarate.htm (accessed 9 April 2007).
90 Cited in Oliver Burkeman, 'Heads in the clouds', *Guardian*, 1 December 2007.
91 See a discussion of this trend in Lucia Zedner, 'Policing before and after the police: the historical antecedents of contemporary crime control', *British Journal of Criminology*, Vol. 46 No. 1, 2006, pp. 78–96.
92 Robert Hill, Defence Minister of Australia, Remarks on the Changing Security Environment, Federal and Young State Liberal Convention, Queensland, 24 January 2004. Online, available at: www.minister.defence.gov.au/HillSpeechtpl.cfm?CurrentId=3461 (accessed 25 March 2005).
93 FATF, *Proliferation Financing Report*, 18 June 2008.

94 *National Strategy for Aviation Security*, Section V, 'Roles and responsibilities'.
95 The White House, *The National Strategy for Maritime Security*, Washington, DC, 20 September 2005, p. 18. Online, available at: www.whitehouse.gov/homeland/maritime-security.html (accessed 22 December 2008).
96 Department of Homeland Security, *Maritime Commerce Security Plan for the National Strategy for Maritime Security*, p. 21.
97 *National Strategy for Aviation Security*, Section II, 'Threats to the air domain'.
98 Robert Joseph, Under-Secretary of State for Arms control and International Security, Remarks at Institute for Defence and Strategic Studies, Singapore, 17 August 2005. Online, available at: www.america.gov/st/washfile-english/2005/August/200508171 74244TJkcolluB0.5095941.html (accessed 30 August 2005).
99 Remarks at Department of Defense News Briefing, Washington, DC, 25 September 2001.
100 Solomon Hughes, *War on Terror, Inc: Corporate Profiteering from the Politics of Fear*, London: Verso, 2007, p. 6.
101 Quoted in 'Bush camp in new attack on Kerry', *BBC News*, 11 October 2004. Online, available at: http://news.bbc.co.uk/2/hi/americas/3733504.stm (accessed 25 October 2004).
102 Quoted in Donna Miles, 'Pace: world recognises terrorist threat, need for cooperation', *American Forces Press Service*, 5 June 2006. Online, available at: www.defenselink.mil/news/newsarticle.aspx?id=16119 (accessed 7 July 2006).
103 Remarks at Department of Defense News Briefing, Washington, DC, 25 September 2001.

Bibliography

Books and journal articles

Acharya, Amitav and Arabinda Acharya, 'The myth of the Second Front: localising the 'war on terror' in Southeast Asia', *Washington Quarterly*, Vol. 30 No. 4, Autumn 2007, pp.75–90.

Adams, J., 'The world's biggest ideas: risk', *New Scientist*, Issue 2517, 17 September 2005, p. 36.

Advani, Asheesh and Sandford Borins, 'Mangaging airports: a test of the new public management', *International Journal of Public Management*, Vol. 4 No. 1, 2001, p. 92.

Albert, Mathias, 'From defending boundaries towards managing geographical risks? Security in a globalised world', *Geopolitics*, Vol. 5 No. 1, 2001, pp. 57–80.

Albright, David, Kathryn Buehler and Holly Higgins, 'Bin Laden and the bomb', *Bulletin of Atomic Scientists*, January/February 2002, pp. 23–24.

Amoore, Louise, 'Biometric borders: governing mobilities in the war on terror', *Political Geography*, Vol. 25 No. 3, 2006, pp. 336–351.

Amoore, Louise and Marieke de Goede, 'Governance, risk and dataveillance in the war on terror', *Crime, Law and Social Change*, Vol. 43 No. 2–3, 2005, pp. 149–173.

Amoore, Louise and Marieke de Goede, 'Transactions after 9/11: the banal face of the preemptive strike', *Transactions of the Institute of British Geographers*, Vol. 33 No. 2, January 2008, pp. 173–185

Amoore, Louise and Marieke de Goede (eds), *Risk and the War on Terror*, London: Routledge, 2008.

Aradau, Claudia and Rens van Munster, 'Governing terrorism through risk: taking precautions, (un)knowing the future', *European Journal of International Relations*, Vol. 13 No. 1, 2007, pp. 89–115.

Aradau, Claudia, Luis Lobo-Guerrero and Rens Van Munster (eds), 'Security, technologies of risk, and the political', Special issue, *Security Dialogue*, Vol. 39 No. 2–3, 2008, pp. 147–154.

Archibugi, Daniel and Matthias Koenig-Archibugi, *Debating Cosmopolitics*, London: Verso, 2003.

Atia, Mona, 'In whose interest? Financial surveillance and the circuits of exception in the war on terror', *Environment and Planning D: Society and Space*, Vol. 25 No. 3, 2007, pp. 447–475.

Atin, Basuchoudhary and Laura Razzolini, 'Hiding in plain sight – using signals to detect terrorists', *Public Choice*, Vol. 128 No. 1–2, 2006, pp. 245–255.

Aviram, Amitai, 'The placebo effect of law: Law's role in manipulating perceptions', *George Washington Law Review*, Vol. 75 No. 1, November 2006, pp. 54–104.

Bailes, Alison, 'Business and security: public–private sector interface and interdependence at the turn of the 21st century', in Alison Bailes and Isabelle Frommelt (eds), *Business and Security: public private sector relationships in a new security environment*, Stockholm: SIPRI, 2004, pp. 1–26.

Baldwin, David, 'The concept of security', *Review of International Studies*, Vol. 23 No 1, 1997, pp. 5–26.

Banks, Christopher, 'Protecting (or destroying) freedom through law: the USA Patriot Act's constitutional implications', in David Cohen and John Wells (eds), *American National Security and Civil Liberties in an Era of Terrorism*, London: Palgrave, 2004, pp. 30–31.

Beck, Ulrich, *World Risk Society*, Cambridge: Polity Press, 1999.

Beck, Ulrich, *What is Globalization*, Cambridge: Polity Press, 2000.

Beck, Ulrich, 'The cosmopolitan state: towards a realistic utopia', 2001, online, available at: www.eurozine.com/articles/2001-12-05-beck-en.html (accessed 14 November 2007).

Beck, Ulrich, 'The World Risk Society revisited: the terrorist threat?', LSE Public Lecture, London, 14 February 2002; 'Terror and solidarity' in Mark Leonard (ed.), *Re-ordering the World*, London: Foreign Policy Centre, 2002.

Beck, Ulrich, *Power in the Global Age*, Cambridge: Polity Press, 2005.

Beck, Ulrich, *Cosmopolitan Vision*, Cambridge: Polity Press, 2006.

Beck, Ulrich, 'Living in a World Risk Society', public lecture at the London School of Economics, 15 February 2006, available in *Economy and Society*, Vol. 35 No. 3, 2006, pp. 329–345.

Beck, Ulrich, 'In the new, anxious world, leaders must learn to think beyond borders', *Guardian*, 13 July 2007.

Beck, Ulrich and Edgar Grande, *Cosmopolitan Europe*, Cambridge: Polity Press, 2008.

Bianchi, Raoul, 'Tourism and the globalisation of fear: analysing the politics of risk and (in)security in global travel', *Tourism and Hospitality Research*, Vol. 7 No. 1, 2007, pp. 64–74.

Biersteker, Thomas and Sue E. Eckert, 'Conclusion: taking stock of efforts to counter the financing of terrorism and recommendations for the way forward' in Thomas J. Biersteker and Sue E. Eckert (eds), *Countering the Financing of Terrorism*, London: Routledge, 2007, pp. 289–304.

Biersteker, Thomas and Sue E. Eckert (eds), *Countering the Financing of Terrorism*, London: Routledge, 2007.

Bigo, D., 'Security and immigration: toward a critique of the governmentality of unease', *Alternatives: Global, Local, Politics*, Vol. 27 No. 1, 2002, pp. 63–92.

Boureston, Jack, 'Al Qaeda's WMD capabilities', *Strategic Insights*, Vol. 1 No. 7, September 2002, online, available at: www.ccc.nps.navy.mil/si/sept02/wmd.asp (accessed 1 February 2003).

Bracken, Paul, Ian Bremmer and David Gordon (eds), *Managing Strategic Surprise: Lessons from Risk Management and Risk Assessment*, Cambridge: Cambridge University Press, 2008.

Braithwaite, John and Peter Drahos, *Global Business Regulation*, Cambridge: Cambridge University Press, 2000.

Butler, Judith, *Precarious Life: The Powers of Mourning and Violence*, London: Verso, 2004.

Byers, Michael, 'Policing the high seas: the Proliferation Security Initiative', *American Journal of International Affairs*, Vol. 98 No. 3, July 2004, pp. 526–545.

Byman, Daniel, *The Five Front War: The Better Way to Fight Global Jihad*, New Jersey: Wiley, 2007.

Castel, Robert, 'From dangerousness to risk' in Graham Burchill, Colin Gordon and Peter Miller (eds), *The Foucault Effect: Studies in Governmentality*, London: Harvester Wheatsheaf, 1991, pp. 281–298.

Clarke, Jonathan and Geoffrey Edwards, *Global Governance in the 21st Century*, London: Palgrave, 2004.

Clarke, Richard, *Against All Enemies: Inside America's War on Terror*, New York: Free Press, 2004.

Clunan, Anne, 'The fight against terrorist financing', *Political Science Quarterly*, Vol. 121 No. 4, 2006, pp. 569–596.

Coaffee, Jon, *Terrorism, Risk and the City: The Making of a Contemporary Urban Landscape*, Aldershot: Ashgate, 2003.

Cohn, Marjorie, *Cowboy Republic: Six Ways the Bush Gang has Defied the Law*, Sausalito, CA: Polipoint Press, 2007.

Coker, Christopher, *Globalisation and Insecurity in the Twenty-first Century: NATO and the Management of Risk*, Adelphi Paper 345, Oxford: Oxford University Press, 2002.

Coker, Christopher, *War in an Age of Risk*, New Jersey: Polity Press, 2009.

Cortwright, David and George Lopez (eds), *Uniting Against Terror: Cooperative Nonmilitary Responses to the Global Terrorist Threat*, Cambridge, MA: MIT Press, 2007.

Cotton, James, 'The Proliferation Security Initiative and North Korea: legality and limitations of a coalition strategy', *Security Dialogue*, Vol. 36 No. 2, 2005, pp. 193–211.

De Goede, Marieke, 'Beyond risk: premediation and the post-9/11 security imagination', *Security Dialogue*, Vol. 39 No. 2–3, 2008, pp. 155–176.

De Goede, Marieke, 'The politics of preemption in the war on terror', *European Journal of International Relations*, Vol. 14 No. 1, 2008, pp. 161–185.

Der Derian, James, 'In terrorem: war, terror, judgement' in Ken Booth and Tim Dunne (eds), *Worlds in Collision*, Basingstoke: Macmillan, 2002, pp. 101–117.

Dewey, John, *The Public and Its Problems*, London: G. Allen and Unwin, 1927.

Diehl, Paul, *The Politics of Global Governance: International Organisations in an Interdependent World*, London: Lynne Rienner, 2005.

Dillon, Mick, 'Underwriting security', *Security Dialogue*, Vol. 39 No. 2–3, 2008, pp. 309–332.

Dixon, John and Rhys Dogan, 'Analyzing global governance failure: a philosophical framework', *Journal of Comparative Policy Analysis*, Vol. 5 No. 2–3, 2003, pp. 209–226.

Dodd, Chris, 'Opening statement: turmoil in US credit markets', Hearing of the Senate Banking Committee, 23 September 2008, online, available at: http://dodd.senate.gov/index.php?q=node/4572 (accessed 23 September 2008).

Drezner, Daniel, 'The new new world order', *Foreign Affairs*, March/April 2007, pp. 34–46.

Duffield, Mark, *Global Governance and the New Wars: The Merging of Development and Security*, New York: Zed Books, 2001, *passim*.

Elbe, Stefan, 'Risking lives: AIDS, security and three concepts of risk', *Security Dialogue*, Vol. 39 No. 2–3, 2008, pp. 177–198.

Ellis, Jason, 'The best defense: counterproliferaton and U.S. national strategy', *Washington Quarterly*, Vol. 26 No. 2, 2003, pp. 115–133.

Ellis, Juan, 'Privatising airports – options and cases', *Public Policy for the Private Sector*, World Bank Note no. 82, June 1996.

Ericson, Richard, 'Ten uncertainties of risk-management approaches to security', *Canadian Journal of Criminology and Criminal Justice*, Vol. 48 No. 3, June 2006, pp. 345–358.

Ericson, Richard, *Crime in an Insecure World*, Cambridge: Polity Press, 2007.

Fallows, James, 'Declaring victory', *Atlantic Monthly*, Vol. 298 No. 2, September 2006, pp. 60–62.

Farah, Douglas, 'Al Qaeda and the gemstone trade', in Thomas J. Biersteker and Sue E. Eckert (eds), *Countering the Financing of Terrorism*, London: Routledge, 2007, pp. 193–205.

FATF, *The 40 Recommendations*, 2003. Online, available at: www.fatf-gafi.org/dataoecd/7/40/34849567.pdf (accessed 12 January 2008).

FATF, *Money Laundering and Terrorist Financing Typologies 2004–2005*, 10 June 2005. Online, available at: www.fatf-gafi.org/dataoecd/16/8/35003256.pdf (accessed 22 December 2008).

FATF, *Annual Review of NCCT 2005–2006*, 26 June 2006. Online, available at: www.fatf-fagi.org/dataoecd/0/0/37029619.pdf (accessed 22 December 2008).

FATF, *Annual Report, 2005–2006*, 23 July 2006. Online, available at: www.oecd.org/dataoecd/38/56/37041969.pdf (accessed 22 December 2008).

FATF, *Annual Report 2007–2008*, Foreword. Online, available at: www.fatf-gafi.org/dataoecd/58/0/41141361.pdf 30 June 2008 (accessed 4 July 2008).

FATF, *Guidance on the Risk-based Approach to Combating Money Laundering and Terrorist Financing*, 2007. Online, available at: www.fatf-gafi.org/dataoecd/43/46/38960576.pdf (accessed 10 January 2008).

FATF, *RBA Guidance for Accountants*, 17 June 2008. Online, available at: www.fatf-gafi.org/dataoecd/19/44/41092947.pdf (accessed 23 July 2008).

FATF, *Money Laundering and Terrorist Financing Risk Assessment Strategies*, 18 June 2008. Online, available at: www.fatf-gafi.org/dataoecd/46/24/40978997.pdf (accessed 5 July 2008).

Finkelstein, Larry, 'What is global governance?' *Global Governance*, Vol. 1 No. 3, 1995, pp. 367–372.

Fisher, David, *History of the IAEA: The First Forty Years*, Vienna: IAEA, 1997.

Forman, Shepard and Derk Segaar, 'New coalitions for global governance: the changing dynamics of multilateralism', *Global Governance*, Vol. 12 No. 2, April 2006, pp. 205–225.

Furedi, Frank, *The Culture of Fear*, London: Cassell, 1997.

Furedi, Frank, *Invitation to Terror*, London: Continuum Press, 2007.

Gardner, Kathryn, 'Fighting terrorism the FATF way', *Global Governance*, Vol. 13 No. 3, 2007, pp. 325–345.

Giddens, Anthony, *Modernity and Self-identity: Self and Society in the Late Modern Age*, Cambridge: Polity Press, 1991.

Giddens, Anthony, *The Third Way: Renewal of Social Democracy*, Cambridge: Polity Press, 1998.

Goldbalt, Jozef, *Can Nuclear Proliferation be Stopped?* Geneva: Geneva International Peace Research Institute, 2007.

Grin, John, 'Reflexive modernisation as a governance issue, or designing and re- shaping structuration' in Jan-Peter Voss, Dierk Bauknecht and René Kemp (eds), *Reflexive Governance for Sustainable Development*, Camberley: Edward Elgar Publishing, 2006, pp. 57–81.

Grossman-Vermaas, Rita, 'Proliferation and development – exposing the link', *NATO Review*, No. 3, Autumn 2007. Online, available at: www.nato.int/docu/review/2007/issue3/english/art3.html (accessed 22 December 2008).

Guilfoyle, Douglas, 'Maritime interdiction of weapons of mass destruction', *Journal of Conflict and Security Law*, Vol. 12, No. 1, 2007, pp. 1–36.

Hagerty, Kevin and Richard Ericson (eds), *The New Politics of Surveillance and Visibility*, Toronto: University of Toronto Press, 2006.

Hainmuller, Jens and Jan Martin Lemitzer, 'Why do Europeans fly safer? The politics of airport security in Europe and the US', *Terrorism and Political Violence*, Vol. 15, No. 4, Winter 2003, p. 1.

Hall, Rodney and Thomas Biersteker, 'Private authority as global governance' in Rodney Hall and Thomas Biersteker (eds), *The Emergence of Private Authority in Global Governance*, Cambridge: Cambridge University Press, 2002, pp. 203–222.

Harbaugh, E., 'The Proliferation Security Initiative: counter-proliferation at the cross-roads', *Strategic Insights*, Vol. 3 No. 7, July 2004. Online, available at: www.ccc.nps. navy.mil/si/2004/jul/harbaughJul04.asp (accessed 22 December 2008).

Haveman, Jon D., Ethan M. Jennings, Howard J. Shatz and Greg C. Wright, 'The Container Security Initiative and Ocean Container Threats', *Journal of Homeland Security and Emergency Management*, Vol. 4, No. 1, 2007. Online, available at: www.bepress. com/jhsem/vol4/iss1/1 (accessed 22 December 2008).

Held, David and Anthony McGrew, 'Introduction' in David Held and Anthony McGrew (eds.), *Governing Globalization: Power, Authority and Global Governance*, Cambridge: Polity Press, 2002, pp. 1–23.

Heng, Yee-Kuang, *War as Risk Management: Strategy and Conflict in an Age of Globalised Risks*, London: Routledge, 2006.

Hewson, Martin and Timothy Sinclair, *Approaches to Global Governance Theory*, Albany, NY: State University of New York, 1999.

Heyman, David, *Lessons from the Anthrax Attacks: Implications for US Bioterrorism Preparedness*, Centre for Strategic and International Studies and the Defense Threat Reduction Agency, April 2002 Online, available at: www.fas.org/irp/threat/cbw/dtra02. pdf (accessed 21 August 2008).

Hobson, John and Leonard Seabrooke (eds), *Everyday Politics of the World Economy*, Cambridge: Cambridge University Press, 2007.

Holmes, James, 'Sea power with Asian characteristics: China, India and the Proliferation Security Initiative', *Southeast Review of Asian Politics*, 1 January 2007.

Hughes, Gordon, *Understanding Crime Prevention: Social Control, Risk and Late Modernity*, Buckingham: Open University Press, 1998.

Hughes, S., *War on Terror, Inc: Corporate Profiteering from the Politics of Fear*, London: Verso: 2007.

Hulsse, R., 'Creating demand for global governance: the making of a global money-laundering problem', *Global Society*, Vol. 21 No. 2, April 2007, pp. 155–178.

Ignatieff, Michael, *The Lesser Evil: Political Ethics in an Age of Terror*, Princeton, NJ: Princeton University Press, 2004.

Jarvis, Darryl and Martin Griffiths, 'Risk and international relations: a new research agenda', *Global Society*, Vol. 21 No. 1, 2007, pp. 1–4.

Johnson, Jackie, 'Repairing legitimacy after blacklisting by the Financial Action Task Force', *Journal of Money Laundering Control*, Vol. 7 No. 1, 2003, pp. 38–49.

Karns, Margaret and Karen Mingst, *International Organisations: The Politics and Processes of Global Governance*, London: Lynne Rienner, 2004.

Kenny, Michael, *From Pablo to Osama: Trafficking and Terrorist Networks, Government Bureaucracies, and Competitive Adaptation*, University Park, PA: Penn State University Press, 2007.

Kern, Alexander, Rahul Dhumale and John Eatwell, *Global Governance of Financial Systems: The International Regulation of Systemic Risk*, Oxford: Oxford University Press, 2006.

Kirchner, Emile and James Sperling, *Global Security Governance*, London: Routledge, 2007.

Kirchner, Emile and James Sperling, *EU Security Governance*, Manchester: Manchester University Press, 2008.

Krahmann, Elke, 'Conceptualising security governance', *Cooperation and Conflict*, Vol. 38 No. 1, 2003, pp. 5–26.

Latham, Robert, 'Politics in a floating world: toward a critique of global governance' in Martin Hewson and Tim Sinclair (eds), *Approaches to Global Governance Theory*, Albany, NY: State University of New York, 1999, pp. 23–54.

Latour, Bruno, 'Whose cosmos, which cosmopolitics? Comments on the peace terms of Ulrich Beck', *Common Knowledge*, Vol. 10 No. 3, 2004, pp. 450–462.

Levi, Michael, 'Lessons for countering terrorist financing from the war on serious and organised crime' in Thomas Biersteker and Sue E. Eckert (eds), *Countering the Financing of Terrorism*, London: Routledge, 2007, pp. 260–288.

Levi, Michael and David Wall, 'Technologies, security, and privacy in the post-9/11 European information society', *Journal of Law and Society*, Vol. 31 No. 2, 2004, pp. 194–220.

Lobo-Guerero, Luis, 'Biopolitics of specialist risk: kidnap and ransom insurance', *Security Dialogue*, Vol. 38 No. 3, September 2007, pp. 315–334.

Lyon, David, *Surveillance Society: Monitoring Everyday Life*, Buckingham: Open University Press, 2001.

Lyon, David, 'Chapter 1: surveillance as social sorting' in David Lyon (ed.), *Surveillance as Social Sorting: Privacy, Risk and Digital Discrimination*, London: Routledge, 2003, pp. 13–30.

Lyon, David, *Surveillance after September 11*, Cambridge: Polity Press, 2003.

McInnes, Colin, *Health, Security and the Risk Society*, London: The Nuffield Trust, 2005.

Mearsheimer, John, 'Back to the future: instability in Europe after the Cold War', *International Security*, Vol. 15 No. 2, 1990, pp. 5–56.

Messner, Dirk and Franz Nuscheler, 'Basic outlines of German development policy' in Saori Katada, Hanns Maull and Takashi Inoguchi (eds), *Global Governance: Germany and Japan in the International System*, Aldershot: Ashgate, 2004, pp. 161–178.

Methuen, Bernadette and Ian Taylor, 'The return of the dogs of war? The privatisation of security in Africa' in Rodney Bruce Hall and Thomas Biersteker (eds), *The Emergence of Private Authority in Global Governance*, Cambridge: Cambridge University Press, 2002, pp. 183–202.

Mythen, Gabe and Sandra Walklate, 'Criminology and terrorism: which thesis? Risk society or governmentality?' *British Journal of Criminology*, Vol. 46 No. 3, 2006, pp. 379–398.

Mythen, Gabe and Sandra Walklate (eds), *Beyond the Risk Society*, Buckingham: Open University Press, 2006.

Mythen, Gabe and Sandra Walklate, 'Terrorism, risk and international security: the perils of asking "what if?"', *Security Dialogue*, Vol. 39 No. 2–3, 2008, pp. 221–242.

Navias, Martin, 'Finance warfare and international terrorism', *Political Quarterly*, Vol. 73 No. 1, 2002, pp. 57–79.

Naylor, R.T., *Satanic Purses: Money, Myth and Misinformation in the War on Terror*, Toronto: McGill-Queen's University Press, 2006.

Nesi, Giuseppe (ed.), *International Cooperation in Counter-terrorism: the United Nations and Regional Organizations in the Fight Against Terrorism*, Aldershot: Ashgate, 2006.

O'Malley, Pat, 'Risks, ethics and airport security', *Canadian Journal of Criminology and Criminal Justice*, Vol. 48 No. 3, June 2006, pp. 413–421.

O'Tuathail, Gearoid, 'Understanding critical geopolitics: geopolitics and risk society', *Journal of Strategic Studies*, Vol. 22 No. 2/3, June/September 1999, pp. 107–124.

Paton, Robert, 'Risk management's role in countering global terrorism', *Rough Notes*, October 2003.

Persbo, Andrew and Ian Davis, *Sailing into Uncharted Waters? The Proliferation Security Initiative and the Law of the Sea*, London: British American Security Information Council, Research Report 2004, June.

Pieth, Mark, 'Financing of terrorism: follow the money', *European Journal of Law Reform*, Vol. 4 No. 2, 2002, pp. 365–376.

Pieth, Mark and Gemma Aiolfi, 'The private sector becomes active: the Wolfsberg Process', *Journal of Financial Crime*, Vol. 10 No. 4, 2003, pp. 359–365.

Power, M., *The Risk Management of Everything*, London: Demos, 2004.

Rasmussen, Mikkel, 'Reflexive security: NATO and international risk society', *Millennium*, Vol. 30 No. 2, 2001, pp. 285–310.

Rasmussen, Mikkel, 'It sounds like a riddle: security studies, the war on terror and risk', *Millennium*, Vol. 33 No 2, 2004, pp. 381–395.

Rasmussen, Mikkel, *The Risk Society at War*, Cambridge: Cambridge University Press, 2006.

Rees, Wyn, *Transatlantic Security Cooperation: Counter Terrorism in the Twenty-First Century*, London: Routledge, 2006.

Renn, Ortwin, *Risk Governance: Coping with Uncertainty in a Complex World*, London: Earthscan, 2008.

Renn, Ortwin and Katherine D. Walker (eds), *Global Risk Governance*, Amsterdam: Springer, 2008.

Reuter, Peter and Edward Truman, *Chasing Dirty Money: The Fight Against Money-Laundering*, Washington, DC: Institute for International Economics, 2004.

Reveron, Derek, 'Old allies, new friends: intelligence-sharing in the war on terror', *Orbis*, Summer 2006, pp. 1–15.

Romaniuk, P., *Global Counterterrorism: How Multi-lateral Cooperation Works*, London: Routledge, forthcoming 2009.

Rosenau, James, 'Toward an ontology for global governance' in Martin Hewson and Timothy J. Sinclair (eds), *Approaches to Global Governance Theory*, Albany, NY: State University of New York, 1999, pp. 287–302.

Rothschild, Emma, 'What is security?' *Daedalus*, Vol. 124 No. 3, 1995, pp. 53–98.

Salter, Mark (ed.), *Politics at the Airport*, Minneapolis, MN: University of Minnesota Press, 2008.

Salter, Mark, 'Imagining numbers: risk, quantification and aviation security', *Security Dialogue*, Vol. 39 No. 2–3, 2008, pp. 243–266.

Schneir, Bruce, *Beyond Fear: Thinking Sensibly About Security in an Uncertain World*, New York: Copernicus Books, 2003.

Scholte, Jan Aart, 'Global capitalism and the state', *International Affairs*, Vol. 73 No. 3, 1997, pp. 427–452.

Sechrest, Larry, 'Privateering and national defense: naval warfare for profit' in Hans-Hermanne Hoppe (ed.), *The Myth of National Defense: Essays on the Theory and History of Security Production*, Auburn, AL: Ludvig Von Mises Institute, 2003, pp. 239–274.

Seidenstat, Paul, 'Terrorism, airport security and the private sector', *Review of Policy Research*, Vol. 21, No. 3, 2004, pp. 275–276.

Senghaas, David, 'Global governance: how could it be conceived?' *Security Dialogue*, Vol. 20 No. 3, 1993, pp. 247–256.

Sharman, Jason, 'Power and discourse in policy diffusion: anti-money laundering in developing states', *International Studies Quarterly*, Vol. 52 No. 3, 2008, pp. 635–656.

Shaw, Timothy, Sandra J. MacLean and David R. Black, 'Introduction: a decade of human security: what prospects for global governance and new multilateralisms?' in Sandra J. Maclean, David R. Black and Timothy Shaw (eds), *A Decade of Human Security: Global Governance and New Multilateralisms*, Aldershot: Ashgate, 2006, pp. 3–19.

Shehu, Adbullahi, 'International initiatives against money-laundering and corruption: an overview', *Journal of Financial Crime*, Vol. 12 No. 3, 2005, pp. 221–245.

Shields, Peter, 'When the "information revolution" and the US security state collide', *New Media and Society*, Vol. 7 No. 4, 2005, pp. 483–512.

SIPRI Yearbook 2007, Stockholm: SIPRI, 2007.

Sopko, John, 'The changing proliferation threat', *Foreign Policy*, No. 105, Winter 1996–97, pp. 3–20.

Spence, Keith, 'World risk society and war against terror', *Political Studies*, Vol. 53 No. 2, 2005, pp. 284–302.

Squassoni, Sharon, 'Proliferation Security Initiative', Congressional Research Service Report for Congress, Order Code RS21881, 14 September 2006.

Stevenson, Jonathan, 'Pragmatic counter-terrorism', *Survival*, Vol. 43 No. 4, Winter 2001–02, pp. 35–48.

Stevenson, Jonathan, 'Demilitarising the "war on terror"', *Survival*, Vol. 48 No. 2, Summer 2006, pp. 37–54.

Stone, Charles and Anne Zissu, 'Registered travellers: the financial value of registering the good guys', *Review of Policy Research*, Vol. 24 No. 5, September 2007, pp. 443–462.

Szyliowicz, Joseph S., 'Aviation security: promise or reality?' *Studies in Conflict and Terrorism*, Vol. 27 No. 1, 2004, pp. 47–63.

Tangredi, Sam, 'Introduction' in Tangredi, Sam (ed.), *Globalisation and Maritime Power*, Washington, DC: National Defence University, 2002, pp. xxi–1.

Taylor, John, *Global Financial Warriors: The Untold Story of International Finance in the Post-9/11 World*, New York: W.W. Norton, 2007.

Thakur, Ramesh and Thomas G. Weiss, *The UN and Global Governance: An Idea and its Prospects*, UN Intellectual History Project, Bloomington, IN: Indiana University Press, forthcoming.

Thomas, Caroline, *Global Governance, Development and Human Security*, London: Pluto, 2000.

Toohey, Kristine, 'Terrorism, sport, and public policy in the risk society', *Sport in Society*, Vol. 11 No. 4, July 2008, pp. 429–442.

Tsingou, Elina, 'Targeting money laundering: global approach or diffusion of authority', in Elke Krahmann (ed.), *New Threats and New Actors in International Security*, Basingstoke: Palgrave, 2005.

Tucker, Jonathan, *War of Nerves: A History of Chemical Weapons from World War 1 to Al-Qaeda*, New York: Pantheon, 2006.

Ulman, Richard H., 'Redefining security', *International Security*, Vol. 8 No. 1, Summer 1983, pp. 129–153.

Valencia, Mark, 'Is the PSI really the cornerstone of a new international norm?' *Naval War College Review*, Vol. 59 No. 4, Autumn 2006, pp. 123–130.

Valencia, Mark, 'The Proliferation Security Initiative: a glass half-full', *Arms Control Today*, June 2007. Online, available at: www.armscontrol.org/act/2007_06/Valencia (accessed 22 December 2008).

Vlcek, William, 'Surveillance to combat terrorist financing in Europe: whose liberty, whose security?' *European Security*, Vol. 16 No. 1, March 2007, pp. 99–119.

Vlcek, William, 'Money, terror and protecting the West', *The Round Table: The Commonwealth Journal of International Affairs*, Vol. 97 No. 395, April 2008, pp. 305–311.

Voß, Jan-Peter, Dirk Bauknecht and Rene Kemp (eds), *Reflexive Governance for Sustainable Development*, Camberley: Edward Elgar, 2006.

Wallis, Rodney, *Combating Air Terrorism*, Washington, DC: Brassey's, 1993.

Wallis, Rodney, How Safe are our Skies? Assessing the Airlines' Responses to Terrorism, Westport, CT: Greenwood Publishing, 2003.

Warde, I., *The Price of Fear: The Truth Behind the Financial War on Terror*, London: University of California Press, 2007.

Wessel, Ramses A. and Jan Wouters, 'The phenomenon of multilevel regulation: the global, EU and national regulatory spheres', *International Organisations Law Review*, Vol. 4 No. 2, 2008, pp. 259–291.

Wilkinson, Paul, 'Enhancing global aviation security?' in Paul Wilkinson and Brian Jenkins (eds), *Aviation Terrorism and Security*, London: Frank Cass, 1999, pp. 147–166.

Wilkinson, Rorden, *The Global Governance Reader*, London: Routledge, 2005.

Williams, Phil, 'Strategy for a new world: combating trans-national organised crime and terrorism', in John Baylis and Steve Smith, *Strategy in the Contemporary World*, Oxford: Oxford University Press, 2nd edition, 2007, pp. 192–208.

Williams, Phil, 'Terrorist financing and organised crime: nexus, appropriation or transformation', in Thomas Biersteker and Sue E. Eckert (eds), *Countering the Financing of Terrorism*, London: Routledge, 2007, pp. 126–149.

Williamson, Eric and David Winget, 'Risk management and design of critical bridges for terrorist attacks', *Journal of Bridge Engineering*, Vol. 10 No. 1, January/February 2005, pp. 96–106.

Wilson, Dean, *Borders, Mobility and Technologies of Control*, Amsterdam: Springer, 2006.

Winner, Andrew, 'The Proliferation Security Initiative: the new face of interdiction', *Washington Quarterly*, Vol. 28 No. 2, Spring 2005, pp. 129–143.

Woodward, Bob, *Bush At War*, London: Pocket Books, 2003.

Woodward, Bob, *Plan of Attack*, New York: Simon & Schuster, 2004.

Yadav, Vikash, *Risk in International Finance*, London: Routledge, 2008.

Zagaris, Bruce, 'The merging of the anti-money laundering and counter-terrorism financial enforcement regimes after September 11, 2001', *Berkeley Journal of International Law*, Vol. 22 No. 1, 2004, pp. 123–158.

Zarate, J.C., 'Bankrupting terrorists', *E-Journal USA*, September 2004. Online, available at: http://usinfo.state.gov/journals/ites/0904/ijee/zarate.htm (accessed 9 April 2007).

Official governmental publications

9/11 Commission, *Monograph on Terrorist Financing*, Washington, DC, August 2004.

Cabinet Office Strategy Unit, *Risk: Improving Government's Capacity to Handle Risk and Uncertainty*, London, November 2002.

Canadian Department of Defence, 'Backgrounder: the Proliferation Security Initiative', 19 May 2006. Online, available at: www.dnd.ca/site/Newsroom/view_news_e.asp?id=1329 (accessed 9 July 2006).

General Accounting Office, *General Aviation Security: Increased Federal Oversight Needed but Continued Partnership with Private Sector is Critical to Long-term Success*, GAO-05-144, Washington, DC, 10 November 2004.

General Accounting Office, *Aviation Security: Risk, Experience, and Customer Concerns Drive Changes to Airline Passenger Screening Procedures, but Evaluation and Documentation of Proposed Changes Could Be Improved*, GAO-07-634, Washington, DC, 16 April 2007.

HM Government, *Countering International Terrorism: The United Kingdom's Strategy*, London, UK, July 2006.

HM Government, *The National Security Strategy for the United Kingdom*, London, UK, March 2008.

National Commission on Terrorist Attacks Upon the United States, *The 9/11 Commission Report*, Washington, DC, July 2004.

US Department of Homeland Security, *National Strategy for Homeland Security*, Washington, DC, July 2002.

US Department of Homeland Security, *Maritime Commerce Security Plan for the National Strategy for Maritime Security*, Washington, DC, October 2005.

US Department of Defense, *Quadrennial Defence Review*, Washington, DC, September 2006.

White House, *National Security Strategy of the United States*, Washington, DC, September 2002.

White House, *National Strategy to Combat Weapons of Mass Destruction (WMD)*, Washington, DC, December 2002.

White House, *National Strategy for Combating Terrorism*, Washington, DC, 2003.

White House, *The National Strategy for Maritime Security*, Washington, DC, 20 September 2005.

White House, *National Security Strategy of the United States*, Washington, DC, 2006.

White House, *National Strategy for Combating Terrorism*, Washington, DC, July 2006.

White House, *9/11 Five Years Later: Successes and Challenges*, Washington, DC, 2006.

White House, *National Strategy for Aviation Security*, Washington, DC, March 2007.

White House, *National Strategy for Homeland Security*, Washington, DC, 2007.

Newspapers, magazines and web-only articles

Armed Forces Information Service News (US Military)
Atlantic Monthly
Christian Science Monitor
Guardian (London)
Hindu (India)
LA Times
New York Times
The Times (London)
TIME
Wall Street Journal
Washington Post
Arms Control Association Fact Sheet, 'The Proliferation Security Initiative at a glance', October 2007. Online, available at: www.armscontrol.org/factsheets/PSI (accessed 15 November 2007).

Beck, Ulrich, 'A new cosmopolitanism is in the air', 20 November 2007. Online, available at: www.signandsight.com/features/1603.html (accessed 12 January 2008).

Gurule, J., 'The global effort to stop terrorist financing', *American Internationalism*, August 2003. Online, available at: http://usinfo.state.gov/journals/itps/0803/ijpe/pj81gurule.htm (accessed 17 November 2008).

Lugar, Richard, 'The Lugar Doctrine', 6 December 2001. Online, available at: http://lugar.senate.gov/bio/doctrine.cfm (accessed 4 February 2002).

Paylor, Anne, 'Wanted: a security standard', *Air Transport World*, June 2006. Online, available at: www.atwonline.com/channels/routesAirports/article.html?articleID=1634 (accessed 22 December 2008).

'The Second Bush–Gore Presidential Debate', transcript available at *Commission on Presidential Debates*, 11 October 2000. Online, available at: www.debates.org/pages/trans2000b.html (accessed 4 April 2008).

Valencia, Mark, 'Bring the PSI into the UN', *Nautilus Institute Policy Online Forum*, 05-101A, 20 December 2005. Online, available at: www.nautilus.org/fora/security/05101Valencia.html (accessed 23 January 2006).

Index